PROFESSOR DERRICK SILOVE is a practising clinical psychiatrist and Director of the Psychiatry Research and Teaching Unit, School of Psychiatry, University of New South Wales.

VIJAYA MANICAVASAGAR is a senior clinical psychologist and is Research Coordinator of the Psychiatry Research and Teaching Unit of the University of New South Wales.

The aim of the **Overcoming** series is to enable people with a range of common problems and disorders to take control of their own recovery program. Each title, with its specially tailored program, is devised by a practising clinician using the latest techniques of cognitive behavioral therapy – techniques which have been shown to be highly effective in changing the way patients think about themselves and their problems. The series was initiated in 1993 by Peter Cooper, Professor of Psychology at Reading University and Research Fellow at the University of Cambridge in the UK whose original volume on overcoming bulimia nervosa and binge-eating continues to help many people in the USA, the UK and Europe. Many of the books in the Overcoming series are recommended by the UK Department of Health under the Books on Prescription scheme.

Titles in the series include:

All titles in the series are available by mail order.
Please see the order form at the back of this book.
www.overcoming.co.uk

OVERCOMING PANIC AND AGORAPHOBIA

*A self-help guide using
Cognitive Behavioral Techniques*

DERRICK SILOVE
AND
VIJAYA MANICAVASAGAR

Robinson
LONDON

Constable & Robinson Ltd
3 The Lanchesters
162 Fulham Palace Road
London W6 9ER
www.constablerobinson.com

First published by Robinson Publishing Ltd 1997
Copyright © Derrick Silove and Vijaya Manicavasagar 1997

The right of Derrick Silove and Vijaya Manicavasagar to be identified as
authors of this work has been asserted by them in accordance with the
Copyright, Designs and Patents Act, 1988

A copy of the British Library Cataloguing in Publication Data for this
title is available from the British Library.

ISBN 978-1-84901-002-3

Important Note
This book is not intended to be a substitute for any medical advice or
treatment. Any person with a condition requiring medical attention
should consult a qualified medical practitioner or suitable therapist.

Printed and bound in EU

Table of contents

Introduction by Professor Peter Cooper

Why a cognitive behavioral approach?

Over the past two or three decades, there has been something of a revolution in the field of psychological treatment. Freud and his followers had a major impact on the way in which psychological therapy was conceptualized, and psychoanalysis and psychodynamic psychotherapy dominated the field for the first half of this century. So, long-term treatments were offered which were designed to uncover the childhood roots of personal problems – offered, that is, to those who could afford it. There was some attempt by a few health service practitioners with a public conscience to modify this form of treatment (by, for example, offering short-term treatment or group therapy), but the demand for help was so great that this had little impact. Also, whilst numerous case histories can be found of people who are convinced that psychotherapy did help them, practitioners of this form of therapy showed remarkably little interest in demonstrating that what they were offering their patients was, in fact, helpful.

As a reaction to the exclusivity of psychodynamic therapies and the slender evidence for its usefulness, in the 1950s and 1960s a set of techniques was developed, broadly collectively termed 'behavior therapy'. These techniques shared two basic features. First, they aimed to remove symptoms (such as anxiety) by dealing with those symptoms themselves, rather than their deep-seated underlying historical causes. Second, they were techniques, loosely related to what laboratory psychologists were finding out about the mechanisms of learning, which were formulated in testable terms. Indeed, practitioners of behavior therapy were committed to using techniques of proven value or, at worst, of a form which could potentially be put to test. The area where these techniques proved of most value was in the treatment of anxiety disorders, especially specific phobias (such as fear of animals or heights) and agoraphobia, both notoriously difficult to treat using conventional psychotherapies.

After an initial flush of enthusiasm, discontent with behavior therapy grew. There were a number of reasons for this, an important one of which was the fact that behavior therapy did not deal with the internal thoughts which were so obviously central to the distress that patients were experiencing. In this context, the fact that behavior therapy proved so inadequate when it came to the treatment of depression highlighted the need for major revision. In the late 1960s and early 1970s a treatment was developed specifically for depression called 'cognitive therapy'. The pioneer in this enterprise was an American psychiatrist, Professor Aaron T. Beck, who developed a theory of depression which emphasized the importance of people's depressed styles of thinking. He also specified a new form of therapy. It would not be an exaggeration to say that Beck's work has changed the nature of psychotherapy, not just for depression but for a range of psychological problems.

In recent years the cognitive techniques introduced by Beck have been merged with the techniques developed earlier by the behavior therapists to produce a body of theory and practice which has come to be known as 'cognitive behavior therapy'. There are two main reasons why this form of treatment has come to be so important within the field of psychotherapy. First, cognitive therapy for depression, as originally described by Beck and developed by his successors, has been subjected to the strictest scientific testing; and it has been found to be a highly successful treatment for a significant proportion of cases of depression. Not only has it proved to be as effective as the best alternative treatments (except in the most severe cases, where medication is required), but some studies suggest that people treated successfully with cognitive behavior therapy are less likely to experience a later recurrence of their depression than people treated successfully with other forms of therapy (such as antidepressant medication). Second, it has become clear that specific patterns of thinking are associated with a range of psychological problems and that treatments which deal with these styles of thinking are highly effective. So, specific cognitive behavioral treatments have been developed for anxiety disorders, like panic disorder, generalized anxiety disorder, specific phobias and social phobia, obsessive compulsive disorders, and hypochondriasis (health anxiety), as well as for other conditions such as compulsive gambling, alcohol and drug addiction, and eating disorders like bulimia nervosa and binge-eating disorder. Indeed, cognitive behavioral techniques have a wide application beyond the narrow categories of psychological disorders: they have been applied effectively, for example, to helping people with low self-esteem and those with marital difficulties.

At any one time almost 10 per cent of the general population is suffering from depression, and more than 10 per cent has one or other of the anxiety disorders. Many others have a range of psychological problems and personal difficulties. It is of the greatest importance that treatments of proven effectiveness are developed. However, even when the armoury of therapies is, as it were, full, there remains a very great problem – namely that the delivery of treatment is expensive and the resources are not going to be available evermore. Whilst this shortfall could be met by lots of people helping themselves, commonly the natural inclination to make oneself feel better in the present is to do precisely those things which perpetuate or even exacerbate one's problems. For example, the person with agoraphobia will stay at home to prevent the possibility of an anxiety attack; and the person with bulimia nervosa will avoid eating all potentially fattening foods. Whilst such strategies might resolve some immediate crisis, they leave the underlying problem intact and provide no real help in dealing with future difficulties.

So, there is a twin problem here; although effective treatments have been developed, they are not widely available; and when people try to help themselves they often make matters worse. In recent years the community of cognitive behavior therapists have responded to this situation. What they have done is to take the principles and techniques of specific cognitive behavior therapies for particular problems and represent them in self-help manuals. These manuals specify a systematic program of treatment which the individual sufferer is advised to work through to overcome their difficulties. In this way, the cognitive behavioral therapeutic techniques of proven value are being made available on the widest possible basis.

Self-help manuals are never going to replace therapists. Many people will need individual treatment from a qualified therapist. It is also the case that, despite the widespread success of cognitive behavioral therapy, some people will not respond to it and will need one of the other treatments available. Nevertheless, although research on the use of cognitive behavioral self-help manuals is at an early stage, the work done to date indicates that for a very great many people such a manual will prove sufficient for them to overcome their problems without professional help.

Many people suffer silently and secretly for years. Sometimes appropriate help is not forthcoming despite their efforts to find it. Sometimes they feel too ashamed or guilty to reveal their problems to anyone. For many of these people the cognitive behavioral self-help manual will provide a lifeline to recovery and a better future.

Professor Peter Cooper
The University of Reading, 1997

PART ONE

About Panic Attacks and Agoraphobia

Prologue

'A day in my life'

As I approach the bus, the symptoms become much worse. It's like being hit by a tornado. My mouth goes dry, my heart starts pounding, I feel sick in my stomach, I can hardly breathe, and my hands are shaking. I am sure that I am going to faint. I don't know how I manage to reach my seat – I feel as if I am just a spectator, everything seems a bit unreal and distant. Am I going crazy? I bet the other people on the bus have noticed. I really can't control my breathing any more, I feel like I am going to suffocate and die. When will it end?

By the time I get off the bus, the symptoms have lessened. Why do these attacks start and stop for no reason? I feel drained, exhausted and weak. I can't think straight. Maybe I should give up taking the bus for a while. Or should I go to the hospital for another check-up? I don't know. I can't cope with this any more. All I know is that I spend most of my time worrying about having another attack. I can't go on like this or my whole life will be ruined.

That night I lie in bed tossing and turning, and the next morning I awake exhausted. It seems ridiculous, but my mind keeps wandering back to those dreadful feelings I had on the bus. What if I have an attack when I'm out shopping? Will I be able to escape before it gets so bad that I can't reach home? I keep checking my body for symptoms. I think about those strange tingling and numb feelings I had in my hands and feet. I have heard that you can have funny feelings down your arms when you are having a heart attack. Perhaps that's what is wrong with me.

At last, I drag myself out of bed. I have that hollow feeling in the pit of my stomach and I feel a bit light-headed. I know the doctor said 'everything is OK,' but it is hard to believe that. There must be something seriously wrong with me. Maybe I should insist on seeing a specialist. They must have more accurate tests to pick up something wrong with your brain or your heart.

I am irritable with the kids at breakfast. They seem bewildered about my moodiness, but I can't tell them about my worries. What if I am seriously ill? It's better to keep it from them until I am sure. Anyway, they will just say the usual things about my worrying too much. I have an extra few cups of coffee to wake me up so that I can cope with the day. We talk about visiting mother in hospital and that seems to upset me even more. She has always been so healthy and now she has suddenly been taken ill. Life seems so unpredictable.

After seeing the kids off to school I rush to get the bus. I notice that the 'clamping' sensation is starting in my chest. I am having difficulty breathing and I feel hot and sweaty. I just hope that I don't have that 'spaced out' feeling on the bus. Why do I keep feeling like this? It seems to be getting worse. Why can't I be confident and in control the way I used to be? I must pull myself together.

1

What are panic disorder and agoraphobia?

Almost everyone feels anxious at some time in their lives. It is common to become anxious in situations such as a job interview, an examination or a public speaking engagement. Mild anxiety is so common that it is regarded as normal, and it is not usually a cause for concern. In fact, a degree of anxiety is necessary to help us perform well in situations requiring concentration, efficiency and skill. For some people, however, anxiety symptoms are so severe and persistent that they become disabling. People with such intense anxiety often are suffering from an anxiety disorder.

Many people suffer from anxiety disorders, yet only a small percentage of them seek treatment. The majority either cope on their own, suffer in silence or use risky methods (e.g. alcohol or drugs) to damp down their symptoms.

In some cases, people develop episodes of sudden and intense anxiety, known as *panic attacks*. They may not realize that they are suffering from an anxiety disorder, but instead believe that they have developed some other illness, like heart disease or stroke – which is understandable, because many of the symptoms of panic are physical. The experience of panic attacks often leads people to avoid situations where they fear experiencing further attacks.

> I began having panic attacks when I was about nineteen, during a stressful time at work. I would become breathless and sweaty, my heart would pound, and I had pains in my chest. I became so frightened that I thought I would have a heart attack or die. After that, attacks came out of the blue, and I noticed that I was avoiding certain situations, such as visiting department stores or travelling on buses. I felt that I couldn't talk to anyone about the problem since they would think I was going crazy.
>
> John

What is a panic attack?

> It starts when I suddenly feel like I can't breathe properly. I then start feeling dizzy and sweaty and notice that my heart is racing. Sometimes I become nauseous or feel like I am going to choke. My fingers go numb and I have a tingling sensation in my feet. I feel strange, as if I am not really 'there', as if I am detached from reality. I start thinking that I am about to lose control or die. This makes me feel extremely frightened . . . Even though the attack only lasts for five or ten minutes, it feels like forever and that I will never get over it.
>
> Christine

A panic attack refers to a sudden burst of acute anxiety, usually accompanied by a number of physical symptoms and catastrophic thoughts. It usually lasts for between two and thirty minutes – but at the time it feels as if it will last for ever, and when it does pass it leaves the sufferer weak and exhausted. Without treatment, panic attacks can occur several times a week or even daily.

The experience of having a panic attack

Every episode is slightly different. At first I used to feel that I was about to vomit or have diarrhea. More recently, I have had this severe choking feeling and sharp pain in my chest. I realize now that those feelings of being detached from myself and the environment are part of the same pattern.

Fay

Panic attacks are particularly frightening because they appear out of the blue, or in situations in which most people do not expect to be nervous or frightened. The speed at which the symptoms occur, their intensity and the fact that they involve so many parts of the body all add to the sense of fear and helplessness. Commonly occurring symptoms include:

- difficulty breathing, or being short of breath;
- a feeling of choking;
- tightness, pressure or pain in the chest;
- shakiness, trembling and weakness;
- sweaty palms and excessive perspiration;
- tingling or numbness in the hands and feet;

- palpitations or a pounding or rapid heartbeat;
- feeling faint, dizzy or unsteady;
- feeling 'out of touch' with your body or your immediate surroundings;
- nausea, chuming or upset in the stomach or lower bowel;
- feeling hot and cold, or flushed.

Together with these physical symptoms of panic, people commonly experience distressing thoughts, such as:

- 'I'm going crazy/insane';
- 'I'm going to lose control';
- 'I'm going to faint';
- 'I'm going to collapse';
- 'I'm having a heart attack';
- 'I'm having a stroke';
- 'I'm going to start screaming and make a fool of myself.

The likelihood of any of these things happening is remote, and when the episode has ended these thoughts often seem silly or irrational; but at the time of the panic attack they can be very strong. Indeed, the fears can be so real during a panic attack that they persist at the back of the mind and lead to more worry and anxiety in between attacks.

How do people feel after a panic attack?

After a panic attack subsides, sufferers often feel exhausted, dispirited and confused. It is an intensely frightening experience, especially when you do not know what is causing it. Many people understandably believe that they are physically unwell and seek medical attention at a hospital or from their local doctor. Others feel ashamed or embarrassed by what they consider to be a lack of self-control, and suffer in silence rather than reveal their problems to others or seek professional help.

What is panic disorder?

Some people have panic attacks repeatedly and the problem begins to interfere with their lives. These people suffer from *panic disorder*. Studies report that approximately 2–4 per cent of us will experience panic disorder at some time during our lives.

Sometimes, people may suffer from just one or two severe panic attacks, and then begin to fear having another attack. Their preoccupation with the problem dominates their minds and their behavior, making them ever more anxious and perhaps causing them to adjust their lifestyles: for example, they may avoid going out for fear of having another panic attack. Such people also suffer from panic disorder, even though they do not experience frequent panic attacks.

Avoiding situations where panic attacks might occur can affect people's lives as much as actually having regular attacks. The experience of worrying that a panic attack will recur is known as *anticipatory anxiety*. Overcoming anticipatory anxiety is one of the key elements in recovery from panic disorder and agoraphobia.

What is agoraphobia?

After a while I became afraid of going shopping in case I couldn't get back home quickly enough. I felt more and more anxious waiting at the check-out, and on one occasion I had to leave my shopping trolley there and hurry home. After that, I could only go to the shops if someone came with me. My fears extended to other situations so that I began to avoid public transport and even driving in the car. Now I can hardly leave the house.

Mavis

People who have had a panic attack in a particular situation may start to find that they avoid that place for fear of having another attack. Someone who has experienced a panic attack in a large department store may begin to avoid going shopping altogether. Using public transport, entering crowded places or being in traffic may remind a person that they have had panic attacks in those situations, so that avoiding those places becomes a way of preventing further anxiety. This kind of behavior is known as *agoraphobia* – literally, translated from the Greek, 'a fear of the market place'. In reality, agoraphobic fears are more extensive than simply a fear of shopping or public places. For some people, being alone at home for any reason is enough to make them very anxious. Agoraphobia is fairly common – over 7 per cent of women and nearly 3 per cent of men suffer from the disorder at some time in their lives.

A person suffering from agoraphobia tends to avoid situations in which escape might be difficult if they have a panic attack, or else tolerates being in that situation only with great dread or apprehension. Sometimes people with agoraphobia find that they only can cope with a feared situation, such as sitting in a car in traffic or going through a tunnel, if they are accompanied by a trusted companion. Others, if they go to see a movie or play, may choose to sit in the aisle seat of the auditorium, as close to the exit as possible, so that they can 'escape' if they become anxious.

Often, these fears extend to include all situations similar to the one in which a panic attack occurred: for example, a panic attack in a restaurant may lead to avoiding all restaurants. In this way avoidance behavior can escalate, restricting people in their movements and activities, even to the point where they may become housebound.

The relationship between panic disorder and agoraphobia is complex. Quite a lot of people with panic disorder develop agoraphobia; but many do not, and they are referred to as suffering from 'pure' panic disorder. Also, agoraphobia can develop on its own or as part of another disorder, such as depression. Agoraphobia also can persist after panic attacks have subsided. If a person who is worried about having a panic attack avoids all feared situations, they may thus prevent any further panic attacks; but the avoidance can continue and become an established way of life.

Examples of situations that people with agoraphobia commonly avoid, or in which they experience anxiety, are:

- driving a car in heavy traffic;
- travelling over bridges or through tunnels;
- visiting the supermarket;
- entering a crowded shopping area;
- taking public transport;
- going out to dinner/parties, shows or movies;
- waiting in line, for example, in a hairdresser's, or in a doctor's surgery;
- being alone at home.

Why do some people develop agoraphobia?

It is not clear why some people with panic disorder develop agoraphobia. Two mechanisms may, however, contribute. First, if you have panic attacks repeatedly in a particular situation, it is natural that you will develop a fear that the anxiety will return if you approach that or a similar situation. In other words, your past experience warns you against approaching places or situations where you have experienced panic. Thus you come to experience a 'fear of fear'. Secondly, other, more automatic 'conditioning' mechanisms may be operating. We have all heard of Pavlov's dog who was conditioned to salivate every time a bell was rung. In the same way, humans can be 'conditioned' automatically to react in an anxious way to otherwise harmless situations if they repeatedly experience anxiety when they approach those places. Thus, without being aware of it, we can come to associate panic with situations where it has occurred in the past, even if those places are not genuinely dangerous. Some people may 'condition' more easily than others. They may need to experience only a few panic attacks in a department store to 'learn' to avoid that place.

The different ways individuals cope with their worries also may influence the likelihood of developing agoraphobia. Assertive persons are more likely to confront their fears, while those who tend to avoid stress tend to withdraw. People with strong fears about separation ('separation anxiety') may tend to cling to others for security, or only to go out in the company of a trusted companion. More women than men with panic disorder develop agoraphobia. One possible explanation for this is that cultural expectations encourage men and women to respond in different ways to severe anxiety. Men are expected (and therefore expect themselves) to 'soldier on' and to fight anxiety (often with the 'help' of alcohol), whereas it may be more acceptable for women to avoid situations that cause fear.

What brings on panic attacks and agoraphobia?

Many people are able to recall several stressful incidents that occurred just before they experienced panic attacks, and some of these 'stressors' may continue or worsen after the attacks have begun. Arguments with a spouse or partner, death of a family member, personal illness or problems at work are commonly reported in the weeks or months before the onset of panic attacks. Stressful life circumstances befall almost everybody and those events do not, on their own, lead to the development of panic attacks. Usually it is a combination of factors, such as being vulnerable physically and/or psychologically together with life stress, that triggers panic attacks. Stress may play a role in causing panic attacks to continue; however, as we shall see in Chapter 3, there are other factors that may cause a vicious cycle of panic to persist.

2

How do panic disorder and agoraphobia affect people's lives?

My life revolves around the fear of having another panic attack. I can't concentrate on my work, which has suffered greatly. My problem has caused family rows. My family think that I should just pull myself together and stop worrying. I have lost my self-confidence and self-respect. I don't like to socialize any more in case I embarrass myself or I am forced to leave in a hurry because of a panic attack.

Patricia

Panic attacks and agoraphobia can have a serious impact on sufferers' lives. Severe anxiety and avoidance interfere with work, studies, family relationships and social life. The constant fear of having another panic attack produces feelings of apprehension, tension and fear, making sufferers overly cautious, unadventurous and constrained in their lifestyles. It is no wonder that people with panic disorder and agoraphobia often become depressed.

Symptoms of depression

Sometimes I would start to cry and cry . . . I felt so hope-less and useless. Other people around me seemed to be able to run their own lives . . . but for me panic attacks were controlling my life. Why couldn't I just snap out of it and be OK? I started feeling more and more depressed and self-critical as I realized that I could not control the panic attacks. I lost my self-confidence, I stopped wanting to socialize, and my friends seemed to withdraw from me. Life became so difficult that the thought crossed my mind that it was not worth going on.

Geoffrey

Some sufferers of panic attacks experience periods of depression in addition to their anxiety symptoms. Between 30 per cent and 70 per cent of people with panic disorder develop depression at some time. Depression may last for hours or days at a time; for some people it may persist for weeks or even months. It may be fairly mild, for example feeling rather sad and tearful at times, or more severe, leading to feelings of hopelessness, worthlessness and failure. The depressed person may no longer feel like working or socializing – not only from the fear of having a panic attack, but also because of the low self-esteem, loss of interest and lack of enjoyment that accompany severe demoralization.

Feelings of depression can be made worse by the sense of shame that accompanies uncontrollable anxiety. Shame makes people secretive about their anxiety, so that they make excuses to avoid social situations rather than having to suffer the embarrassment of revealing their problem to their friends. This may lead to a vicious cycle of avoiding enjoyable activities (like seeing a movie with friends, or going out for dinner), thus increasing feelings of isolation which worsen depression and lead to further loss of motivation. The person may begin to feel helpless and hopeless and then become more self-critical and withdrawn. People with agoraphobia are likely to become depressed because of their greatly restricted activities. In this way symptoms of anxiety, avoidance and depression interact to cause greater suffering and disability. It is important to recognize these vicious cycles and to attempt to break them in the process of recovery.

People suffering from panic attacks may feel quite desperate at times. It may seem impossible to improve their situation. They may begin to overeat, to use alcohol excessively or to take drugs in the attempt to forget about their problems or blot out their symptoms. When panic symptoms are complicated by severe depression or other problems, there is a risk of serious self-harm, even suicide. Clearly, it is important to take steps towards recovery long before such a level of desperation is reached.

For most sufferers of panic disorder and agoraphobia, depression lifts when anxiety symptoms are brought under control. In those few instances where depression lingers after the anxiety has improved, it is important to seek specific professional help. Some people suffer a mixture of anxiety and depressive symptoms; in others, depression is the main problem, with anxiety symptoms being secondary. If you are in doubt as to which is the main problem – anxiety or depression – you should consult your doctor or the local mental health service.

Effects on social life

My anxiety problem has taken over my whole life. Even though I have a close family, I can't talk to any of them about it since they don't understand what I am going through. My problem has created a wall between me and my husband. Also, I become terribly embarrassed with my friends when I start developing panic symptoms. I can't face seeing people.

Joanne

Panic attacks can have a profound effect on family and social life. Often, the situations in which panic attacks occur are those that involve being out of the house among other people. It is understandable that a person who experiences panic attacks at a movie or in a restaurant will be apprehensive about returning to such places and may even avoid them. Sufferers may make excuses not to go on social outings, especially if it means entering situations in which they fear they might panic. Friends and family may become frustrated and offended when their invitations are regularly turned down. On the other hand, some panic sufferers who have disclosed their symptoms to those close to them find that their problems are not taken seriously and that they are given superficial advice, for example 'pull yourself together' or 'be strong'. These responses may seem insensitive, but it must be remembered that most non-sufferers have very little knowledge about panic attacks and agoraphobia, and they may not understand how difficult it can be to overcome these problems. It is common for people to believe that because it is common to experience anxiety, everyone should be able to cope with it by using will-power.

Severe anxiety can disturb intimate relationships. Anxiety can cause a sufferer to be irritable, preoccupied, withdrawn or in need of repeated reassurance. Sufferers may come to depend heavily on their spouses or partners to carry out everyday chores such as shopping, banking or collecting the children from school. A sufferer may feel that the problem is not understood by a spouse or partner, who in turn feels baffled, frustrated and helpless. Thus a vicious circle of misunderstanding can set in.

The social and personal relationships of those who suffer from panic attacks and agoraphobia commonly are transformed when they recover from the acute symptoms and learn how to master their anxiety. They often feel much happier within their family and social networks, and their spouses or partners are greatly relieved. Occasionally, because the family's lifestyle has adapted gradually to the sufferer's restricted activities, recovery will require other family members to change their own habits and expectations. The household has to adjust to a member who is more active, assertive and independent than they are used to. Such adjustments can cause tension and uncertainty within the family. There are some advantages in having a parent or spouse who is always at home!

3

What causes panic and agoraphobia?

A number of factors act together to cause panic attacks and panic disorder. The particular combination will vary from one person to another. It is useful, however, to think of a chain of factors of broadly three types that together progressively build up to produce panic.

- First, some people are *vulnerable* as a result of the way they are built (their constitution) or because of experiences they have had in early life.
- Then there are immediate stresses or *triggers* that bring on a sudden panic attack.
- Finally, there are a number of influences (*perpetuating factors*) that keep the process going, often leading to a vicious cycle in which panic attacks are made worse or brought on more frequently.

This chapter will outline how these *vulnerability, trigger* and *perpetuating* factors are at present understood.

Vulnerability to panic attacks and agoraphobia

Are some people more vulnerable than others to developing panic attacks and agoraphobia? Certainly there seem to be physical, psychological and social factors that put some of us at greater risk. Some of these factors relate to early life, and others to adulthood.

Risk factors in early life

> When I was young I was very afraid of the dark. I hated being alone and worried that I might be kidnapped. If my parents went out I kept thinking that they would be killed in an accident or attacked. These thoughts made me very insecure.
>
> Paul

In some (but not all) instances, panic disorder runs in families. This can be a matter of genetic inheritance and/or the nature of family relationships – whether openly affectionate or cold, supportive or demanding, etc. Identical twins share similar levels of 'trait anxiety' – that is, the temperamental tendency to worry or be nervy – which suggests that, to some extent, we inherit our tendency to develop symptoms such as panic. Many adults with agoraphobia recall their family environments as being somewhat cold and unsupportive. Some children who are vulnerable to later panic disorder have high levels of 'separation anxiety' in early life which makes them clingy, insecure, afraid of being alone and sometimes unwilling to go to school. Clearly, interactions between children and their parents are always complex, and it is important not to blame one or the other for creating anxiety. It is difficult to be sure whether, for example, parental overprotectiveness causes the child to feel insecure or whether some anxious children demand more and are less satisfied with the attention they receive from their parents.

Children who are exposed to shocking events, abuse and trauma in early life appear to run an increased risk of panic disorder as they grow up. Indeed, such experiences make children vulnerable to a wide range of emotional difficulties in adulthood, of which panic disorder is just one. However, some events may be particularly significant for later panic symptoms: for example, events that cause difficulty in breathing in early life (e.g. near-drowning, suffocation, severe attacks of asthma) may sensitize the nervous system to changes in blood gas levels. If someone who has had such an experience becomes anxious, or hyperventilates, in later life, he or she may be more likely to develop full-blown panic attacks.

Factors in later life

Psychological factors

Why can't I control myself? Perhaps I should stop going out altogether. That way I can make sure that I won't have any more of these terrible attacks. I am sure that something terrible is going to happen during one of these attacks. My life seems to be completely out of control.

Walter

People who are prone to having panic attacks often think in particular ways. They are more likely to interpret bodily sensations (e.g. a racing heartbeat) in a catastrophic way, jumping to the conclusion that they are having a heart attack. Most people are able to counter unrealistic fears with more positive, reassuring thoughts ('That twinge of pain in my lower chest is probably just a bit of indigestion'). People who are prone to catastrophic interpretations, on the other hand, tend to believe that they are unable to control their lives or the world around them. They may slip quickly into thinking that problems are too great to tackle and beyond their capacity to solve. This means that they are more likely to become worried and stressed when they encounter real-life problems. A negative thinking style may grow out of a family setting in which a child was not reassured enough or encouraged to develop confidence. Or again, it may become established where a vulnerable person has suffered a major disruption in the family or other severe trauma in early life which has undermined his or her self-esteem. Events like this often seem uncontrollable at the time, leading to the feeling that life is worryingly unpredictable and that problems are impossible to solve.

Such negative thinking may affect the way you deal with stress. Different people have different ways of coping with stress or stressful situations. Some methods are more helpful than others, and some individuals cope better than others in similar situations. Coping skills are largely learnt and become a habit by repeated use. Children often learn ways of coping with stress from the people around them – parents, teachers and friends.

Some negative coping styles include:

- giving up or becoming frustrated when you face obstacles in life;
- avoiding situations that cause discomfort;
- becoming tense and irritable if you cannot get your way immediately;
- depending too much on others for help;
- taking excessive amounts of alcohol or drugs to dampen unpleasant feelings.

If you are susceptible to anxiety, negative coping styles like these can actually make the symptoms worse. Breaking old coping habits and learning new, more helpful ones can be difficult and requires a lot of practice.

Social factors

I have been working day and night for the exams and have had little time to go out with Sam. It is hard to know why things are so cold between us. Is it because I am so busy or are the attacks I am having making me more irritable? He seems confused about our relationship but I am scared to tell him about the attacks in case he thinks I am crazy or weak. At the same time, I need his support even more now that my confidence is so low.

Yvonne

People from all walks of life develop panic attacks and panic disorder. However, women are at greater risk than men. Why this should be so remains unclear. The answer may have something to do with the role of women in modern society, or with genetic or hormonal factors, or – partly, and in some cases – to the stress of childbearing and childrearing. It has been suggested that women are pulled in opposite directions in the modern world, finding it hard to be both a home-builder and also a breadwinner. Difficulties in relationships appear to be important in panic disorder – but, as we have already seen, this is a complex area. Although chronic stress within marriages and other long-term partnerships may be an important factor, many people who develop panic attacks are single. It is not always easy to be sure whether the stress within the family is a cause or a result of one member having panic disorder. For example, if a partner is 'dominant' this may be to compensate for the panic sufferer's insecurity, or it may be a factor that is increasing the sufferer's level of anxiety and dependence. It may even be both.

Physical factors

I had spasms in my chest in which I felt that I could not breathe, that my chest was in a vice, and that pins were being stuck into my heart. I kept going back to the hospital, but they said they could find "nothing wrong". The symptoms were so real, I was sure they were missing something serious like a heart attack.

Frank

People who suffer from panic attacks commonly ask whether their symptoms are real or just a result of their 'imagination'. To begin to understand panic attacks, it is important to consider the normal 'stress response'. A sudden shock or threat causes extreme fear in anyone. Think how you would react if a car suddenly turned a corner at high speed and narrowly missed you as you crossed the street; or if someone unexpectedly slammed a door behind you. You are suddenly very alert and vigilant; your skin crawls, your heart may pound, and you may become a bit shaky. You may jump up, shout or get angry. This is the normal '*fight or flight*' response which helps us to take defensive action when we feel threatened. The response is controlled by the centres of the nervous system buried deep in the brain. These centres control the involuntary (or 'automatic') nervous system, which controls the muscles of the internal organs and glands of the body. The involuntary nervous system is activated immediately when the brain receives a threatening message from the outside world. It responds instantaneously and without any conscious prompting from us. When those nerves send out an alarm signal, the muscles of the heart contract faster, leading to rapid beats or palpitations, the muscles of the chest wall contract, causing you to breathe more quickly, and the perspiration glands squeeze more sweat on to the skin. The involuntary nervous system also activates hormone glands which release chemicals such as adrenalin into the blood. Those chemicals prepare the body for rapid action by sending more blood to the muscles, by releasing sugar to give you more energy and by making you alert to the environment.

This fear reaction is essential and could save your life in an emergency. The associated physical sensations are caused by actual physiological changes, and usually pass after the threat has disappeared. However, in panic disorder, the 'fight or flight' response is activated inappropriately, when there is no direct threat present. It may be that some people have a lower 'trigger' threshold or that their control mechanism in the nervous system for bringing the fight or flight response to an end is less efficient. Temperamental factors, such as an ingrained tendency to worry, together with continuing stress over a period of time, may increase the general level of bodily tension so that you are operating closer and closer to the trigger threshold. Even minor events may then set off the fight or flight response, leading to panic. Because, as we saw above, vulnerable people interpret upsetting experiences or bodily sensations as more threatening than others, they keep sending 'false alarms' to the centre that triggers the fight or flight reaction. It is when the fight or flight response is triggered inappropriately in situations that, although stressful, are not really dangerous, that you experience the symptoms of a panic attack. The fight and flight response itself is a normal and useful mechanism aimed at protecting the body from danger. Thus, for people who are otherwise healthy, the physical symptoms of panic, although frightening, are not directly damaging to your health. This is a very important point to grasp, as one of the greatest fears that beset panic sufferers is that the attacks themselves are doing them harm.

Anxiety mechanisms in the nervous system

A lot of research has been done into what goes on in the brain immediately before and during extreme anxiety and panic attacks. It is known that certain chemicals, called 'neurotransmitters', pass messages from one nerve to another in the brain. A number of these chemicals are thought to be important in the nerves that transmit fear, alarm and anxiety 'messages'. It is still not clear how these 'messenger' systems may differ in anxiety sufferers; but it nevertheless seems that many of the medications that affect anxiety (see Chapter 4) act to alter the actions of these neurotransmitters or the way the nerve endings respond to these 'messengers'. If there are differences in the nervous system of panic sufferers, then these are of a very subtle kind and probably relate to the fine balance of certain chemicals and their actions in particular brain pathways. In other words, ordinary tests (such as X-rays or brain scans) invariably are normal in sufferers of panic disorder. If abnormalities are detected, then the person is likely to be suffering not from a primary panic disorder but from one of the relatively rare physical illnesses that sometimes can mimic panic.

Physical illnesses that can cause panic-like symptoms

Rarely, physical illness can mimic panic disorder. For example, people who have problems with their thyroid gland (which normally regulates the body's temperature and the rate at which chemicals are processed) may experience symptoms that are very like those of anxiety and panic. Usually, other accompanying symptoms will make it clear that a physical disorder is present. Occasionally, anxiety-like symptoms will be the first sign of such an underlying illness.

Some conditions that may cause panic-like symptoms include:

- irregular heart rhythms, and occasionally, disease of the heart blood vessels;
- disorders affecting your breathing;
- excessive use of certain medications, e.g. for asthma;
- rare disorders of the glands that produce hormones and other chemicals in the blood;
- unusual types of epilepsy;
- excessive use of or withdrawal from caffeine, drugs or alcohol.

If you have any concern that you may have a serious physical illness, it is important for your doctor to take a full medical history, to examine you, and to carry out some investigations such as blood tests. If there is any likelihood of heart disease, then an electrocardiogram, a 'stress test' and some blood tests can usually identify if there is an active problem. Most likely, these tests will show that you are physically healthy and you can then be quite certain that your symptoms are due to anxiety. If these tests do show some sort of physical illness (e.g. thyroid disease), it is very likely that treatment of this problem will also reduce your anxiety-like symptoms. It is possible to suffer from both a physical illness (for example, asthma or heart disease) and panic disorder, and anyone in this situation will require treatment for both conditions. In the majority of sufferers, however, no associated physical illness is found.

While it is very seldom that panic disorder is caused by physical illness, the symptoms can be so dramatic that it is difficult for the sufferer to believe that there is no physical condition underlying the problem. Consequently, he or she may visit several doctors or insist on repeating blood tests or on having more complicated investigations. The procedures themselves may cause stress and reinforce the fear that there 'must be something wrong'. It is helpful to remember that one of the common symptoms of panic disorder is an uncontrollable worry about having a physical illness. If tests performed by the doctor rule out a physical illness, then it is best to reassess the situation and to focus on managing the anxiety symptoms rather than to have unnecessary additional tests.

What sets off a panic attack?

Hyperventilation and panic symptoms

A common 'trigger' of panic symptoms in those who are susceptible to them is 'overbreathing' or 'hyperventilation'. Many people who suffer from panic attacks notice that their breathing rate increases and becomes shallow while they are in the midst of an attack. Vulnerable people may in fact be hyperventilating chronically, but this may not be obvious. Signs of hyperventilation include shallow, frequent breathing, gasping, sighing, yawning or panting. Two common signs of chronic hyperventilation are excessive sighing and yawning. Few people realize that yawning may not be caused by boredom or sighing by sadness, but that both may be signs of anxiety! If you notice that you are sighing and yawning through the day, you may be chronically overbreathing and therefore at risk of provoking panic symptoms and panic attacks. Normally, there is a balance between the gases oxygen and carbon dioxide in the blood. Hyperventilation causes more than usual amounts of carbon dioxide to be breathed out, making it difficult for the red blood cells to release oxygen to the body. In other words, the harder you breathe, the less oxygen you are delivering to the brain! Hyperventilation thus results in typical symptoms of panic such as unsteadiness, dizziness, feeling 'spaced out' and weakness. Hyperventilation increases under stress and, in chronic overbreathers, may trigger a panic attack. Once the panic attack starts, breathing then becomes more rapid, and the 'hyperventilation – panic' cycle begins. Also, catastrophic misinterpretation of the physical symptoms of hyperventilation can lead to greater anxiety and panic. Thus a vicious cycle results, as shown in Figure 1.

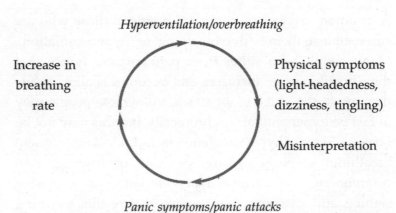

Hyperventilation/overbreathing

Increase in breathing rate

Physical symptoms (light-headedness, dizziness, tingling)

Misinterpretation

Panic symptoms/panic attacks

Figure 1. The connection between hyperventilation and panic symptoms

Misusing alcohol, drugs and medications

I found that if I had a few beers before going out, then I was less likely to have the attacks. Over time, I needed to drink more to control the attacks. I found that I woke up shaky in the morning and I needed to have a drink immediately to calm down. I then lost track whether I was still having panic attacks or just needed another drink.

Bill

One of the most important physical factors contributing to anxiety in panic sufferers is the misuse of alcohol, drugs or other stimulants. People with panic disorder may attempt to comfort themselves by smoking or drinking cups of coffee or strong tea, but in reality they are provoking their nervous systems with strong stimulants. The excessive use of these stimulants can lower the panic threshold and make it more likely that further attacks will occur. Panic attacks also can be triggered or made worse by the use of marijuana, cocaine, amphetamines and other stimulant drugs.

If you suffer from panic attacks it can be very tempting to turn to alcohol and sedative drugs (such as barbiturates) in an attempt to dampen symptoms of panic or to give you the courage to go out. But as many sufferers who have tried this 'cure' will know, the positive effect is only short-lived; excessive alcohol or drug use makes anxiety worse in the long run. As the amount of alcohol you need to control your anxiety increases, so you are more likely to experience withdrawal symptoms (such as the 'shakes') when you are not drinking. Sedative drugs can have the same effects. These withdrawal effects are very similar to symptoms of panic and therefore complicate the underlying anxiety disorder.

As with many of the other contributory factors we have discussed, the relationship between alcohol or drug use and panic disorder is complex. It is important to decide which came first, the anxiety or the alcohol. It may be clear that panic attacks or anxiety symptoms were experienced before heavy drinking began. In such cases, even though alcohol use is a secondary problem, it can cause dependence as well as damaging organs of the body (for example, the liver, stomach and brain), leading to physical illness and psychological problems including anxiety. If, on the other hand, panic symptoms are secondary to alcohol dependence, then the anxiety symptoms will improve when the drinking is brought under control. Even if the anxiety is primary, the alcohol problem may have become entrenched, and if this is the case it will need treatment in its own right, It is rarely possible to overcome panic disorder if alcohol abuse is continuing.

What keeps the vicious cycle going?

Many people have one or two panic attacks in their lives when they are under extreme stress. Although the experience is very unpleasant, it is soon forgotten and does not continue to affect their lives. For some people, though, a self-perpetuating mechanism or vicious cycle is set up which causes panic attacks to recur like a chain reaction. The factors that may cause this reaction can be divided into psycho-logical, social and physical factors.

Psychological factors

As we have already seen, 'fear of fear' and 'fear of illness' can greatly increase the risk that one panic attack may lead to another. In some ways, sufferers and their nervous systems are tricking each other. Initially, a vulnerable person may be under great stress, perhaps from work or home life, so that without being aware of it, she is very close to the tension threshold for triggering a panic attack. A small added stress, such as noise, light, crowding and the frustrations of going shopping, pushes her over that threshold, and she has a panic attack. In other words, the automatic nervous system has been 'fooled' into a state of emergency. It should be remembered that the auto-matic nervous system's responses are crude and primitive, since this mechanism developed very early in human evolution to protect us from wild animals and other obvious dangers. It was not designed to make fine judg-ments about how dangerous a supermarket may be! Once it is triggered, the full fight or flight response occurs, with the automatic nervous system 'assuming' that if the tension level is so high, the situation must be dangerous. Because the actual final stress is only minor, the person is not consciously aware of any immediate danger in the environment. As a result, the person experiencing panic for the first time is bewildered by the powerful impulse to 'fight' or 'run away' and understandably interprets these weird feelings as signs of going mad or losing control. The physical sensations (palpitations, sweating, tingling in the hands and feet) seem to have nothing to do with the environment, so that it is natural for her to think that these feelings must be symptoms of some serious physical or mental illness. It is not surprising that once the early attacks have subsided, sufferers are left with strong lingering fears that they are ill, about to die or experiencing early signs of mental illness. Background factors keep these fears alive and even make them worse. If a person is prone to catastrophic thinking then the fears of imminent death or loss of control will be magnified. Every physical sensation is taken to be a sign that the 'illness' is coming back or getting worse.

The situation is made worse by the powerful conditioning effects of having a fight or flight response in a particular situation. To protect you from future 'danger', your nervous system 'remembers' what the situation was in which the emergency reaction occurred: then it 'warns' you by producing early anxiety symptoms every time you approach that or a similar situation. In this way the vicious cycle of fear, avoidance and agoraphobia is set up.

Some ways of 'coping' with the situation in fact make it worse. Some people may become more pressured in their activities under stress and then manage their time poorly, leading to more pressure and anxiety. Others who have a strong need for approval, and thus find it difficult to say 'no' for fear of rejection, may accept too many tasks to compensate for the difficulties caused by fear and panic attacks, and try to meet too many demands. Again, the result is more pressure and more anxiety. Yet others will tend to avoid 'risky' situations or to give up and retreat once they have had their first few panic attacks. They are likely to withdraw into themselves and become despondent, losing their self-esteem and confidence. Others, by contrast, may be so determined to overcome the problem that they force themselves repeatedly into difficult situations without using appropriate techniques to overcome their anxiety. This leads to an escalation of stress, frustration and the likelihood of having further panic attacks.

Social factors

The social crises that lead to a build-up of tension before the onset of panic disorder may continue after the attacks begin, causing the sufferer continuing and increasing stress. Pressures at work or at home may be longstanding and difficult to resolve. The internal stress (worrying about having another panic attack) adds to the external stress at work or at home, leading to a mounting spiral of tension and creating a high risk of panic attacks recurring. To try to cope with immediate problems at work, suffers may give up their social, leisure and sporting activities. Instead of relaxing and enjoying recreational outings with their spouse, partner or family, they bring work home to try to 'get on top' of the pressure. They may not realize that the increasing pressure they are putting themselves under is actually making it more likely that they will suffer further panic attacks. Once this vicious cycle is established, it becomes difficult for panic sufferers to see clearly whether the stress is coming from 'outside.' or 'inside'.

Physical factors

Bouts of illness such as the flu can mimic anxiety and thus intensify panic symptoms. Viral infections cause fever, sweating, tiredness, light-headedness and weakness, so that it is easy for the sufferer of panic disorder to mistake these symptoms for worsening anxiety. As discussed earlier, it is relatively rare for a serious physical illness to mimic panic disorder, but if any such disease is discovered it should be treated actively.

Most of the physical factors that can lead to panic disorder also may keep it going. The hyperventilation-panic cycle, discussed earlier, can strongly increase the risk of further attacks, especially in a person who remains in a state of worry and stress. Poor general health, loss of fitness and inadequate sleep – often provoked by the stress of having panic attacks – only make the situation worse. A pressured lifestyle increases the risk of overexertion (e.g. running up stairs to get to your office early), producing sensations such as sweating, rapid heart rate and heavy breathing which can be mislabelled as panic, making the sufferer believe that the situation is worse than it really is. In such circumstances the sufferer may try to dampen symptoms or improve performance by using alcohol, drugs or other stimulants. As discussed earlier, the risk of complicating panic disorder by misusing alcohol or drugs cannot be overemphasized.

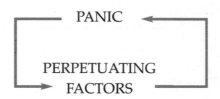

Psychological factors	Social factors	Physical factors
ongoing stress	chronic stress	hyperventilation
poor coping with stress	pressured lifestyle	poor sleep
		overexertion
fear of illness	family tension	poor general health
fear of further panic attacks	reduction in leisure time	alcohol
negative thinking:	social isolation	drugs
• catastrophic thinking		
• loss of sense of control		
• loss of self-esteem and confidence		

Figure 2. What keeps panic disorder going: a summary

4

How can panic disorder and agoraphobia be treated?

There have been impressive advances in the treatment of panic disorder since the early 1980s. Several carefully designed studies, together with the extensive clinical experience of experts, indicate that with guided practice most sufferers of panic disorder should make a good recovery. Most of the studies conducted have investigated people who have full symptoms of panic disorder, with or without agoraphobia, but there is no reason to suspect that sufferers of less intense panic attacks will not benefit from these techniques. Treatments that have been evaluated across the world include both psychological interventions, particularly techniques which fall under the broad heading of *cognitive behavioral therapy*, and medications, especially using drugs called the tricyclics and the minor tranquilizers (or benzodiazepines).

The emphasis in Part Two of this book is on a cognitive behavioral approach to self-management. In this chapter a brief outline of relevant medications is first provided: more details can be sought from your doctor. Then the cognitive behavioral approach to therapy is outlined. Other methods of therapy offered around the world include traditional psychotherapy based on psychoanalytical principles; family and marital therapy; and various newer psychotherapies. Readers who wish to inquire about those approaches should discuss the possibilities with their doctor or local mental health service

Medications

Experts differ somewhat in their views about the use of medication for panic disorder. Several studies have shown that medications such as the minor tranquilizers (known as the benzodiazepines) and the tricyclics (traditionally used to treat depression) are effective in reducing symptoms of panic. Those therapists who are concerned about the use of medications raise the following issues:

- many sufferers do not wish to take medication;
- medications have side-effects which can themselves be upsetting;
- some medications encourage dependence after long use, and the ensuing withdrawal symptoms may mimic anxiety;
- taking medication does not help the sufferer gain control over the problem;
- people may suffer a relapse after they cease taking medication;
- in some cases, medication may interfere with attempts to learn techniques of self-control.

Medications may be useful in the short term, for example where anxiety is very severe, where the person is not in a state to commence practicing anxiety management techniques, or in other circumstances that make it difficult to use psychological treatments. Wherever possible, however, non-drug approaches to treating panic disorder should also be attempted, to lessen the sufferer's need to take medication. Where medication is used, it should be under the direct supervision of an experienced medical practitioner. This will ensure that the dose is carefully monitored, that possible side-effects will be detected and that the drug can be gradually withdrawn over time if appropriate.

Types of medication

Tricyclic medication

Tricyclic medications are a group of drugs that were first introduced to treat depression, but have subsequently been found to be effective in the treatment of several other conditions including panic disorder, obsessive-compulsive disorder and chronic pain. Donald Klein observed that the tricyclic imipramine reduced symptoms of panic disorder, and further studies have confirmed the effectiveness of imipramine and related tricyclic medications in treating panic. These drugs appear to increase the effect of certain natural chemicals in the brain, called neurotransmitters, which transmit signals across nerves. Reactivating these nerve pathways appears to stabilize anxiety.

These medications generally are taken at night, and the dose is increased gradually. Beneficial effects can take between one and three weeks to become apparent. Possible side-effects include sedation (which is why the dose is better taken at night), a dry mouth, blurred vision and, occasionally, dizziness on standing up. Sometimes people with panic disorder notice that they feel jittery and tense when they start to take medication of this type. By building up the dose very gradually, the side-effects can be minimized; and if they do occur, they tend to subside after a few weeks of treatment. Although these drugs are safe for those who are healthy, they may not be suitable for some people suffering from major physical diseases such as heart or kidney problems. Also, there are risks if excessive doses are taken, or if the medication is taken in combination with alcohol or other drugs.

Newer groups of medications used in the treatment of panic disorder which also increase the effects of neurotransmitters in the brain include the SSRIs or selective serotonin reuptake inhibitors (e.g. fluoxetine, paroxetine and sertraline) and the reversible MAOIs or mono-amine oxidase inhibitors (e.g. moclobemide). They tend to be safer for people with physical illnesses than the older drugs and cause fewer side-effects. They are usually taken in the morning since they may cause sleep disturbance in the initial stages of treatment. Other possible side-effects include headaches and nausea, but these tend to subside after the first few weeks. Although these drugs show promise, further studies are needed to confirm that they are useful in panic disorder.

Benzodiazepines or minor tranquilizers

The group of medications called the benzodiazepines are commonly prescribed for panic disorder. The most extensively studied drug in this group for panic disorder is called alprazolam, which is as effective as imipramine. It does have side-effects, of which the most important are sedation and interference with concentration. The main drawbacks of this group of medications are the development of tolerance – in other words, over time the dose may need to be increased to achieve the same effect – their tendency to cause dependence, and the risk of unpleasant effects if the medication is withdrawn too rapidly. These withdrawal effects can mimic panic symptoms, thus discouraging people from attempting to stop taking the medication. Reducing the dose should therefore be monitored closely by an experienced doctor. Many doctors favor using these drugs selectively and for a short period only, with the aim of substituting non-drug methods to control anxiety in the long term.

Other medications

Occasionally, doctors will prescribe a beta-blocker (which is usually used to treat high blood pressure and some other heart problems) to counter some of the physical symptoms of panic, especially tremor and rapid heartbeat. This medication has little effect on the psychological symptoms that occur during a panic attack, although some people find that when the physical symptoms are less prominent they are able to cope more effectively with their attacks.

Buspirone is another agent that has been successfully used to treat various types of anxiety, though most often 'generalized' anxiety rather than panic. As with the anti-depressant medications discussed above, the effect may be delayed, so that the medication needs to be taken for a few weeks to achieve maximum benefit.

Psychological treatments

Several types of psychological approaches are used for the treatment of panic disorder. The techniques outlined in this book are drawn mainly from the principles of cognitive behavioral therapy, since these approaches have been used extensively over the last few decades and researchers have shown convincingly that the methods – if systematically applied – can make a major impact on problems such as panic and agoraphobia. One of the great advantages of these techniques is that they lend themselves well to a self-help approach which emphasizes self-directed practice and methods for exerting self-control over anxiety.

Cognitive behavioral therapy is based on the principles of *learning theory*, which suggests that many behaviors, and the symptoms that they cause, develop as a result of a repeated pattern of responses to conditions in our environment. In other words, we can develop faulty habits in the way we respond to environmental stress, and these learnt behaviors can in themselves lead to symptoms of distress. If these habits can be *learnt*, then it is possible to *unlearn* them and to *relearn* better methods of coping which do not cause distress and difficulties in living. Cognitive behavioral therapy thus offers the sufferer from panic disorder and agoraphobia the possibility of learning by practice and repetition new ways of dealing with difficult situations and the anxieties that they may cause.

As we have already seen, there are several types of learning. Unhelpful learning may lead to habits which produce symptoms of anxiety. Conditioning can occur, so that a particular response such as extreme fear is produced every time you are exposed to a particular situation. For example, if you repeatedly experience panic in a supermarket, then you become conditioned to feel afraid whenever you go into a supermarket, even if you are not actually being threatened. By avoiding the situation, you also avoid the unpleasant emotions associated with fear. The relief you feel further reinforces avoidance of the situation and increases the risk that your agoraphobic symptoms will worsen. Once established, avoidance can be difficult toundo. That is why the method that is used has to be practiced systematically over time. The method is called *gradual exposure* or *systematic desensitization*, and involves approaching feared situations in a step-by-step manner, giving yourself time to allow any feelings of fear and anxiety to settle before leaving. This ensures that *counter-conditioning* occurs: that is, the connection between the situation and the fear response is broken, and instead the situation or place becomes associated increasingly with feeling at ease. Of course, this transition usually takes time and practice to achieve, and over-rapid exposure to feared situations may make the anxiety worse.

That is why the exposure needs to be gradual, starting from the least anxiety-provoking situations to those that cause most fear. Regular practice as part of a systematic program is also important to achieve good results: if the exercises are practiced only occasionally, then there is time for the old habits to strengthen again between attempts.

Our inner thought processes or what are known as *cognitive mechanisms* also play an important role in learning. The *A-B-C* model is useful in understanding this form of learning. *A* refers to the situation, place or event in the outside world, *B* to the way we interpret or think about that event and *C* to our emotional or behavioral response. According to cognitive theory, component *B* is critical to human learning: often it is not the outside event itself that makes us feel depressed or anxious, but the way we interpret that event. We can all see from our own experience that the same event affects people in very different ways. If the boss is in an angry mood, some workers may immediately assume that it is their fault, that they have done something wrong and that they must work harder to mollify the boss. Others may simply shrug and assume that something probably has gone wrong in the boss's private life and that her bad mood has nothing to do with them. Predictably, the first group will become anxious, worried, and guilty, and might work longer hours, whereas the second group will simply continue with their normal work in the expectation that the boss's mood will improve.

Applying cognitive techniques helps us to identify, reconsider and if necessary alter unrealistically negative interpretations of events or situations. Often we make ourselves anxious by 'overpredicting': that is, we anticipate the worst outcome. In other words, even before we enter a situation or place, our thought processes may be warning us that we will become stressed or anxious, or may even have a panic attack. As a result we fear the situation and avoid it. By monitoring and systematically trying to change these negative thoughts, it is possible to reduce the anticipatory anxiety that may build up into a panic attack. Cognitive techniques also allow you to challenge the typical catastrophic thoughts associated with panic, so that it is possible to shorten an attack and to reduce its impact on your emotional state.

Cognitive behavioral therapy therefore allows the sufferer from panic and agoraphobia to recognize and examine exactly how symptoms are produced and to practice systematic methods to prevent or control these symptoms. By approaching the problem from both a cognitive and a behavioral perspective, the sufferer is able to use a combination of techniques to beat the problem.

In summary, the principles guiding recovery involve:

- understanding the nature of panic attacks and panic disorder and the 'fear of fear' and 'fear of illness' cycles;
- learning the skills required to combat the symptoms of panic attacks and anxiety;
- practicing exercises to replace unhelpful or catastrophic thoughts with more helpful ones;
- developing an approach to dealing with bodily

symptoms that trigger anxiety and learning to evaluate more realistically the meaning of those sensations;

• gradually facing the situations previously avoided in order to overcome agoraphobia.

Combination treatment

For some sufferers, a combination of psychological techniques (especially cognitive behavioral approaches) and appropriate medications may be useful. A person who is suffering from severe or frequent panic attacks may have such high levels of anxiety that he is not able to put psychological techniques into practice straight away. In these situations, it may be helpful to consider medication in the short term to reduce the levels of anxiety sufficiently for cognitive behavioral strategies to be applied. It may then be possible to reduce the medication gradually, using cognitive behavioral treatment to maintain improvement.

Will treatment help?

Sufferers from panic disorder may be afraid that they will never recover. This fear in itself can hamper recovery. Fortunately, over 80 per cent of people (some studies indicate even higher rates) report significant and lasting improvement from using cognitive behavioral approaches. In other words, once people with panic disorder learn how to control and then prevent panic attacks, they can remain symptom-free for long periods, often several years. Even if they experience some symptoms at a later stage, these usually are less severe and more easily controlled. So it *is* worthwhile helping yourself by learning to manage your anxiety. You will feel the benefits not only immediately, but for years to come.

5

A short technical note

Although agoraphobia has been recognized for a long time, it was not until 1980 that panic disorder was added to the American classificatory system, the *Diagnostic and Statistical Manual of Mental Disorders*, third edition *(DSM-III)*. Prior to that, panic disorder was considered to be part of 'anxiety neurosis', which included many different types of anxiety.

The definition of panic attacks and panic disorder

The fourth and most recent edition of the *DSM* (*DSM-IV*) requires that at least four of a list of thirteen symptoms be present for a panic attack to be diagnosed (see Table 1). Most sufferers experience more than four symptoms, and the same person may experience different types of symptoms on different occasions. In order to fulfil the criteria for panic disorder, sufferers must have regular panic attacks *and* have a period of at least one month in which they fear having further panic attacks (see Table 2).

The definition of agoraphobia

Panic disorder is classified by the American Psychiatric Association as occurring with or without agoraphobia. The defining features of agoraphobia are set out in Table 3. Some people may suffer from agoraphobia without ever suffering from panic disorder, or they may suffer from some other underlying disorder such as depression.

Table 1: The defining features of panic attacks

A panic attack is a discrete period of intense fear or discomfort in which four (or more) of the following symptoms develop abruptly and reach a peak within ten minutes:

1. Palpitations, pounding heart or accelerated heart rate
2. Sweating
3. Trembling or shaking
4. Sensations of shortness of breath or smothering
5. Feeling of choking
6. Chest pain or discomfort
7. Nausea or abdominal distress
8. Feeling dizzy, unsteady, light-headed or faint
9. Derealization (feelings of unreality) or depersonalization (being detached from oneself)
10. Fear of losing control or going crazy
11. Fear of dying
12. Paresthesias (numbness or tingling sensations)
13. Chills or hot flushes

Source: adapted from American Psychiatric Association, *DSM-IV*, 1994.

Table 2: The defining features of panic disorder

Both (1) and (2) must be present:
1. Recurrent unexpected panic attacks (see Table 1); and
2. At least one of the attacks is followed by one month (or more) of one (or more) of the following:
   (a) persistent concern about having additional attacks;
   (b) worry about the implications of the attack or its consequences (e.g. losing control, having a heart attack, 'going crazy');
   (c) a significant change in behavior related to the attacks.

Source: adapted from American Psychiatric Association, *DSM-IV*, 1994.

Table 3: The defining features of agoraphobia

Anxiety about being in places or situations from which escape might be difficult (or embarrassing) or in which help may not be available in the event of having a panic attack

The situations are avoided or else are endured with marked distress or with anxiety about having a panic attack, or require the presence of a companion

Source: adapted from American Psychiatric Association, *DSM-IV*, 1994.

How common are panic disorder and agoraphobia?

About 10 per cent of the general population experience at least one unexpected panic attack in their lifetime. Although figures vary, approximately 2–6 per cent of the population suffer from panic disorder at some time in their lives. About two-thirds of sufferers are female. About 60 per cent of people with panic disorder also develop agoraphobia.

Most commonly, panic disorder begins in the mid to late twenties, although it can begin at any age. Many sufferers do not seek treatment at all; those who do usually do so in the mid-thirties.

Panic, agoraphobia and other anxiety disorders

Panic attacks can occur in specific situations and be caused by other anxiety disorders. For example, people may develop panic symptoms when exposed to specific objects or situations (spiders, heights, air travel), in which case they are suffering from specific *phobias*. People who suffer from *social phobia* experience intense anxiety when in a situation of scrutiny, for example when eating in public or having to make a speech. People with *obsessive-compulsive disorder* may become very anxious if they see a risk of becoming contaminated, or if they cannot complete their rituals of checking, counting or washing. Those suffering from *post-traumatic stress disorder* following a life-threatening shock may startle easily or become extremely anxious if exposed to reminders of their trauma.

The syndrome known as *generalized anxiety disorder* (GAD) may be associated with panic disorder. GAD is a condition in which a person suffers from anxiety symptoms most of the time and tends to worry excessively or unnecessarily about many things. In its pure form it does not include acute attacks of panic. While there may be a great deal of overlap between the two conditions, most research studies have found differences between them in terms of family history, inheritance patterns and response to specific treatments.

Although all these conditions belong to the 'family' of anxiety disorders, and they may overlap or coexist in the same person, it is worth trying to be accurate in diagnosing which form of anxiety is most prominent. General stress management techniques are valuable in most forms of anxiety, but it is increasingly apparent that specific techniques are most useful for each disorder. In other words, the closer the match between diagnosis and management, the better the outcome.

After working through the self-help program for panic disorder and agoraphobia in Part Two of this book, you may find it useful to gather more information about the treatment of general stress and anxiety symptoms. Refer to the self-help book on stress management in this series, or consult your family doctor or local mental health service for other treatment programs.

PART TWO

Dealing with Panic Attacks: A Self-Help Manual

Introduction

At first, when the attacks started, I thought they would just go away by themselves. When they lasted for a few months, I began to realize that I had to do something about them. I never considered that this would require psychological treatment. The symptoms seemed so physical, like I was having a heart attack or something, and I just wanted a fast cure. I wanted to find a way to stop the attacks immediately.

Lorraine

There are a number of techniques that can be used to control and even eliminate panic attacks. Some sufferers may not be aware that such techniques are available or effective. Others may give up practicing the techniques because they expect immediate results which do not materialize, or because they feel unsupported in their efforts.

A self-help approach

The important message is that it is possible to learn effective skills to manage panic. These skills may be acquired from a self-management book such as this one; for some people, the book may best be used in conjunction with more intensive treatment provided by a professional in mental health. Either way, this book should offer a first step in combating panic attacks and agoraphobia, whether or not further professional help is sought.

Who will benefit from this self-help manual?

Reading this self-help manual should benefit a range of people who are interested in finding out more about panic disorder and agoraphobia. There are broadly four groups of people who should find this book helpful:

1. Those people currently suffering from panic attacks, with or without agoraphobia, who are interested in learning specific skills to combat anxiety. For some, this book may be sufficient on its own to teach them the necessary skills to control panic symptoms and agoraphobia. Those already involved in treatment programs should find that this book is a useful supplement to their individual or group treatments.

2. Those who have suffered from panic attacks in the past and who wish to learn techniques to prevent the symptoms coming back. Detecting early symptoms and knowing how to combat them will help the ex-sufferer to feel confident about preventing relapse.

3. Those who are familiar with the basic principles of anxiety management but who have not incorporated these skills into a structured program. If skills are used in a haphazard manner or without the

necessary practice, they are likely to be less effective. The six-step program outlined in this book provides a systematic method for overcoming and preventing panic attacks.

4. Relatives and friends of sufferers who wish to gain a fuller understanding of panic disorder. People who are close to sufferers often want to help but feel unable to do so because they do not know what to do or what to suggest. Relatives and friends who take an active interest can be very helpful as long as the advice and support they offer are appropriate and constructive.

Who should seek further assistance?

Not all people with symptoms of panic will be helped by this book, and some may need additional assistance. Special attention will be necessary for six groups of people in particular:

1. Those who have any of the rare physical disorders that mimic panic attacks. This manual is designed for the treatment of panic attacks that stem from stress-related psychological factors. In Part One of this book we described a number of medical conditions that (although rare) may produce symptoms similar to panic. If there is any suspicion that you may have one of these conditions you should consult your family doctor.

2. Those suffering from severe agoraphobia, especially if that disorder is unrelated to symptoms of panic.

These people need a thorough assessment and intensive assistance from an experienced mental health professional. This book is intended for people suffering primarily from panic disorder who may or may not have some degree of agoraphobia. If avoidance of situations or places is your main difficulty then you should consult your doctor or your local mental health service for further advice.

3. Those suffering from severe depression associated with panic disorder, who may not have the necessary motivation to work through a self-help book on their own. They may need to seek treatment for their depressive illness before they can start to work actively to combat anxiety symptoms such as panic attacks. Depressed persons may require antidepressant medication to life their mood and to enable them to concentrate enough to embark on this program. A brief guide to the management of depression is provided at the end of the book.

4. Those who lack the confidence to work on their own, who may decide at the outset that a self-help program such as this is not enough. If practice of the suggested techniques is halfhearted, the results will not be satisfactory. If your motivation is low through lack of confidence, working with a therapist may help you to summon up the necessary energy to embark on change.

5. Those who have strong resistance to lifestyle change. In some cases, especially when panic disorder has become entrenched, sufferers may reorganize their

lives to accommodate the problem. The notion that recovery will require a change in lifestyle can seem threatening and may be actively avoided. Panic disorder and agoraphobia can become a way of life which is difficult to overcome. A more thorough review of the motivation to change may be needed, with the help of an expert therapist.

6. Those for whom panic attacks and agoraphobia are only one aspect of wider emotional, social or personality problems. For example, people who respond to stress by misusing drugs or alcohol may need to seek counselling for substance abuse before (or at the same time as) trying to overcome panic disorder. For a person who has panic attacks and is also severely mentally disturbed, for example in a state of severe depression or psychosis, this book will be of little use and the help of a mental health professional should be sought.

Early hurdles to self-management

Understanding the factors that may undermine efforts at self-help can be helpful in overcoming these obstacles.

Fear of change

The six-step programme that follows this chapter recommends ways of changing those elements of your life that cause and perpetuate panic attacks and agoraphobia. For many people, these changes in lifestyle and daily routine may seem daunting. It may seem safer to keep things as they are – indeed, the very thought of change may cause a temporary increase in anxiety! It is important to confront the reality that although limitations in your lifestyle – like avoiding going to the city or taking a train – may make your life more 'comfortable,' in the long term such restrictions are very disabling.

Lack of support

Sometimes, friends or relatives whom you tell of your intention to pursue a self-help program may be discouraging. Occasionally, others may be dismissive and express disbelief that a book can help. Relatives may be overly cautious or protective. Those close to you may be fearful of any changes that they may have to make in their own lifestyles once your condition starts to improve. Whatever the reason for their lack of support, it is important to realize that the choice to change is an individual decision that you make for yourself. Although it is helpful to elicit the support of friends and family, it is not critical to your success that you obtain the support of everyone around you before you start putting this self-help program into practice.

Making a commitment to change

As a first step, it may be useful for you to consider the potential benefits and drawbacks of overcoming panic attacks and agoraphobia. Making a list and rating each item from -10 to +10 in terms of its importance in improving lifestyle may help to focus your thinking on the reasons for making changes. A minus score indicates a negative impact of making a lifestyle change; a score of 0 indicates 'no effect on lifestyle' or a 'neutral' effect of making a change; and a plus score indicates a beneficial effect. An example of this exercise is shown in Table 1.

Table 1: Working out the benefits of change			
Benefits of change	Impact on lifestyle (-10 to +10)	Consequence of no change	Impact on lifestyle (-10 to +10)
Able to go to supermarket alone	+7	Have to wait for friend/mother to go out with me	-3
Able to find a job	+9	Forced to stay at home and watch TV	-5
Able to go to the movies with friends	+5	Have to wait for DVD version to be released	-4
Could throw a dinner party	+8	Can't socialize with groups of friends	-4

Listing the benefits of change in this way gives you a reminder of why it is so important to overcome panic attacks and agoraphobia. Rereading your list may also help you when, at times, the effort to change seems too great, or if there have been temporary setbacks in your program.

Overcoming panic attacks must be regarded as a worthwhile and necessary pursuit, as important as any other commitment, such as pursuing a career, studying for a diploma or caring for your family. People who want to overcome panic attacks and agoraphobia may wish for an immediate 'magic cure' or a 'fast-acting pill' that will get rid of their anxiety symptoms immediately. If it were that easy, then you would not be reading this book! In reality, beating panic disorder and/or agoraphobia requires time, some hard work and a determination to succeed. If you are prepared to treat each small success as a step towards overcoming the problem, and if you accept that there may be small setbacks along the way, then you eventually will succeed.

Dealing with setbacks

Setbacks may occur in any treatment program. At the beginning it can be difficult to control all sources of stress and all triggers of panic attacks. Sometimes a number of small stresses occur in rapid succession, making it difficult to implement the intended changes to your daily life. A single major life event, such as the death of a family member or a serious illness in a close friend, may result in a recurrence of panic attacks and agoraphobia. There are also particular times in people's lives when setbacks are more likely to occur. For example, overwork, poor sleep or a viral infection may cause anxiety symptoms to flare up. If these stresses occur before anxiety management skills have been mastered it becomes harder to control symptoms.

The way in which these minor setbacks are dealt with can make a great impact on long-term progress. You may feel totally demoralized by a minor setback and decide that it is useless to go on with the program; you may then give up trying and resign yourself to becoming increasingly agoraphobic and dependent on the people around you. On the other hand, you may decide that minor setbacks provide the opportunity to practice your anxiety management skills in new situations, and thus learn to regard new forms of stress as a challenge rather than as a catastrophe.

The urge to quit

For most people, there will be several moments during this program when they feel like quitting. Falling back on the same safe routines, however restrictive they are, may seem more comfortable than keeping up the effort required to change.

If you are faced with the urge to quit, try one or more of the following:

- reading through your 'benefits of change' table (see Table 1) to remind yourself that it is worth continuing;
- talking to a close, supportive friend or family member about the benefits of overcoming anxiety, again to remind yourself of the reasons for continuing with the self-help program;
- accepting that a break in the program is not a disaster and being willing to return to an earlier step when you feel ready to begin again;
- recognizing that you may have tried to progress through the program too rapidly and that you have not had enough time to practice the skills introduced

in the earlier stages; slowing down progress from one step to the next may help consolidate what you have learnt;
- visualizing or imagining a panic-free lifestyle and all the activities that then will become possible to rediscover the incentive to continue.

Self-questions that undermine your efforts

You may find you ask yourself the same self-defeating questions over and over again, thereby undermining your confidence. It is worth considering some of these at the outset.

Why can't I just stop panicking?

This question is asked regularly by people with panic disorder. Although the first panic attack may have occurred out of the blue, it is important to realize that the stresses that eventually led to the onset of panic attacks may have been building up over several months or even years. Your body's physiological processes have been adapting gradually as your levels of tension have been rising. Once the 'habit' of triggering panic has set in, it takes time to reset the body's mechanisms to a normal level, where the prevailing degree of tension is not so close to the 'fight or flight' trigger. Thus a process of physical 'realignment' must occur; you cannot just 'decide' not to panic any more.

The expectation that panic attacks can be stopped simply by willpower places unnecessary pressure on the sufferer to get better quickly. Sheer effort of will without the skills to apply the necessary techniques unfortunately does not automatically guarantee success. Such expectations of immediate recovery lead people to become disappointed and to blame themselves, creating additional pressure. This added pressure may fuel further panic attacks and create more feelings of demoralization.

Nearly everyone who has had a panic attack remembers what the first episode felt like, even years later. It is a powerful experience that usually sensitizes sufferers to any sensations that remind them of that first attack. Trying to forget the initial experience of panic is difficult and unhelpful. It is more important to place those memories in the past, where they are no longer threatening.

Repeated panic attacks undermine self-confidence, so that after a series of attacks you become unsure of yourself and worry about embarrassing yourself in front of others. Previously easy tasks such as driving through heavy traffic, waiting for a bus or buying tickets to a movie become major ordeals. Many sufferers find themselves having to rely excessively on other people; or they may feel isolated and incompetent. Regaining self-confidence usually takes time and patience as you slowly attempt to overcome your anxiety in different situations. As with most practical tasks, some attempts will be successful while some may be disappointing. Eventually, as more tasks are successfully accomplished, self-confidence will improve, but the process is a gradual one.

Why am I different?

You may notice that your relationships with people close to you have changed since you began to have panic attacks. Unfortunately, some of these changes may not be healthy or satisfying. Sufferers may notice that their partners, children or friends treat them differently because they cannot leave the house or participate in social activities without experiencing distress. Some friends may even desert them. Relatives may offer simple and thoughtless 'advice', or even try to bully sufferers into overcoming their anxiety and avoidance behavior. After anxiety and panic attacks have subsided, some former sufferers notice that their relationships with others have not changed accordingly: that is, other people continue to treat them as if they were still suffering from panic disorder. This may be especially so if they have reorganized aspects of their own lifestyles to accommodate the sufferer. Re-educating friends and family to behave differently may take time and patience.

Not all the after-effects of suffering from panic disorder are negative. Often, people who have suffered from panic disorder and agoraphobia are more sensitive to other people's distress and tension and better able to understand the difficulties and anxieties that others may experience. They are usually able to suggest helpful techniques and skills to assist those around them to control anxiety.

Many of the skills used to overcome panic attacks and agoraphobia can be applied to other stress-related problems. These skills can be a sound investment for dealing with other stressful events that may occur later in life.

About the self-help program

The program outlined in this manual is designed to provide the basic skills necessary to control panic attacks and to overcome agoraphobia. Several years of research and clinical experience have shown that the techniques outlined here are effective. Not all the skills presented will be appropriate for everyone, but most people will find at least some of them helpful. It is best to reserve judgment as to whether each step will be of benefit to you until you have practiced the techniques for some time. Like most skills, anxiety management techniques take time to learn, and the benefits may not be apparent immediately.

It is possible for most people to work through this manual in six to eight weeks. This is only a rough guide since it is most important to work through the six steps systematically and not to progress to the next step until the previous ones have been practiced and mastered. Some people may need longer than a few weeks. It is important not to work through the program as fast as possible but to understand the techniques and to practice the skills, no matter how long it takes.

How to use this manual

The best approach to using this manual is first to skim through the six steps, getting an idea of the skills and tasks involved. This will make the whole program less formidable and should reduce anxiety about what may lie ahead. Once you have familiarized yourself with the manual in this way, then work through each of the six steps in turn, first reading right through the step before attempting the tasks or exercises suggested. Make sure you have grasped each step and are comfortable practicing the techniques it introduces before moving on to the next step. When you have worked through the six steps systematically, you may want to reread the manual to reinforce the skills you have learnt.

Recruiting a helper

You may wish to get a friend or relative to help you through the six-step program. This can be a good way to make sure that you practice the skills and to keep you motivated to work through the book. A reliable helper can support you through those difficult times when you may be tempted to give up, or become temporarily discouraged. He or she can also help you to acknowledge your successes, especially when you may not recognize them as significant achievements yourself. On the other hand, there will come a point when you need to carry out tasks independently to achieve full recovery. This needs to be recognized by you and your helper in advance, and you will need to discuss the issue with each other regularly so that the point of independence is not delayed.

Step 1. Recognizing when you are anxious and identifying panic triggers
(learning accurately to monitor physical and psychological symptoms of panic and sources of stress)

Step 2. Lifestyle factors that may be contributing to anxiety and panic attacks
(changing aspects of lifestyle to reduce the likelihood of panic attacks occurring)

Step 3. Controlling panic attacks
(learning techniques to control and eliminate panic attacks)

Step 4. Changing unhelpful thinking styles
(identifying, challenging and learning to change negative thinking styles)

Step 5. Reducing sensitivity to physical sensations
(learning not to be fearful of 'normal' physical sensations)

Step 6. Putting these skills into practice
(overcoming agoraphobia and establishing a new lifestyle)

Figure 1. The six steps of the self-help program outlined in this manual

The six steps

The six steps outlined in this self-help program are as follows.

In **Step 1** you will get to know your particular stress symptoms and to identify the 'triggers' that set off your panic attacks. It focuses on learning to monitor symptoms so that you will be able to distinguish between actual anxiety symptoms and those symptoms that seem like anxiety but are really due to other factors.

Step 2 focuses on lifestyle factors that may be increasing the risk of panic attacks. In particular, it examines the importance of diet, exercise, sleep and relaxation to your psychological health.

Step 3 introduces some specific techniques to control panic attacks and other anxiety symptoms when they occur. Being able to control these symptoms will increase your self-confidence and should enable you to tackle situations that you may have been avoiding.

Step 4 considers the negative thinking patterns that may be contributing to anxiety symptoms. There is little doubt that our attitude to and thoughts about ourselves, our bodily sensations and outside events can influence the way we feel and behave. By changing some of these attitudes, it is possible to change the way we feel about ourselves, our lives and our feelings, thus influencing the levels of anxiety and stress we experience.

Step 5 examines the way in which physical sensations trigger fearful thinking and thus increase the risk of further panic. Labelling physical sensations more accurately helps to reduce this tendency.

Step 6, the last step in the program, focuses on applying skills in a wide range of situations to overcome agoraphobia and to establish a healthy lifestyle. Learning to control anxiety and to overcome panic disorder means more than just keeping symptoms at bay: it eventually means enjoying your life to the full and not focusing constantly on the fear of having another panic attack.

A review section at the end of each step will help you to monitor your improvement and to set the pace for further progress. You may need to re-read certain sections or re-attempt some exercises before you progress to the next step.

Some advice about eliminating anxiety symptoms

Before you start working through the six steps, it may be helpful to consider the following points. You may also find it useful to read this section again as you work through each of the six steps.

Normal anxiety and panic

This program is aimed at helping you to stop having panic attacks in situations such as shopping, driving or waiting your turn at a bank; but remember that there are some situations where sensations identical to panic are entirely normal. For example, some fairground rides such as the roller-coaster or Big Dipper excite people by stimulating feelings which are very similar to panic but which are enjoyable – for some! Heightened tension is also normal and indeed necessary to ensure that you perform at your best in testing situations such as during examinations or while giving a talk. And if you were to stand in front of an oncoming truck you would experience symptoms of arousal and fear which would be normal – and part of the 'fight or flight response' discussed earlier. Even after you have mastered all the techniques for controlling panic attacks and eliminating anxiety symptoms, some situations will still evoke these powerful emotions. It is worth bearing this in mind: your goal is not to eliminate anxiety completely. It is important to set realistic goals for yourself in managing your anxiety and in overcoming panic attacks.

Preventing anxiety and panic attacks from developing

Most people find that it is easier to stop a panic attack when it is in its early stages than to try to bring it to an end when it is already in full swing.

At the first sign of panic, it is important to apply the techniques you have learnt without delay. In time and with regular practice, these skills will come into play almost automatically, so that controlling the symptoms before they escalate becomes increasingly easier.

A final note

I kept surprising myself how easy it was to do the things that I previously feared. There were so many changes in my lifestyle once I started going out again. I could drive around, visit my friends, pick up the kids from school and go shopping. Best of all, I could start looking for a job, something I've always wanted to do but couldn't consider because of my panic attacks. My relationship with my husband has improved because we don't fight like we used to about my reliance on him. I've even started going out to the club with my girlfriends every Wednesday night. I really feel like I am living again.

Joan

At all times, try to keep in mind that you are embarking on this program for yourself, for your future lifestyle and for the people you care about. There may be several times during the program when you feel like giving up. When these low periods occur, try to keep in mind all the positive changes to your lifestyle and to your relationships that overcoming panic disorder and agoraphobia will deliver.

Step 1

Recognizing when you are anxious and identifying panic triggers

It may seem strange to have to learn about symptoms of anxiety when you have suffered from them for a long time. Most people assume that they can tell the difference between symptoms of anxiety and those caused by physical illness, but many in fact confuse the two. For example, people who suffer from panic attacks often assume that pains in their chest or shortness of breath mean that they are suffering from a physical illness. Though they find it difficult to believe, these symptoms could be caused by anxiety. Also, anxiety symptoms can occur without our being aware of the stresses that give rise to them, seeming to come 'out of the blue', and this can reinforce the belief that they are caused by physical illness.

In panic disorder, especially, it is common for people to think they are suffering from heart disease, a stroke or a brain tumour because of symptoms such as tightness in the chest, difficulty in breathing or strange feelings of unreality. People who suffer from panic attacks may have undergone several physical checkups, cardiac stress tests and numerous blood tests in an attempt to detect a physical cause for their symptoms. It is not uncommon for people suffering from panic attacks to be admitted to hospital for a suspected heart attack.

Pinpointing the symptoms of panic

How, then, do you know when you are experiencing symptoms of panic rather than a physical illness? When health professionals make a diagnosis, they do so by identifying several symptoms that are known to occur together in a regular pattern. In the same way, we tend to recognize our emotions according to a regular pattern of experiences. For example, the emotion of anger is associated with flushing of the face, tension in the jaw, shallow breathing and hostile thoughts. When we feel depressed, we may notice changes such as poor concentration, preoccupation with pessimistic thoughts, disturbed sleep and lack of energy. Of course, no one experiences feelings in exactly the same way or with the same intensity as anyone else. Sometimes the pattern may vary slightly even for the same individual. Nevertheless, when an emotional state develops into a serious problem, the particular pattern of symptoms is sufficiently consistent for a diagnosis to be made.

As an exercise, try describing to yourself the general pattern of symptoms that you have experienced in the past when you felt despondent or depressed.

Your pattern of symptoms when you are depressed:

1.

2.

3.

4.

5.

Extending this exercise to anxiety, we can examine the common patterns of symptoms that people experience when they are stressed or anxious. Once again, it is important to remember that not everyone is the same and that each person will experience a slightly different pattern of symptoms.

Think back to the last time you had symptoms of panic and, in the spaces below, list the major symptoms that you experienced.

Your major symptoms of panic:

1.

2.

3.

4.

5.

Once you have completed the list, try to recall the last three times when you experienced that group of symptoms. On each occasion, did you think you were suffering from a physical illness at the time? Were you baffled by the symptoms, or did you immediately recognize that they were a result of anxiety? The next time you experience these symptoms, try to remember that they are symptoms of anxiety rather than an indication of serious physical illness.

Identifying and monitoring panic triggers

It is worth monitoring your panic attacks over the course of this program so that you can identify major panic triggers. Keep a diary of your panic attacks, noting when and where each attack happens and what the trigger seemed to be, and giving each attack a rating between 0 and 10, where 0 indicates 'minimal symptoms' and 10 indicates the 'worst possible symptoms'. You may also find it useful to rate your level of coping with each panic attack, again using a rating scale from 0 to 10, where 0 indicates the 'poorest level of coping' and 10 your 'best or most effective level of coping'. An example of a few entries in such a diary is given in Figure 2.

Common situations where panic attacks are likely to occur are when driving a car, taking public transport, visiting a busy shopping centre or attending a social function. You may find that there are other situations that are regularly stressful for you.

Date	Situation	Anxiety symptoms (0–10)	Coping (0–10)
4 May	At sister's house with her family	7	4 Had to leave the room
12 May	Waiting In line at the bank	8	2 Left the bank in a hurry
6 June	Taking the dog for a walk	5	6 Managed to complete the walk
10 June	Speaking to my mother on the telephone. I felt criticized	6	7 Continued talking but could not concentrate

Figure 2. Example of diary entries monitoring panic attacks

You also may find that your anxiety is very specific: for example, you may become anxious in the company of some but not all acquaintances.

Use the 'monitoring from for panic attacks' given here to monitor your panic attacks over the next few weeks. (Extra blank copies of this form, and of the other forms used in later steps of the program, are printed at the back of the book.) If you wish, you can add another column and write down how you would have liked to have coped with each particular situation. When rating your level of anxiety, it is important to recognize the normal range of anxiety. Some situations are anxiety-provoking for most people. For example, having to attend a job interview or to give a speech are two situations where some degree of anxiety is to be expected. It may help to discuss your level of anxiety with someone else so that you develop a realistic picture of the types of situations that cause most people to become anxious.

Common sources of anxiety for people with panic disorder

When you describe situations in which you feel anxious, try to be as specific as possible. This will help you to pinpoint particular types of situations that seem to trigger panic attacks. You will probably find that a number of situations can be grouped together because they share certain characteristics or trigger particular fears. Some of these common features are listed below. See how many you can identify as relevant to you and your anxiety symptoms.

Monitoring form for panic attacks

Date	Situation	Anxiety symptoms (0–10)	Coping (0–10)

- *Escape not possible* For many people suffering from panic disorder, the feeling that they cannot escape easily from a situation can trigger intense anxiety symptoms and panic attacks. These situations typically involve crowded places such as shopping centres, sports stadiums or restaurants.

- *Embarrassment* People with panic attacks may be particularly sensitive to others noticing their symptoms of distress. Once you have started experiencing panic symptoms, feeling under scrutiny can add another source of anxiety. Sometimes this extra 'laycr' of anxiety is enough to trigger off a full-blown panic attack.

- *Help not available* People with panic disorder need to feel that 'help' is close by in case they have a panic attack. Some find that their anxiety subsides when they are with people whom they trust, or when they are close to places where they can obtain help, such as a hospital or a doctor's surgery.

- *'Going crazy'* Sometimes people believe that when they start to suffer a panic attack the symptoms will get worse and worse until they faint, 'go crazy' or suffer from a heart attack. These catastrophic thoughts add to the experience of anxiety and tend to worsen the symptoms, thereby prolonging the attack or triggering another attack.

- *Losing control* Having a panic attack understandably makes sufferers feel that they are losing control. This fear may be extended to believing that they are about to lose control over their behavior, that they may run amok, hurt someone or act in a bizarre and embarrassing way. Some situations, like crowded places, intensify this fear because there are people around who would witness such behavior. In reality, panic sufferers do not harm others or act dangerously, but the fear of this, along with the fear of embarrassment noted above, can make the sufferers particularly anxious about certain situations.

Use the checklist below to identify the triggers of anxiety that make your symptoms worse in particular situations and that increase the likelihood of experiencing a panic attack. Perhaps you can think of other repetitive fears or worries that you have whenever you feel anxious; if so, list them on a separate sheet of paper and use the same format to pinpoint which situations are more likely to trigger such thoughts.

Checklist for monitoring situations that trigger common fears

Situation	Escape not possible	Embarrass- ment	Help not available	Going crazy/fear of collapse
_____	☐	☐	☐	☐
_____	☐	☐	☐	☐
_____	☐	☐	☐	☐
_____	☐	☐	☐	☐
_____	☐	☐	☐	☐

Identifying and monitoring agoraphobic symptoms

You may find that you are actually avoiding situations or are entering certain situations only with great reluctance because of your anxiety. What are some of the situations or activities that you have been avoiding? List all those situations or activities in the checklist below. When you have completed the list, rate each of these situations or activities in terms of the difficulty you experience approaching or entering them. Once again, you may wish to use a '0' to '10' scale where '0' indicates 'no anxiety' or 'no difficulty and '10' indicates 'extreme anxiety' or 'severe difficulty'.

Checklist for monitoring situations or activities that you may be avoiding

Situation	Anxiety rating (0–10)
_____	☐
_____	☐
_____	☐
_____	☐
_____	☐
_____	☐

Review of Step 1

After monitoring your panic attacks and avoidance behavior for a few days, you should be able to see particular patterns emerging. Identifying these patterns will help you to focus on applying your anxiety management skills to problematic situations. Ultimately, this will help you to overcome panic attacks and agoraphobia.

- At the beginning of the chapter, you were asked to write down your own pattern of symptoms when you become depressed. Next you were asked to write down your pattern of symptoms when you become anxious. Could you detect a specific pattern of symptoms? Can you list all the symptoms you experience? Next time you experience some or all of these symptoms, try to say to yourself 'these sensations probably mean that I am anxious' rather than jumping to the conclusion that you are suffering from a serious physical illness, going 'crazy', or are about to collapse.

- The second exercise aimed to identify what types of situations and associated fears are likely to trigger panic attacks. Have you noticed that your panic attacks tend to occur at particular times of the day or night? Are there particular situations that are more difficult for you than others? By monitoring your panic attacks, you will be able to focus on some of the factors that may be contributing to your anxieties. For example, if you tend to have panic attacks at the end of the day, it may be that tiredness is playing an important role. If you tend to have attacks at night, you may find that you are dwelling on the day's worries before you go to sleep, or that you are drinking too much coffee before going to bed. Withdrawl symptoms from alcohol misuse could also be a factor.

- The third exercise aimed at helping you become aware of the situations that could worsen your symptoms. You were asked to note the situations which are most likely to trigger fearful thinking. Do you tend to have specific fears and worries in certain situations? What are they? Ways of overcoming these fears and worries will be discussed in detail in Step 4; however, it is helpful to become aware of them early in the program so that you can begin to confront them.
- Exercise four was about monitoring agoraphobic avoidance and rating the severity of your symptoms in those situations. Rating your response in this way will enable you to set realistic targets in trying to confront your fears. By working through the list slowly, from easiest to most difficult, over the course of this program you will gradually be able to overcome your avoidance of those situations.

Try to make a fixed time each week to review your progress and your monitoring forms. Make sure that you are using all these monitoring forms for at least one week before moving on to Step 2, which focuses on lifestyle factors that may be contributing to your panic attacks.

Step 2

Changing lifestyle factors that contribute to panic attacks

Life stress and anxiety: a vicious cycle

A stressful lifestyle can contribute to anxiety symptoms and panic attacks in susceptible people. Most people who suffer from panic attacks can recall several stressful incidents in their lives just before the attacks began. Some of these stresses may continue or worsen with the onset of panic attacks. Problems in any area of life become much more difficult to solve when you are suffering from panic symptoms. Thus you may face a vicious cycle in which life stress makes panic worse and vice versa. For example, if the problem you face relates to your work, then you may respond by working longer hours, skipping meals and neglecting to take exercise. This attempt to 'solve' the backlog in work commitments may instead increase your susceptibility to panic attacks. Or you may find that arguments or difficulties with a spouse or partner have arisen since you began to have panic attacks. Once again a vicious cycle of anxiety symptoms may be set up, as the added relationship stress leads to a worsening of panic attacks, and that puts more pressure on the relationship. The stress may be increased by poor sleep and insufficient time being reserved for leisure and relaxation, raising your level of tension even further.

These everyday stresses can hamper your recovery from panic disorder, especially if you do not have the skills to handle or control your symptoms. Furthermore, if your lifestyle itself is stressful because of poor diet, lack of recreational time or disturbed sleep, then it is likely that your recovery will be slower. On the other hand, you cannot avoid all sources of stress while you recover from panic disorder. A more realistic goal may be to solve problems where you can and to learn how to rid yourself of unnecessary tension by increasing your resilience to life stresses which cannot be fully resolved. A note on problem-solving is added at the end of Step 6.

Step 2 is about building up your resilience to everyday stresses such as those described above. It focuses on simple lifestyle changes that may help to lower your vulnerability to panic attacks, concentrating on four major areas of lifestyle: exercise, nutrition, sleep and relaxation. All four areas are vital in reducing anxiety and in overcoming panic attacks.

Types of stress: the mind–body link

It is useful to divide the common sources of stress into two categories:

- The first type of stress is 'mental stress', which is characterized by fears and worries. You may worry excessively about work, family or friends; or your worries may focus on having another panic attack, coping with public transport, or waiting in line.

- The second type of stress is called 'physical stress', since it relates to your physical health. If your diet is poor and you sleep badly and take too little exercise, then you are placing your body under physical stress. This form of stress can make people more susceptible to fatigue, minor illnesses and irritability. Being 'run down' or physically unfit can make you more vulnerable to other stresses and therefore more likely to suffer from such symptoms as tiredness, headaches and muscle tension.

Because the mind and body are so closely linked, any symptoms of physical ill-health can 'feed back' in a circular fashion resulting in mental ill-health as illustrated in Figure 3. For example, if you are feeling run down and have not slept well for several days, you are more likely to experience poor concentration and irritability. This in turn can affect your self-esteem and confidence, ultimately worsening feelings of anxiety or depression. For some, this kind of physical stress may be enough to trigger panic attacks.

BODY
(symptoms include stomach upsets,
muscle tension and headaches)

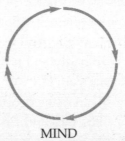

MIND
(symptoms include fears and worries,
poor self-esteem and loss of confidence)

Figure 3. The stress cycle

You may have noticed that after an episode of flu or another physical illness you experience a short period of feeling 'down', exhausted or stressed. This is to be expected, especially if you have not taken enough time off from your usual chores to recover fully. We often have to learn to make time for ourselves, to look after our physical and mental health, and to do so can be a challenge in itself.

Recognizing the link between the mind and body can be helpful in preparing to reduce your levels of stress. Just as chronic physical fatigue can make you more vulnerable to stress, so improving your physical health can make you more resistant to stressful situations. Many people notice that after a good night's sleep followed by a healthy and nutritious breakfast they are able to perform much more effectively in completing their daily chores, whether at home or at work. Similarly, we tend to find that it is difficult to concentrate or apply ourselves efficiently if we are short of sleep or hungry.

Targeting your physical health

As noted above, four main areas of physical stress are targeted in this chapter (exercise, nutrition, sleep and relaxation). You may find that one or several are particularly relevant to you in reducing your vulnerability to stress.

Exercise

Exercising regularly can increase our mental tolerance of stressful situations. Exercise can be a good way of 'working off' tension and boredom, especially if you are spending most of your day at a desk or sitting down in one spot. People who are physically fit also tend to sleep better than those who have not been taking regular exercise. Exercise also can be a good way to meet people or to broaden your daily activities. Joining an exercise club or gym, going for a swim or playing tennis are all ways of becoming fit. Mixing with a new group of people also can take your mind off your worries and concerns, and may help you to direct your attention away from your anxiety symptoms.

Individuals, of course, differ in their physical make-up, in their level of stamina and in the types of exercise they enjoy. Sometimes, exercising with a friend can be both enjoyable and helpful, especially on those days when your motivation may be low. Others enjoy exercising alone. When starting to exercise, make sure you choose a program that you enjoy rather than one that you only carry out as a sense of duty. If you cannot think of any particular exercise you enjoy, think back to when you were younger and probably fitter. What exercises did you enjoy when you were at school? What exercises did you enjoy as a young adult?

If you have not been exercising regularly, avoid over-exerting yourself. Start off with a few minutes of walking every day, then build this up to longer periods of light exercise. If you have not exercised for several months, have a medical check-up before you begin an exercise program.

The following points may help you establish and maintain an exercise routine:

- choose an exercise that you enjoy;
- make sure that you have the right equipment and clothing;
- start with light exercises and only gradually work up to more vigorous ones;
- exercise with a friend if that suits you;
- try to exercise every day or every other day at the same time: establish a routine;
- reward yourself for exercising during the first two weeks if you are just beginning;
- be tolerant of disruptions to your exercise routine: go back to your exercise plan as soon as possible.

Once you notice your fitness level and tolerance level increasing together, of course, this will help to keep you motivated!

People with panic disorder worry that exercise might bring on some of their panic symptoms. While it is likely that exercise will make you feel hot and flushed, raise your breathing and heart rate, and cause you to perspire, it is important to remember that these are normal reactions associated with physical activity. So although these sensations may remind you of having a panic attack, remember that they are not anxiety-related since they have occurred in the context of physical activity. It is helpful to label these physical sensations as healthy, natural bodily responses to exercise.

If you feel hesitant about starting an exercise program, try some very light exercise, like slow walking, every day. Even this will increase your fitness level, and as you become fitter you may notice that you do not feel breathless so often, and are less aware of an increased heart rate. When you feel more confident about your level of fitness, you may then embark on a more vigorous exercise program. Remember that gentle regular exercise is far better than no exercise at all.

Anxiety about leaving the house may limit your choice of exercise at first, especially if you suffer from agoraphobia. If this applies to you, you could ask a friend or member of the family to accompany you; or if this is not possible, you could do some exercise at home until you have built up your confidence to the level where you are ready to leave the house.

Nutrition and Drugs

Physical health, as we have already seen, is closely linked with mental health. Eating sensibly according to your body's needs is a first step in combating stress. If your eating is usually erratic, try to ensure that you have regular meals so that you do not experience wide swings in blood sugar levels. Major fluctuations in blood sugar levels can produce symptoms similar to those of anxiety.

Drinking too much coffee, tea or cola drinks, or eating too much chocolate or foods with high levels of caffeine or other stimulants, can make you feel 'hyped up' and increase the risk of panic attacks. It is not always necessary to drink a lot of tea or coffee to have this effect: if you are one of the few people who are sensitive to even small quantities of these stimulants, you will feel the effect after even moderate amounts.

Nicotine is a powerful stimulant that can increase anxiety. If you smoke, giving up can have a marked beneficial impact on your physical and mental health. If you are a heavy smoker and choose to give up, try to get help from a health professional. He or she can give you a withdrawal program designed to avoid unpleasant symptoms which could worsen your anxiety.

We have already seen how important alcohol can be in provoking panic attacks. Monitoring your alcohol intake and ensuring that you are drinking well below the recommended level for your sex and weight are critical to recovery from panic disorder. Current recommended maximum levels are two standard drinks a day for women and four standard drinks a day for men. (One standard drink equals one glass of wine, one bar measure of spirits or half a pint of beer.)

To summarize, try to establish a healthy diet by following these guidelines:

- make sure you are eating enough fruit and vegetables;
- drink plenty of fluids, especially water, throughout the day;
- if you are trying to lose weight, aim to do so gradually; avoid crash diets and fasting;
- eat regular meals and try not to go for long periods without food;
- try to limit the amount of coffee and tea you drink;
- keep your alcohol consumption below the recommended limit for your sex and weight;
- if you are a smoker, consider quitting with the assistance of a health professional;
- avoid stimulant or mood-altering drugs unless they are prescribed by your doctor.

Sleep

Most people require between seven and nine hours of sleep every night. Some people can make do with less, while others may need more in order to function well. Even members of the same family may have very different sleep requirements. Lack of sleep (or too much sleep) can make you tired, irritable and less able to cope with the demands of daily living. People also differ from one another as to whether they function better in the mornings or in the evenings. Some people find that they can concentrate or work best late at night, others that they work better in the early morning. Individuals also differ in how deeply they sleep. While some may enjoy a long stretch of unbroken sleep, others may have to get up regularly to go to the bathroom or to have a drink during the night: yet both groups may report 'a good night's sleep'. Some people sleep more soundly than others who awaken at every slight sound in the house. Some toss and turn in their sleep, while others hardly move at all throughout the night.

Sleep cycles of this nature are thought to be 'inbuilt', so that trying to alter them substantially, although it is possible, often is difficult to accomplish in the short term. The important point here is that each of us has our own individual sleep habits. There are no fixed 'rules' about the right time to go to bed, how deep your sleep should be, or the number of hours that you need to sleep. What is important is whether

Date	Sleep rating	Problem area(s)
June 3	6	Awakened by a loud storm outside; afraid of thunder and lightning
June 4	4	Had too much to drink the night before
June 5	2	Worried about work, couldn't fall asleep

Figure 4. Example of a sleep diary

you feel refreshed after waking up. If you do not, then you may need to examine your sleep pattern more closely. For example, do you have difficulty falling asleep or staying asleep? Do you suffer from repeated nightmares or sudden awakenings at night? Do you wake too early in the morning? If the answer is 'yes' to any of these questions, you may need to keep a 'sleep diary' which will help you pinpoint the precise problem.

An example of a sleep diary is provided in Figure 4. Following this pattern, each morning write down how refreshed you feel, rating this feeling on a ten-point scale where 0 is 'extremely unrefreshed' and 10 is 'very refreshed'. You will also need to jot down the problem areas so that you can work out how to deal with them in order to improve the quality of your sleep.

There are some basic strategies we can use to improve our chances of sleeping well. You may already have discovered your own personal way of ensuring a refreshing night's sleep; some of the more common remedies are:

- try not to engage in any vigorous activity or tasks needing intense concentration in the hour before going to bed;
- have a relaxing warm bath or shower before bedtime;
- drink a glass of warm milk before going to bed (*not* coffee);
- try to avoid alcohol just before bedtime;
- listen to music or engage in a relaxing activity before bedtime;

- try to 'switch off the day's worries and stresses: you can think about them the next morning;
- use a relaxation exercise or tape (see section on 'Relaxation' below).

Relaxation

Taking time for relaxation and enjoyable activities is important to maintaining a sense of well-being. Finding some time every week simply to enjoy ourselves is necessary to allow us to unwind and recharge our batteries.

We all differ in what we find enjoyable. Meditation may be the best way to relax for some, while for others going to a movie may be an effective distraction. Others may enjoy going to the beach, gardening or fishing. Some people may prefer to engage in leisure activities for a short period in every day, while others prefer to save up their time so that they can enjoy themselves at more length once a week. Whatever your preference, it is important to set aside some time regularly, whether daily or weekly, to do something you enjoy.

In choosing relaxation activities, make sure they really are ones *you* enjoy, and that you are not participating in them just to please someone else. In the space below, list some of the relaxing activities that you enjoy. They may be things you haven't done for a while, or things you have often thought you would like to do one day, as well as things you already do sometimes.

Relaxing activities	How often do you do them?
1.	
2.	
3.	
4.	
5.	

Another method of relaxing is to use a technique known as *progressive muscle relaxation*. This exercise, if practiced regularly, will help to reduce muscle tension and other stress symptoms. The technique involves progressively tensing and relaxing the major muscle groups in the body while maintaining your breathing at a slow rate. The exercise needs to be practiced at least once a day in order to be effective. If you can find the time to do it twice a day, the benefits will be greater. Most people find that they notice positive effects after two to three weeks of regular practice. When you begin, find a convenient time of the day to ensure that you can perform the exercise regularly. The most suitable times usually are in the morning when you first wake up and just before retiring for the night. You can use the self-monitoring form on p. 80 to remind yourself to be regular in carrying out the exercise. There are extra forms at the end of the book.

There are several commercially available relaxation tapes that can help you to learn the technique. If you choose to use a tape, try practising without it as well, so that you can perform the exercises independently.

Once you have mastered this technique, try applying a mini-relaxation exercise in situations where you cannot carry out the full exercise. Even on a bus or a train, you can close your eyes, practice your slow breathing, mentally say 'relax', and gently tense and relax the muscles of either your hands or feet. With practice, this mini-relaxation exercise can be almost as effective as the full-scale method.

Review of Step 2

In Step 2 we have examined some of the ways in which you can improve your physical health and thereby reduce your vulnerability to stress. Now that you have read the chapter, try to answer the following questions about your current lifestyle and how you might improve it:

- Are you currently engaging in any regular exercise? If not, what type of exercise could you start doing on a regular basis?
- Is your diet adequate? Are you eating regular meals? Have you reduced your intake of coffee, tea and chocolate? Are you on a program to stop smoking? Are you ensuring that your alcohol consumption is reduced to safe levels?
- Are you experiencing difficulties in falling asleep or staying asleep? Are you waking too early? What can you do to improve your sleep?

- Are you allowing yourself enough time for relaxation and recreation? If not, how can you reorganize your schedule so that you can make sufficient time?
- When can you practice the progressive muscle relaxation exercises? How are you going to ensure that you practice them at least once and preferably twice a day?

Altering your lifestyle so that it becomes less stressful may take several weeks or even months. There may be several barriers to change. However, if you start with small changes to your lifestyle, then the larger changes may not seem so threatening or overwhelming. Make sure that you are not attempting to change too many aspects of your lifestyle too quickly, and that you accept that there may be interruptions and distractions. The important message is to treat any setbacks as temporary and to resume your program as soon as possible.

- Find a comfortable, quiet place to sit or lie down, and try to ensure that you will not be interrupted for about twenty minutes. It may be necessary to tell the people that live with you that you do not want to be disturbed, or organize time to be alone in a quiet room.
- Close your eyes and focus on your breathing, keeping it slow and even. Say the word 'relax' to yourself a few times as you breathe out.
- Tense your right foot, squeezing your toes together and pointing them downwards. Focus on that tension. Slowly release that tension as you breathe out, saying the word 'relax' to yourself.
- Now tense your right calf muscle and hold the tension for a while. Slowly release the tension as you breathe out.
- Progress through your body, working through the muscles of your right leg, left leg, buttocks, back, abdomen, chest, shoulders, left arm, left hand and fingers, right arm, right hand and fingers, neck, jaw, lips, eyes, and forehead, tensing and relaxing for each group of muscles in the same way.
- Scan through your body and make sure that most of the tension has been released. If some areas are still tense, spend extra time relaxing those muscles.
- Slowly open your eyes. Try to maintain that feeling of relaxation for the rest of the day; or, if it is evening, as you go to bed and prepare for sleep.

Figure 5. Progressive muscle relaxation: the technique

Daily self-monitoring form for muscle relaxation exercises

Effectiveness rated from 0 to 10 where 0 = not at all effective and 10 = very effective

	Monday	Tuesday	Wednesday	Thursday	Friday	Saturday	Sunday
✓ A.M.	☐ ☐	☐ ☐	☐ ☐	☐ ☐	☐ ☐	☐ ☐	☐ ☐
Effectiveness rating							
Comments							
✓ P.M.	☐ ☐	☐ ☐	☐ ☐	☐ ☐	☐ ☐	☐ ☐	☐ ☐
Effectiveness rating							
Comments							

Step 3

Controlling panic attacks

In Step 2, we considered ways of reducing your overall stress levels by making changes in your lifestyle. We discussed approaches to improving your physical health that could reduce your vulnerability to stress symptoms and panic attacks. Changing lifestyle can take time, so that you should continue with your program to improve your sleep, exercise, diet and relaxation patterns at the same time as you begin to practice specific exercises to combat symptoms of panic. Like any new skill, learning to control your panic attacks may take time, and you may need quite a lot of practice before you feel confident in using the techniques. Remember that achieving control over panic symptoms will help you to participate in activities that you may have been avoiding because of a fear of having panic attacks; this in turn may help your physical well-being and so start you on a 'benevolent' cycle away from stress and anxiety.

Step 3 deals with specific ways to control symptoms of panic. You may already be familiar with some of these techniques; others may be completely new to you. By practising these techniques regularly, you will equip yourself to prevent the debilitating symptoms of panic and to control minor symptoms of anxiety when they do occur.

Controlling overbreathing or hyperventilation

You may find yourself breathing faster for several reasons such as when you have a fever, during strenuous exercise or after you have experienced a sudden shock. In these situations an increased rate of respiration is a perfectly normal response. Some people, however, develop a habit of over-breathing, especially when they are stressed or worried. Overbreathing itself can trigger a panic attack, as discussed earlier. Once the panic attack starts, breathing becomes difficult or irregular and the 'hyperventilation – panic' cycle begins.

In Part One, Chapter 3, we discussed how hyperventilation causes unpleasant physical sensations by changing the balance of gases in the bloodstream. These effects can be reversed simply by slowing your breathing rate so that you increase the amount of carbon dioxide in the blood. By reversing the process of hyperventilation, you will find yourself feeling less aroused, less anxious and less likely to experience symptoms of panic.

We focus here on two ways of increasing the amount of carbon dioxide in the bloodstream in order to prevent a panic attack. You can use these techniques individually or in combination to control your panic attacks. Try both.

Slow breathing

This techniques may be used anywhere and takes only a few minutes. The aim of the exercise is to slow your breathing rate to about eight to ten breaths per minute when you feel anxious or panicky. If you practice the exercise regularly, and learn to keep your normal breathing rate at the correct level, you will be more able to control your breathing when you notice early symptoms of panic.

- Begin by focusing your attention on your breathing. Try not to control your breathing rate just yet, but concentrate on the sensation of breathing. If your mind wanders off to other things, gently redirect your attention back to your breathing.
- Practice 'abdominal' breathing. Place one hand over your stomach and gently expand the muscles in that region every time you breathe in. At the same time try to reduce movements in your chest and shoulders during breathing. If necessary, watch yourself in the mirror to ensure that your shoulders hardly move. This technique stops you from taking gasping, sharp breaths.
- Now, on your next breath in, hold your breath to the count of ten (for ten seconds). Do not take an excessively deep breath. If holding your breath to the count of ten is too difficult, try holding your breath to the count of eight.
- Now slowly exhale.
- Now breathe in to the slow count of three and then out to the slow count of three. Keep breathing in and out to the count of three, trying not to take overly deep breaths. Try pacing your breathing so

that it takes three seconds to inhale and three seconds to exhale.

- Continue breathing at this rate for at least one minute.
- If you still feel panicky, hold your breath for a further ten seconds and repeat the exercise. Continue practising the exercise until the sensations of panic subside.

If you practice this exercise regularly and frequently, five or six times a day, you will find that you can control your breathing at all times. Turn it into a secret 'game' you play on the bus, at traffic lights, or whenever you have an idle moment. With practice you will be able to use this exercise to control panicky sensations before they turn into full-blown panic attacks.

The paper bag technique

This method of controlling overbreathing increases the amount of carbon dioxide in the bloodstream simply by restricting the amount of oxygen that enters your lungs and increasing your intake of carbon dioxide as you breathe back in air you have already exhaled. (Don't worry: you are still absorbing ample amounts of oxygen!) The method does not involve as much practice as the slow breathing technique, but obviously is less easily used in public.

- When you feel panicky, place a small paper bag over your mouth and nose. Keep the bag firmly in place by holding it close to your face with your hands. Try not to allow any gaps where air can escape.

- Now breathe slowly and regularly into the bag. Keep breathing in and out into the bag until the panic attack begins to subside and your breathing becomes easy.
- A similar effect can be achieved by cupping your hands around your nose and mouth and breathing slowly.

To use this technique, you will need to carry a paper bag with you in your handbag or pocket. In public, the hand-cupping technique is more convenient. If you find a private place where you can use the paper bag, however, the technique will help you restore the balance of gases in your blood quickly and so help to control your anxiety.

Distraction techniques

Focusing your attention on your symptoms usually makes them worse and increases the severity of the panic attack. There are a number of techniques that can help you to take your mind off the sensations of panic. You probably have found some of your own already. Four that have been found particularly useful by panic sufferers are outlined here. Try them all to see which ones work best for you.

1. *The rubber band technique* Wear a rubber band loosely around your wrist. When you feel a panic attack

starting, stretch the rubber band out and let it snap back on to the inside of your wrist. Often the short, sharp sensation of pain will be enough to redirect your attention away from the beginning of panic symptoms. This can give you time to begin using some of the other techniques for controlling anxiety, such as the slow breathing technique. Sometimes the rubber band technique by itse If is enough to stop a panic attack from developing.

2. *Counting* Some people find that if they focus on counting objects in their environment, they can distract themselves from an imminent panic attack. You could count the number of red cars passing by on the road or the number of windows in a building. Or you could multiply numbers in your mind. There are several possible ways of distracting yourself using the counting technique.

3. *Visualizing* It can be relaxing to imagine yourself in a pleasant or enjoyable setting, away from the cares of daily life. When you begin to experience early signs of anxiety, try imagining a pleasant scene from your memory, or from a movie or book. For example, try visualizing a warm summer day at the beach, or a walk through a beautiful park. Think of a scene that is special for you alone, and try to make the details (sounds, sights, smells) as real as possible. Practicing the same scene over and over will help you slip more easily into the exercise when necessary.

4. *Intellectualizing* Another method of distraction is to 'intellectualize' the symptoms of panic. This

involves acknowledging the symptoms in an objective manner. For example, while feeling anxious you can note down all the symptoms and fears you experience and rate their severity. This technique suits some people who can step back from themselves and their anxieties to 'self-examine' and record their experiences. The panic attack becomes an external 'thing' that you can examine from a distance rather than an event that seems to be controlling you.

Simple, everyday activities like talking to a friend on the telephone, listening to the radio or watching television can also help to distract you from your panic sensations.

A package of coping techniques to deal with panic attacks

It is important to learn which techniques work best for you when you feel anxious so that you will be better prepared to face difficult situations, armed with the confidence of knowing how to combat your anxiety. Make a list of distraction techniques you have tried and consider how effective they were. Give them each a rating out of 10. This exercise may help you select more carefully which techniques to use in the future.

It may be helpful to write down all the techniques that help you to control your panic attacks, perhaps on a card which you can carry around in your purse or wallet. By doing this you will be able to remind yourself quickly about what to do whenever you feel anxious or panicky.

For example, you might write the following instructions on a small card:

- hold breath for ten seconds;
- do slow breathing exercise;
- focus attention on counting technique.

Or:

- snap rubber band on wrist;
- put paper bag over nose and mouth;
- breathe slowly;
- visualize peaceful scene.

Once you begin to feel the panic attack subsiding, try to remain where you are and to continue what you were doing, but at a slower pace. For example, if you have a panic attack in the shopping centre, try to stay there for a while after the attack has subsided even if you are only walking around slowly. Escaping from a situation because of a panic attack may make it difficult to go back to that situation later. Try to reward yourself for coping with the panic attack by treating yourself to something you like or by praising yourself for handling the event as well as you did.

Review of Step 3

Step 3 has described some important techniques for preventing and controlling panic attacks. With regular practice of these techniques, you will be better able to overcome symptoms of panic and to resume the activities that you may have been avoiding. Of course, there may still be times when you experience symptoms of anxiety despite practising these skills. The occasional panic attack or anxiety symptom is only to be expected during recovery from panic disorder. Try treating the recurrence of anxiety as a minor setback that allows you to practice your skills further. Keep repeating to yourself that you are on the path to recovery and that the occasional slip along the way does not mean that you are falling back to the beginning.

Review your progress in Step 3 by asking yourself the following questions:

- Are you managing to slow down your breathing rate?
- Are you practicing your chosen breathing exercise regularly?
- Which distraction techniques work best for you?
- Have you written down those helpful techniques on a card, using the card promptly when needed?
- Are you managing to remain in difficult situations at least until the anxiety begins to subside?

When you are able to answer 'yes' to all these questions, you are ready to progress to the next step. Step 4 examines thinking styles that may be contributing to anxiety and panic attacks.

Step 4

Changing unhelpful thinking styles

Most of us have experienced periods in our lives when we have been extremely worried – about our health, our families or our friends, our jobs, our finances or our futures. Worrying about things is normal and even useful, since it enables us to anticipate and solve problems. Excessive worry, however, can become a problem in itself and may prevent us from focusing on the positive aspects of our lives. If worry becomes intense and prolonged, we are likely to experience physical symptoms such as muscle tension, sweating, churning in the stomach, and dryness of the throat and mouth. In some people, increasing tension may trigger panic attacks. As we have already noted (Part One, Chapter 3), physical symptoms of anxiety in themselves often cause worry about health, creating fears of serious illness and hence increasing anxiety.

In Step 2, we saw how physical factors such as tiredness, low levels of fitness and poor health could worsen symptoms of stress and anxiety. We also discussed the mind-body link to demonstrate how lack of sleep, poor diet and other physical factors reduce our resistance to stress. In Step 3 we discussed how hyperventilation can trigger panic attacks and looked at some methods of coping with panic symptoms. In Step 4 we will explore how you can deal with worrisome thoughts or negative thinking styles that can make you more vulnerable to suffering from anxiety and panic attacks.

There are three stages in considering and managing negative thinking styles. The first stage is learning to identify your negative thoughts; the second stage is learning how to challenge them, and the third stage is changing them to more positive, constructive thoughts that will reduce unnecessary anxiety. This three-step process is summarized in Figure 6.

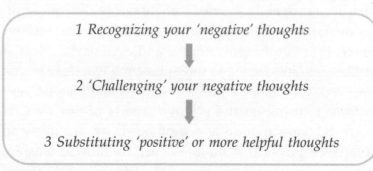

Figure 6. Overcoming negative thinking

Identifying negative thinking

How we interpret experiences, situations and sensations influences the way we feel about them and hence our emotional states. For example, if you think that you are going to suffer from a panic attack in a shopping mall, you may find yourself becoming very nervous every time you go shopping. As mentioned in Part One of this book, this is called *anticipatory anxiety*. What this means is that, just by predicting anxiety, you increase the risk of a panic attack actually happening. When the attack occurs, it strengthens the belief that you always will have a panic attack in that situation, and you become convinced that anxiety is unavoidable and uncontrollable. In effect, you are giving yourself a negative message: 'I told you so!'

In this way our ideas, thoughts and beliefs can lead to unpleasant emotions like anxiety, anger or depression. Because these emotions are so unpleasant, we may begin to avoid those situations where we predict that these feelings are likely to occur. We are made upset not so much by *actual* places or events as by our *interpretations* and *expectations* of places or events.

Most situations can be interpreted in different ways. We may be in the habit of interpreting situations in a way which regularly creates feelings of anxiety and panic. By practising alternative (but realistic) interpretation of these situations, we can reduce our anxiety reactions.

Some examples of negative thoughts are:

'I know for sure that I will have a panic attack if I go into any department store.'
'I'm definitely going to faint and no one will help me.'
'This pain in my chest must be a heart attack. I am going to die.'
'Everyone will laugh at me if I have a panic attack here.'
'Once panic starts, nothing can stop it.'

Unhelpful thoughts such as these may arise repeatedly in certain situations. These 'automatic' thoughts appear suddenly in our mind, sometimes without our even being fully aware of them. It is as if we have a 'hidden commentator' in our minds predicting gloom and doom. This tendency to interpret situations negatively arises from many influences including our upbringing, the expectations of those around us and the impact of the society in which we live.

A particularly unhelpful aspect of these interpretations is that they are overgeneralizations. For example, after having a panic attack on a bus, you may assume that you will have similar attacks on all forms of transport. These ideas cause a vicious cycle: because we tend to avoid the situations that we predict will lead to anxiety and fear, we avoid testing out these overgeneralizations and so are never able to find out how unhelpful or untrue they really are. If you have stopped going to department stores, it is difficult to know whether you will still have panic attacks in that environment. This vicious cycle effectively locks the sufferer into a restricted life of fear.

Figure 7 shows two examples of negative thoughts and the situations in which they occur. Fill in the blank spaces with negative thoughts that you have had in difficult situations.

Examples of negative thinking styles

There are several types of negative or faulty thinking styles, all of which serve to increase anxiety levels or to make us feel despondent

Situation	Negative thought
Shopping in a department store	'I can't cope with this anxiety'
Appointment at the hairdresser	'What if I have a panic attack and can't get out quickly?'

Figure 7. Examples of negative thinking

or demoralized. Below are some examples of faulty thinking styles observed by Albert Ellis, a therapist specializing in methods of challenging negative attitudes. See if you recognize some of these thinking styles in yourself.

1. *Black-and-white thinking*, or seeing an event as either total success or total failure, with no gradations in between. For example: 'If I experience any anxiety symptoms when I go shopping, then I have failed completely in managing my anxiety.'

2. *Generalizing* from one situation to the next. If one situation does not work out well, then we may decide that all similar situations will also be difficult. For example: 'I was feeling panicky at the train station so I know I will be panicky whenever I try to take public transport' or 'I am still experiencing

some panicky symptoms when I go out so I know I can't go anywhere anymore.' We have already noted how overgeneralizing can set up a vicious cycle of avoidance.

3. *Magnifying unpleasant experiences or focusing only on negatives.* For example: 'I chaired a meeting and caught up with all my paperwork, but I then became panicky when I could not find a folder. The whole day was a complete write-off.'

4. *Overestimating failure and underestimating success.* For example: 'So what if I am a successful journalist? I am a worthless person because I suffer from anxiety symptoms' or 'Everyone thinks that I am a total failure because I have panic attacks.'

5. *Setting unrealistic expectations* and not allowing yourself to make any mistakes. For example: 'I am practicing all my anxiety management skills so I expect never to suffer from a panic attack again' or 'I expect to be cured by next week.'

6. *Taking responsibility for others' feelings.* For example: 'It's my fault that the party was a failure – it must be because I was anxious' or 'it's my fault that my anxiety symptoms make my family upset.'

7. *Mind-reading other people's thoughts* or assuming certain outcomes without checking the facts. For example: 'They think I am stupid because I suffer from panic attacks' or 'I know for sure that I will have a panic attack if I try to drive over the bridge.'

You may be using some of these negative thinking styles without being fully aware that you are doing so. Remember, these thoughts can become habitual, flashing through your mind quickly, upsetting you without your realizing exactly why.

Every time you become upset or anxious, even if only slightly, say to yourself 'STOP'. Then try to assess exactly what the train of thought was that led to that feeling. See if you can link the negative thoughts to anything that has happened or been said recently. Can you detect a particular pattern in your negative thinking?

Challenging negative thoughts

Having identified your negative thinking habits, your next step is to learn how to change those thoughts to more positive, appropriate ones. This involves critically examining those thoughts and considering how accurate they really are. There are three ways of challenging your negative thoughts:

1. *Questioning the evidence for the negative thought*
   You may need to examine the probability of a negative thought being true all of the time. For example, to challenge the thought 'I am sure to have a panic attack. if I go into the department store,' you may need to consider whether you *automatically* have panic attacks in *all* department stores. What evidence do you have that suggests that you will *definitely* have a panic attack in this situation? Recall the

times that you did *not* have an attack, or had only minor symptoms while shopping.

Another way of questioning the evidence for a negative thought is to check whether your expectations of yourself are unrealistic. Are you expecting yourself *never* to experience *any* symptoms of anxiety when you go shopping?

2. *Checking out other possibilities before jumping to a conclusion* Before deciding that your negative interpretation of yourself or of a situation is the only 'correct' one, consider alternative ways of interpreting the same situation. For example, if you experience sensations such as not feeling 'with it', slight dizziness, weakness or feeling hot, try to consider other possible causes: did you stand up too quickly after sitting for a long time? Were you feeling excited? Was the room overheated? Were there other factors (strenuous exercise, hot weather, tiredness, viral illness) that could have produced some of those sensations?

3. *Asking others for their interpretation of a situation* This can be a useful method, especially if there is someone who can provide an accurate account of a particular event. Close friends, work colleagues, spposes or relatives often can help you to see a situation from a different and possibly more realistic perspective.

Try challenging some of your own negative thoughts by completing the exercise set out in Figure 8. Look at the two examples in the figure. Now select three recent instances when you felt anxious. Identify the situations you were in.

Consider the negative thoughts you experienced on each occasion. Try challenging those thoughts using the strategies of 'questioning the evidence' and 'checking out other possibilities'. Do you notice that your anxiety level changes when you start challenging your negative thoughts?

Situation	Negative thought thought	Challenging and considering an alternative
Going to supermarket on a hot day and experiencing panic symptoms	'I'll never get better'	'It was hot and I was rushing. Next time I will take it slower, choose a less busy time and make sure to stop for a drink. I have already made some progress and if I continue to improve I will eventually get better.'
Visiting family and having a heated deated discussion; feeling dizzy and experiencing rapid heartbeats	'I'm going to have a heart attack'	'I have been through several medical investigations and there is nothing wrong with my heart. My symptoms improved as soon as we left. I must have become overexcited. I know that

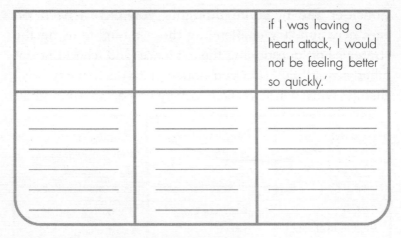

Figure 8. Challenging negative thoughts

Changing negative thoughts to positive thoughts

In the last two sections we considered how negative thoughts about ourselves and our ability to cope in different situations can lead to anxiety symptoms and panic attacks, and how the act of challenging these thoughts can reduce anxiety by making our excessive worries less 'believable'. The next stage in overcoming negative thoughts is to substitute more positive thoughts for the unpleasant, unhelpful ones.

Rather than thinking those gloomy or fearful thoughts that may result in anxiety symptoms, what would you like to be able to say to yourself instead? Most people would like to be able to say to themselves 'I can cope with this' or 'I'll be all right.' What sorts of encouraging thoughts would you like to say to yourself the next time you encounter a difficult situation? Look at the examples in Figure 9 and then add some of the things you would like to think in the situations that worry you.

Situation	Positive thought
Department store	'I can handle my anxiety'
Hairdresser	'I am going to enjoy having my hair cut'

Figure 9. Examples of positive thinking

Now try the three-step process for yourself. Think back to the last time you felt anxious or panicky and try to recall the kinds of negative thoughts that were going through your mind. First describe the situation.

Situation: _____

Now write down any negative thoughts, either about yourself or about the situation, that you remember.

Negative thoughts: _____

What can you say to yourself to challenge those negative thoughts? Try questioning the evidence for them, using the techniques discussed in the previous sections of Step 4. What could you say to yourself to make the negative thoughts less 'believable'?

Challenging thoughts: _____

_____

Now that you have challenged those negative thoughts, do you notice that your anxiety about the situation has decreased? Have you managed to make your negative thoughts less 'believable'? If you have, then the final stage is to substitute more positive, helpful thoughts about the same situation. What encouraging things could you say to yourself?

Positive thoughts: _____

_____

At first, this exercise may seem a little difficult. However, with practice you will find that you are better able to recognize and challenge negative thoughts and finally to substitute more helpful, positive thoughts about yourself and the activities you undertake. Use the monitoring form opposite to help you practice this technique further. (There are extra forms at the end of the book.)

Self-monitoring form for changing negative thoughts

Rate anxiety level from 0 to 10 where 0 = not at all anxious and 10 = extremely anxious

Day/date	Negative thought	Anxiety level	Challenging thought	Positive/appropriate thought

Further ways to help change negative thoughts

How many times have you thought to yourself that you can give others good advice about coping with stress but cannot solve similar problems of your own? You could try to 'advise' yourself on how to change your negative thoughts by treating yourself as a good friend whose problems you understand very well. What would you say to someone who is seeking your advice about anxiety and panic attacks?

Another technique is to imagine someone you know who always manages to look on the bright side of a difficult situation. How would this person interpret a situation that you find difficult? What sorts of positive, encouraging thoughts would this person think? Sometimes, just putting yourself in someone else's shoes can help you to look at a situation differently, especially if that person has a positive outlook on life.

You can also check your own thoughts about a situation with someone who is close to you and knows you fairly well. Develop the habit of discussing the way you see a situation with someone else if that situation makes you feel tense or anxious. Another person might immediately see the negative aspect of your perception when it is not obvious to you. This could help you practice 'thinking straight' by looking at alternative explanations for situations you find difficult. Try not to hold on to particular negative interpretations of yourself and of the situations you encounter. Instead, get into the habit of looking at a situation from different angles.

'Cue cards' can be a useful way to remind yourself of positive, encouraging thoughts. These are small cards that can be carried in your purse or wallet and read whenever you feel yourself slipping back into negative thinking styles. Write a single positive thought on each card and use as many cards as you need. Whenever you feel the need to remind yourself of positive thoughts, read through these cards. You can use them when out shopping, while using public transport, or in any other situation that may be difficult for you. With repeated practice, these positive thoughts will become 'second nature' to you and you may not need to use the cards any more.

Review of Step 4

By now you are better able to recognize your negative thoughts, and to challenge and change them to more positive, helpful thoughts. Remember that thinking styles are learned over time. Like any other habit, they take time and practice to change. Rewarding yourself for overcoming each negative thought can be a helpful way to break the habit of thinking negatively. Try to reward yourself whenever you 'think straight' and manage to overcome your anxiety.

Review your progress by answering the following questions:

- Can you identify some of your negative thoughts that may be leading to anxiety and panic?
- Are you being effective in challenging your negative thoughts?
- What positive or encouraging thoughts would you like to substitute for those negative thoughts?

- Have you developed a list of cue cards to use when you feel anxious?
- Are you using your cards regularly?

If you are able to answer 'yes' to the above questions, proceed to Step 5, which deals with your anxieties about the physical sensations of panic.

Step 5

Dealing with physical sensations

For many people who suffer from panic disorder, physical sensations that remind them of symptoms of panic may increase their worry and anxiety. If these health concerns are particularly severe or prolonged, they may in turn trigger panic attacks. In this way a vicious cycle is created in which physical symptoms trigger panic attacks and panic leads to a greater focus on physical sensations.

Have you noticed that certain changes in your bodily sensations (such as a rapid heartbeat while walking) make you concerned that you might be having a panic attack? If so, then you are among the many sufferers who have started to fear 'normal' physical sensations, mistaking them for signs of imminent panic.

Which physical sensations remind you of symptoms of panic? In the space below list the ones that you associate with feelings of anxiety and panic:

1. _____

2. _____

3. _____

4. _____

5. _____

What activities do you avoid because they are more likely to lead to these symptoms? Many people suffering from panic disorder avoid strenuous activity and regular exercise for this reason. For example, a swim might cause temporary shortness of breath. This lack of exercise can result in poor physical fitness and an increased vulnerability to stress. People suffering from panic disorder also tend to avoid confrontations with family members, friends or colleagues. Arguments and disagreements can produce high levels of emotional arousal, causing flushing of the face, shallow breathing, and a dry throat and mouth. These sensations are very similar to those experienced during a panic attack. To avoid these sensations, people suffering from panic disorder may find it easier to 'give in' or to agree with friends or members of their family too easily simply to keep the peace. Unassertive behavior can become a habit leading to other problems in your personal and social life, such as not standing up for yourself when necessary.

To break this chain of negative effects, it is important to recognize the activities or situations that you may be avoiding so as not to become too aroused. In the space below list some of the situations that you avoid for fear of triggering physical sensations that remind you of panic:

	Activity	Physical sensations
1.		
2.		
3.		
4.		
5.		

Learning not to be fearful of 'normal' physical sensations

Two methods are suggested here to help you overcome fears about 'normal' physical sensations that remind you of panic attacks. If you practice both, you should find that you become able to accept these feelings without anxiety.

Desensitization of exposure

The first technique involves allowing yourself to experience normal physical sensations of arousal while controlling your anxiety levels. It is difficult to remain anxious if you experience the same sensation repeatedly without suffering any negative effects. In Step 3 we discussed a breathing technique aimed at helping you to control your anxiety and panic attacks. The same technique can be used to help you overcome your fears of physical sensations.

Go back to your list of feared physical sensations. Can you think of ways to produce these sensations? Below is a list of suggested ways of experiencing those sensations that remind you of panic symptoms:

Physical sensations	How to produce this sensation
Rapid heart rate	Physical activity such as walking, slow jogging, walking up and down stairs, or doing push-ups or sit-ups
Sweating	Physical activity as listed above or walking about in hot weather, taking a hot bath, wearing warm clothes
Trembling or muscle weakness	Make a fist and squeeze hard: hold the tension in your hand for a few minutes and suddenly release it
Shortness of breath, panting	Exercise such as fast walking, slow jogging or swimming
Dizziness	Spin slowly around with your eyes open, or spin slowly on a swivel chair

For any of the sensations that are not produced by vigorous exercise, you can use the slow breathing technique described in Step 3 to control your anxiety levels. Slow breathing will be effective for controlling anxiety when you experience sensations of sweating, dizziness or muscle weakness. For the fears associated with rapid heart rate and shortness of breath, it is best to wait these out or to use the technique described in the next section to control your anxiety level.

You may also choose to use the muscle relaxation exercise described in Step 2 to reduce your overall level of arousal while you 'wait' out these sensations.

Use a gradual step-by-step approach that can be included in your exercise program. For example, choose a walk through a park where you know that there are benches at regular intervals. Gradually increase your pace of walking daily until you experience some sweating, increase in heart rate and in the rate of breathing. Then sit down at a bench and practice your minimuscle relaxation exercise, noting that the sensations fade gradually as you relax and rest.

Challenging catastrophic thoughts

In Step 4 of this book you learned how to identify, challenge and change the negative thoughts associated with anxiety and anxiety-provoking situations. Now you need to apply the same principles to overcoming your fears of physical sensations.

Physical sensation	Fearful thought
1. Rapid heart rate	'I'm having a heart attack'
2. Light-headedness	'I'm going crazy'; 'I'm going to faint'
3.	
4.	
5.	

Figure 10. Examples of catastrophic thinking

Physical sensation	Negative thought	Challenging thought	Positive thought
Sweating	'I'm going to have a panic attack'	It's a hot day, I must be hot. I'm only sweating because of the heat. I'll just remove my jacket'	This isn't a panic attack. My sweatiness will go away as I cool down. I can cope'

Figure 11. Challenging and changing negative thoughts

What are your thoughts when you experience these physical sensations? Figure 10 gives a couple of examples. Use the space in the figure to write down some of your own thoughts.

In Step 4 we saw how negative thoughts can be challenged by questioning the evidence, checking out other possibilities before jumping to conclusions, and asking others about their interpretations of the same situation. Use these techniques now to challenge your fears of physical sensations. What could you say to yourself to make these fears less believable? What would be a more sensible way of interpreting your physical sensations? The last stage of changing unhelpful thinking styles is to substitute more rational, encouraging thoughts. Try substituting positive, helpful thoughts in those situations where you previously tended to think negatively about physical sensations. Use the chart in Figure 11 to challenge and change your negative thoughts to more positive, helpful ones, using the example for guidance.

If you practice both these techniques regularly, you will become more effective in challenging the negative thoughts that tend to turn a normal physical sensation into a symptom of panic. Use both methods whenever you find that your anxiety is being triggered by physical sensations. You may need to produce some of those sensations repeatedly to become skilled in using a combination of slow breathing, relaxation and thought challenging to overcome your anxiety. Think up exercises that will help you get used to physical sensations and work out the combination of anxiety-reducing techniques that is most useful for you. Using 'cue cards', as described in Step 4, will help to remind you of the techniques to use when you begin to overreact to your physical sensations. Remember, these small cards can be carried around with you and used whenever you feel yourself slipping into anxiety.

Review of Step 5

In Step 5 we have considered ways of preventing fear of normal sensations associated with physical arousal. We have set out two techniques that can help overcome unnecessary anxiety associated with these sensations.

Review your progress by asking yourself the following questions:

- Have you made a list of the physical sansations that mimic panic?
- What methods can you use to produce those sensations?
- What are your negative thoughts associated with those sensations?
- Can you challenge those negative thoughts?
- Have you developed a list of positive, helpful thoughts to substitute for those negative thoughts?
- What other anxiety management techniques can you use to control the anxiety caused by mislabelling physical sensations?
- Have you written out cue cards to use when you start to react to your physical sensations?
- Are you using your cards regularly?

If you can answer 'yes' to all these questions, you are ready to start putting all the skills into practice. When you feel confident in applying these skills, you are ready to move on to Step 6, which deals with overcoming anxiety and agoraphobia in difficult situations.

Step 6

Overcoming agoraphobia and troubleshooting problem areas

By now you should be familiar with a number of techniques to control your anxiety symptoms. These skills will help you to return gradually to those activities that you may have been avoiding. As we have already seen, some people avoid or retreat from situations in which they become anxious so that they participate less and less in activities that they previously enjoyed. For example, if you fear driving you may avoid visiting friends, going shopping or looking for a job. In this way, a fear of driving can lead to major life problems like losing touch with friends, relying on family members for transport, or financial hardship. Although avoidance or withdrawal from stressful situations may be one way of reducing your anxiety in the short term, it always leads to other difficulties which greatly affect your lifestyle. Other ways of coping are possible, as you will have learned from working through this program.

The principles of gradual exposure

As discussed in Part One, Chapter 4, gradual exposure or systematic desensitization is an effective technique for overcoming fears or phobias of situations that are not really dangerous. Repeated exposure uncouples the 'fight or flight' response from the previously feared situation.

Several principles should be kept in mind when applying gradual exposure techniques:

1. It is important to work out and write down a hierarchy of feared places and situations, ranking them according to the level of anxiety that they provoke.
2. It is best to work through the list from least to most feared situations in a systematic way. It may be necessary to break down each task into a series of smaller ones, so that you overcome the fear step by step. It may be necessary to repeat the first step several times before your anxiety level falls enough to proceed to the next step. It is also best if you remain at your destination long enough for your anxiety to fall to comfortable levels before returning.
3. Don't try to rush up the scale of feared situations. It is important to progress at the rate which is right for you as an individual, so that wherever you are on the scale the level of anxiety you feel is never more than moderate and therefore is always manageable. It is better to progress slowly and steadily than to try to take bigger steps than you can manage and then feel discouraged by setbacks.

4. A number of tactics can be used to make exposure easier in the early stages of the exposure program. Select the most useful techniques from the anxiety management strategies you have learned. Not all will be useful in every situation, so try to plan ahead, noting which are likely to be the most useful for each situation.

5. A trusted companion such as a close friend or family member may be very helpful in the early stages of the exposure exercises. It is important, though, that the companion fully understands the purpose of the exercises and agrees to withdraw gradually during the program to allow you to develop full independence in approaching previously feared situations. It is critical that both sides of the partnership accept this and are open about it, as the companion may expect quicker progress than is possible, or you may be tempted to 'hold on' to the security provided by the companion for too long.

6. The most important principle is to remember that you are trying to work systematically. This means being committed to the program as a priority in your life, approaching the tasks one step at a time, practicing the exercises regularly, and being willing to take one step back if you have a setback. If you practice the exercises haphazardly, or give up for days at a time because you had a 'bad' outing, then progress will be much slower. Using the monitoring forms and plotting your progress week by week helps you to monitor your improvement and to see

that even if small setbacks occur, they do not necessarily mean that you are not making headway overall.

Making a ranked list of stressful situations

Drawing up a list of anxiety-provoking situations is the first step in overcoming the fear of them. Once you have done this you will be able to see more clearly the kinds of situations that lead to anxiety, as we discovered in Step 1. Remember that this list is specific to you: what you find distressing may not be so distressing to someone else. Listing these situations also will help you to focus on when and how to use your newly learned anxiety management skills. Remember, it is best to practice your stress management skills on 'easier' or 'less stressful' situations first. List the situations that are stressful to you on the form opposite and, in the space provided, rate the level of anxiety associated with each situation from 0 to 10, where 0 = no anxiety and 10 = highest level of anxiety. Examples may include:

- being alone at home;
- walking down the road;
- visiting the supermarket;
- driving over a bridge in heavy traffic;
- telling the kids to clean up their room.

You can then use this form to record the progress you make in reducing the 'anxiety ratings' of the various situations.

List of anxiety-provoking situations

Situation	Rating (0–10) (0 = no anxiety, 10 = highest level of anxiety)	Change in rating	
		Week 1	Week 2
1.			
2.			
3.			
4.			
5.			
6.			
7.			
8.			
9.			
10.			

Catching a bus: an example of gradual exposure

People with agoraphobia often have difficulty catching a bus, even though they were once quite able to do so. This offers a simple example of how gradual exposure can be carried out. Catching a bus may rate 4–5 on your list in terms of the level of anxiety it causes, so it is not too difficult a task to start with. You may decide that it is best to break the task down into three

segments: walking to the bus stop, catching the bus for one stop; and then catching the bus over the bridge to the shopping centre. It might be best to try stage 1 over three or four days, at first with the help of a companion. The first day, the companion accompanies you to the bus stop and you sit together in the bus shelter, waiting for your anxiety to diminish. (You may find it useful to practice your mini-relaxation exercise, as described in Step 2, while you are there.) You then return home together. The next day, you may repeat the same exercise, noting the decrease in your anxiety. The following day, your companion might follow you at fifty paces, then join you at the bus stop. Within a few days, you may find that you can walk to the bus stop and back on your own. The procedure is then repeated for catching the bus one stop, beginning with your companion accompanying you, then sitting a few rows behind you, and then seeing you off at the bus stop and meeting you at the next stop. In this gradual way, you can progress to catching the bus on your own and taking it to the shops. Of course, with modifications, the same sequence can be applied to driving a car, catching a train, walking to a shopping mall or going out to a restaurant.

Remember, learning to cope with anxiety is a gradual process that requires practice. If possible, start practicing your anxiety-controlling techniques in less distressing situations. Once you become more confident in applying these skills, you can apply them to more difficult situations.

Applying anxiety management techniques

In the following sections we will examine how to combine stress management skills to work through more complex situations that cause anxiety. Remember, there is no single set of steps that applies equally well for everyone, and each person must work at his or her own pace. You will need to discover the combination of techniques that is most helpful in managing your own stress levels effectively, and a comfortable pace to proceed at.

Often a combination of techniques that works on your physical as well as your psychological state is most effective in overcoming stress and anxiety. In Step 2, we discussed looking after your physical well-being by exercising, maintaining a good diet, and ensuring that you have enough sleep. We also discussed muscle relaxation exercises as an effective method for reducing tension. In Step 3, we considered various ways to help you control panic attacks, such as slow breathing and distraction techniques. Step 4 examined how to change negative thinking styles that can lead to symptoms of anxiety and to loss of confidence. These techniques can now be used individually or in combination to control your anxiety in a wide range of situations.

The next two sections look at how you might apply the skills you have learnt in two situations many panic sufferers find stressful: going to the supermarket and visiting the dentist.

The supermarket

Let us imagine that going to the supermarket rates 6 on your list of stressful situations. You may want to start the day by doing a brief muscle relaxation exercise before you leave the house. You may also need to use the slow breathing technique in the car park outside the supermarket to ensure that you are feeling calm and relaxed. You may then need to challenge your negative thoughts associated with supermarket shopping. Writing them down before you leave home may make this task a little easier. For example:

'I will have a terrible panic attack and lose control'
'I will look so anxious that other people will think
I am crazy'

These negative thoughts can be challenged in a number of ways:

'I do not always have panic attacks in supermarkets,
and even if I did get panicky, I know how to control my
symptoms'

'I have never lost control or started screaming when I go to the supermarket, and it is unlikely that I will do so now'

'I look anxious, it is unlikely people will take special notice of me. Even if they do notice me looking anxious, they will not automatically think I am crazy. Lots of people look stressed in the supermarket'

Finally, try substituting more positive, encouraging thoughts that will reduce your anxiety about going to the supermarket.

'I can cope with this'
'I know how to keep my anxiety under control'
'It will be over soon'

If you have made up 'cue' cards to remind yourself of how to challenge your negative thoughts, you may want to look at them before going into the supermarket. Once inside, keep your breathing slow and even. Try pacing yourself so that you do not rush through the supermarket feeling overwhelmed and frantic. If you do get anxious, simply stop and focus on slowing your breathing while reading your 'cue' cards that help to challenge negative thoughts. While waiting at the checkout you might use distraction techniques like counting or visualization.

Finally, when you have completed your supermarket shopping, reward yourself with a small treat for having coped with the situation.

The dentist

Another commonly feared situation is going to the dentist for a check-up, a task which you may have rated 6. You could start preparing for this situation by making sure that you have a good night's sleep. Before leaving the house, practice your muscle relaxation exercise. Give yourself plenty of time to reach the dentist's surgery so that you do not feel rushed or flustered.

As with going to the supermarket, you may need to examine your negative thoughts before the visit. Write down some of your negative thoughts about going to the dentist. Your list may look something like this:

'I will scream or lose control when the dentist examines me'
'I will be so anxious that I may faint and the dentist will think I'm crazy'

Remember, the next step in modifying these negative thoughts is to begin to challenge them. You may want to start questioning your negative thoughts as follows:

'I have never screamed or lost control when I have gone to the dentist in the past and it is unlikely that I will do so now'
'I have never fainted at the dentist's surgery and it is unlikely that I will faint now. If I do feel faint, I can tell the dentist and she will give me time to recover'
'The dentist sees many patients who are anxious and it is unlikely that she thinks they are all crazy'

The last step is to substitute more positive thoughts that
will help you to control your anxiety about going to the
dentist:

> *'Even though it is uncomfortable visiting the dentist, it
> only last for half an hour. I can manage that'*
> *'I have ways of controlling my anxiety symptoms'*
> *'I can cope with going to the dentist. I am prepared for
> this visit'*

In the dentist's waiting room, scan through your body
to detect any muscle tension. Ask yourself whether your
body feels rigid or stiff. Carry out a quick muscle relaxation exercise by focusing on those areas that feel especially
tense and then relaxing them. As you breathe out, say the
word 'RELAX' to yourself. Do this a few times until you
begin to feel those muscles actually relaxing and the tension
reducing. Focus on your breathing, remembering to keep
your rhythm slow and even. If you feel anxious, use your
breathing control technique until you start to feel yourself
relax. Try to maintain a feeling of calmness for as long as
possible.

Mention to the dentist that you feel anxious and that you
may need a little time between procedures to regain your
equilibrium. Also, ask the dentist to explain each procedure to you and say how long it will take. Most dentists
will agree beforehand to stop a procedure if you lift your
hand up to signal the need for a break.

When the visit is over, reward yourself with a small treat
for having coped with your anxiety.

Trouble-shooting problem areas

Some situations trigger panic in a high proportion of people with panic disorder, especially those who also suffer from agoraphobia. In addition, there are individual anxieties that are specific to each person. Some of these personal triggers may be obvious and immediate, such as problems at work, at home, or in a relationship. Other problems may be more complex and have their roots in earlier experience. Dealing with such deeper problems is beyond the scope of this book. If you believe that you need help in that area, you would be best advised to seek counselling.

All of us have to deal with problems every day. The way in which we go about tackling these problems varies from person to person and from one situation to the next, and there is no 'best' way of solving problems; nevertheless, some ways of solving problems are better than others, especially in the long run.

Not dealing with problems as they arise can lead to feelings of helplessness and frustration, and may eventually lead to a worsening of panic symptoms. Some common but ineffective ways of coping with problems are:

- ignoring them, hoping that they will go away or that they will magically 'sort themselves out';
- relying on someone else to come up with a solution;
- worrying repeatedly about what has caused the problem rather than thinking of any possible solutions;

- relying on fate or luck to sort things out;
- becoming too distressed to deal with the problem.

If you find yourself resorting to any of these 'methods', you may be keeping yourself in a stressed state for longer than is necessary.

A more effective way of dealing with problems is to try to solve them yourself in a step-by-step way. An example of structured problem-solving follows.

Step 1: Define the problem
First, try to define what the problem area is. Be as specific as you can: this makes it easier to think of possible and appropriate solutions. For example:

I get anxious whenever I argue with my daughter about her excessive use of the telephone.

Once you have thought about what the problem is, write down as many solutions to this problem as you can think of. Be as imaginative or outrageous as you like.

Look through your list of solutions and rate each solution from -10 to +10, where -10 indicates a very poor solution and +10 indicates an extremely good solution. A middle rating of 0 indicates a solution with equal advantages and disadvantages.

Step 2: Define solutions   *Rating*
1. Leave the house whenever my daughter
   uses the telephone   -9

2. Disconnect the telephone   -5
3. Make her pay for her use of the telephone
   if it exceeds 'normal' usage   +7
4. Consider what types of negative thoughts
   may be contributing to my anxiety about her
   use of the telephone   +8
5. Install a separate extension for her to use in
   her room   +4

Now look through your list once again and decide which is the best solution to that particular problem. You may decide that there is more than one solution, or that a combination of solutions will work best. Write down your chosen solution or solutions to this problem.

Step 3: Best solution or combination of solutions
   1. Install another telephone and make her pay for
      her own telephone calls
   2. Examine my attitude about her use of the tele-
      phone and try to challenge any irrational thoughts
      that are causing unnecessary distress

Now consider how you will implement your solution to this problem. What is the best time to carry out your plan? Does the solution involve particular people or apply to certain places?

Step 4: How and when will you implement this solution?
Wait for the weekend when we are both at ease and

then talk to my daughter in her room about this problem and the solutions I think would be best.

Finally, once you have tried a particular solution, it is important to review your efforts. How well did you manage to discuss this solution? Was it effective? If not, how can you modify it? Mark your solutions on a simple scale.

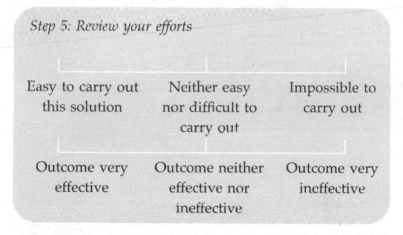

Step 5: Review your efforts

Easy to carry out this solution — Neither easy nor difficult to carry out — Impossible to carry out

Outcome very effective — Outcome neither effective nor ineffective — Outcome very ineffective

Effective problem-solving can prevent small problems from growing into major sources of stress which could make your panic symptoms worse. Try practicing this exercise on important problems you can identify in your life.

Review of Step 6

This step has involved your considering various combinations of techniques that work for you in different situations. Relaxation exercises beforehand and use of the breathing exercise may help to settle yourself in at the dentist's surgery. Challenging and substituting negative thoughts, and practicing slow breathing, may be useful in the supermarket. The most important thing is to identify and use the techniques that work best for you.

- We have seen, too, that another useful way of preparing for a situation is by practicing it in your mind, challenging the negative thoughts that can arise and imagining the stressful situation while you use your coping strategies to control your anxiety. In this way you can proceed through the imagined situation step by step and plan ahead which anxiety management strategies you will use at each point. When you have successfully practiced coping with a particular situation in your mind, you can try it out in 'real life'.

- Don't forget to reward yourself when you succeed at reducing your anxiety. You can go back to your original list and rerate each item as you lessen the worry it causes you. As you overcome your anxiety in a range of situations, your ratings will start to decrease to more manageable levels.

- Remember to work through your list of stressful situations slowly. Do not move on to the harder items until you feel some degree of confidence in completing the easier tasks. Keep practicing your coping skills regularly, as it is easy to become disorganized or confused when you are anxious. Try to use the structured problem-solving technique described above to help overcome some of your sources of stress.

- Once again, remember that effective stress management takes time and practice. Don't be discouraged if your anxiety remains high even after practicing all these skills. Be patient and learn from your experiences, even the ones that may not turn out exactly the way you want them to. Remember, it is virtually impossible to remain anxious if you expose yourself repeatedly to a situation that is not really dangerous.

Preventing setbacks

The six-step program described in Part Two focuses on various ways of coping with stress and panic attacks. Regular practice will make the techniques progressively easier to use; yet sometimes, despite all your efforts, it may seem as if you are going backwards rather than continuing to improve. It is easy to become demoralized by such setbacks, especially when they occur after you have been making progress for some time. This last section of the book considers ways of preventing these setbacks and overcoming them if they occur.

Understanding the pattern of recovery

Recovery from panic disorder and agoraphobia often follows a fluctuating course, and at times it may seem that you have reached a plateau or even that your anxiety has worsened. This pattern is part of the 'normal' recovery process, which can be depicted on a 'recovery graph' (see Figure 12). From this graph you can see that over a period of time, your symptoms tend to improve; however, there may be

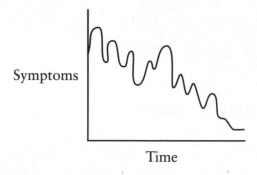

Symptoms

Time

Figure 12. The normal pattern of recovery from panic disorder and agoraphobia

days, or even weeks, when your symptoms may flare up, just as there also may be times when symptoms improve rapidly, even more than expected. The important point to remember here is that despite fluctuations in the intensity and/or frequency of symptoms, if you practice your techniques, the level of anxiety will gradually follow a downward course and symptoms will diminish or disappear completely.

What is relapse?

Relapse is a more serious setback or recurrence of panic disorder. In other words, the symptoms that you managed to overcome or control may start to reappear for a variety of reasons. As a first step, it is important to distinguish 'relapse' from the normal recovery process which tends to have 'ups' and 'downs' over time. Answering the questions

	Yes	No
1. Are you experiencing full-blown panic attacks?	☐	☐
2. Have your symptoms returned at the same intensity as when they first occurred?	☐	☐
3. Are the symptoms increasingly interfering with your usual daily routine?	☐	☐
4. Has the frequency of these symptoms increased to the same level as when you first started experiencing panic attacks?	☐	☐

Figure 13. Checklist for relapse

shown in Figure 13 may help you to check whether you are experiencing a relapse of your symptoms. If you answer 'yes' to any of these questions, you may be experiencing an early stage of relapse and you may need to consider systematic ways of preventing the symptoms from worsening. In the following sections we examine ways of preventing setbacks from developing into a fullblown relapse.

Why do people relapse?

Usually, a combination of factors leads to relapse. This can include the recurrence of external stresses, difficulty coping with these problems, and insufficient or irregular practice of stress management techniques. Also, people who have suffered from panic disorder may continue to have trouble 'labelling' normal anxiety correctly, even after they have recovered, and so may mistake normal levels of stress (e.g. before an examination or a public speech) as signs of relapse. The worry about symptoms returning may itself provoke the recurrence of panic.

External stress is more likely to lead to a return of panic under certain conditions. You may be particularly vulnerable to stress because of lack of sleep, poor diet or physical illness. Low self-esteem and lack of confidence also may increase your vulnerability to anxiety symptoms. You may have given up practicing your anxiety-reducing techniques too early, or stopped taking your prescribed anti-anxiety medication too soon: suddenly ceasing medication can leave you vulnerable to anxiety symptoms. On the other hand, if your symptoms have changed in character, or you have any doubt about what is wrong, you should visit your doctor for a thorough reassessment.

Preventing relapse

There are many strategies that you can use to prevent relapse if you begin to feel stressed. Look back at the questions in Figure 13 earlier in this chapter. If you answered 'yes' to any of them you may find it useful to consider the following questions too, which may help to pinpoint ways of preventing yourself from relapsing.

Are there new stresses in your life, or are you becoming overly sensitive to minor anxiety symptoms leading you to worry unnecessarily?

You may need to refer back to Step 1in this program in order to refresh your memory about anxiety symptoms and sources of stress. Try to list the factors that may have contributed to your increased anxiety symptoms. Are any of the stresses similar to the ones you listed in Step 1, or are there new stresses that are adding to your worries?

Are you attempting to overcome your anxiety or avoidance of situations too quickly?

If you suddenly experience a full-blown panic attack after weeks or months of minimal anxiety symptoms, it may be an indications. that you are attempting too much too soon or without adequate preparation. If you have been trying concentratedly to overcome your avoidance of difficult situations, you may be pushing yourself a little too hard. Perhaps you need to rethink how much preparation you need before undertaking more difficult situations.

If you are becoming anxious about a new life challenge or change (e.g. a new job) assess the situation carefully before plunging into it. Use the techniques you have learnt to help you cope with the heightened tension that may be provoked by considering these options. If you do not feel ready for a particular challenge, do not force yourself to undertake it unless it is essential. The timing of new undertakings can be critical. If you do embark on a new venture, make sure that the rest of your lifestyle and stress management program are not disrupted.

Are you still maintaining a healthy lifestyle?

It is easy to forget about those lifestyle factors that may be affecting your anxiety levels, especially if you have had a long panic-free period. Re-examine your lifestyle, checking that you are eating a healthy diet, taking regular exercise and limiting your intake of stimulants like tea, coffee and cigarettes. Remember, an increase in alcohol intake may lower your threshold of panic.

Resume your relaxation exercises and slow breathing techniques if you have stopped doing them, and keep them up even when you do not feel especially anxious. All these techniques take time to master, and lack of practice can result in some loss of skills. You will be less able to control your anxiety if your stress management skills are rusty.

Have you suddenly stopped taking your prescribed medication, or been varying the dose?

Suddenly ceasing medication or changing the dose can lead to a resurgence of anxiety symptoms and panic attacks. Even if you feel a great improvement, it is best to keep taking your medication as prescribed until both you and your doctor decide to reduce the dosage. If your doctor has changed your medication and you are now experiencing increased anxiety or panic attacks, consult your doctor to try to work out whether these symptoms are likely to pass quickly or whether you need to return to the original dose.

Are you lapsing into unhelpful ways of thinking?

Remember to use the thinking exercises outlined in Step 4 to maintain a positive frame of mind. Challenge and re-evaluate any negative interpretations of events, your feelings and your physical sensations. Reinstitute your systematic program of substituting positive thoughts for any negative ones you have detected. Poor self-esteem and lack of confidence are directly related to negative thoughts, and vice versa. Remember to reward yourself for coping with your anxiety symptoms and to acknowledge your successes.

By systematically working through these questions, you will be better able to prevent yourself from slipping backwards. Go back to the exercises you learnt in Steps 1–6 to refresh your memory of how to overcome anxiety symptoms and panic attacks. If panic attacks continue, it may be useful to discuss the situation with your family doctor and perhaps seek referral to a mental health professional who specializes in the treatment of panic disorder. Remember that setbacks need not mean a return to your previous levels of anxiety symptoms. If you apply your techniques energetically to deal with temporary setbacks, you usually can put yourself back on the road to recovery very quickly.

A note on depression

For many people, depression and anxiety go hand in hand. For most people suffering from panic disorder, depressive feelings are fleeting or relatively minor: these people are able to sustain the energy and motivation to continue working on overcoming panic attacks and agoraphobia. For others, however, depression may become overwhelming. When this happens, it is necessary to seek professional help.

For minor bouts of depression, lasting a few hours or days, a self-help approach can be effective. An initial step is to write down what stresses may be contributing to the depression and then take a step-by-step approach to solving the immediate problems that you face. A further strategy may be to use distraction techniques (see Step 3) to focus your mind on pleasurable, non-stressful activities. This is especially effective if the cause of the depression cannot easily be eliminated. It may also be useful to examine whether negative thoughts or attitudes are contributing to depressive feelings. Learning to challenge these thoughts (see Step 4) is a useful skill that could be developed through further reading on the topic of depression.

If these techniques do not help to alleviate depression, or you are feeling hopeless or desperate, do seek professional help. Antidepressant medication together with regular counselling sessions may be required to overcome the depressive episode. In the unusual instance of depression being very severe, a period in hospital may be necessary, especially if the depression is so bad as to raise the risk of self-neglect or self-harm.

The recommended steps in dealing with depression are summarized in Figure 14.

Write down the stresses you face and try to work out step-by-step strategies to deal with them

⬇

Engage in distracting, pleasurable and non-stressful activities

⬇

Examine whether your thoughts about yourself, your situation and the future are excessively negative. Challenge these negative thoughts and try to replace them with positive ones

⬇

If symptoms persist, or if you feel desperate and are unable to cope, seek professional help

↙ ↘

Regular counselling sessions   *Hospitalization*

Figure 14. Dealing with depression: a summary

A final note

Now that you have worked through this self-help book, you are in a better position to take charge of your panic attacks and to participate fully again in all the activities you have avoided. Reread the book slowly if you feel yourself slipping back to the old lifestyle or thinking patterns that could increase the risk of panic attacks recurring.

If you find it difficult to maintain your motivation, you could consider joining a support group. For many people suffering from anxiety disorders, meeting other people who suffer from the same problems can be extremely helpful. To find out more about support groups, contact your family doctor or local mental health service. Attending a support group may be particularly beneficial if you suffer from panic disorder with agoraphobia.

Finally, remember that your experience of anxiety, although painful, has taught you valuable lessons about the impact of stress on your health and about the need to monitor and deal with stress when it occurs.

Useful books

There are a number of other books that you may find useful in understanding panic disorder and agoraphobia. Some of these take a broad-based approach to dealing with stress in general. The more reading you do, the greater the likelihood of picking up some useful skills for coping with panic attacks and agoraphobia. On the other hand, as in your use of this book, you need to be selective and critical in deciding which techniques work best for you.

The following titles may be helpful.

Dr Lee Baer, *Getting Control*, London, Little Brown, 1996.
Dancing with Fear, London, Jason Aronson, 1996.
Mark Greener, *The Which? Guide to Managing Stress*, London, Which? Books, 1996.
Gerlad L. Klerman *et al.* (eds), *Panic Anxiety and Its Treatments: Report of the World Psychiatric Association Presidential Educational Task Force*, New York, American Psychiatric Association, 1993.
Professor Isaac Marks, *Living with Fear*, New York, McGraw-Hill, 1978.

Joy Melville, *Phobias and Obsessions*, London, Macdonald Optima, rev. ed. 1991.

Reneau Z. Peurifoy, *Anxiety, Phobias and Panic: Taking charge and conquering fear*, New York, Warner Books, 1995.

Stanley Rachman and Padmal de Silva, *Panic Disorders: The Facts*, Oxford, Oxford University Publishing, 1996.

Shirley Swede, *Panic Attack Recover Book*, New York, New American Library-Dutton, 1989.

Robert E. Thayer, *The Origin of Everyday Moods: Managing energy, tension and stress*, Oxford University Publishing, 1996.

Shirley Trickett, *Coping with Anxiety and Depression*, London, Sheldon Press, 1989.

Useful addresses

United Kingdom

British Association for Behavioural and Cognitive Therapies
Victoria Buildings, 9–13 Silver Street
Bury
BL9 0EU
Tel.: 0161 7974484
Fax: 0161 7972670
Email: babcp@babcp.com
www.babcp.com

British Association for Counselling and Psychotherapy
BACP House, 15 St John's Business Park
Lutterworth, Leicestershire
LE17 4HB
Tel.: 0870 443 5252
Email: bacp@bacp.co.uk
www.bacp.co.uk

First Steps to Freedom
22 Randall Road
Kenilworth
Warwickshire CV8 1JY
Helpline: 01926 851608

Institute for Neuro-Physiological Psychology
Warwick House
4 Stanley Place
Chester CH1 2LU
Tel.: 01244 311414

Lifeskills
Bowman House
6 Billetfield
Taunton
Somerset TA1 3NN
(No telephone number available)

MIND: The National Association for Mental Health
Granta House
15–19 Broadway
Stratford
London E15 4BQ
Tel.:0181 519 2122 (can also give you details of local tranquil-
lizer withdrawal support groups)

No Panic
93 Brands Farm Way
Randlay
Telford
Helpline: 01952 590545

Open Door Association
447 Pensby Road
Heswall
Wirral
Merseyside LR 9PQ
(No telephone number available)

Phobic Action
Hornbeam House
Claybury Grounds
Woodford Creen
Essex IG8 8PR
(No telephone number available)

Phobics Society (a self-help network)
4 Cheltenham Road
Chorlton cum Hardy
Manchester M21 9QN
Tel.: 0161 881 1937

Relaxation for Living (courses and information to combat stress)
Dunesk, 29 Burwood Park Road
Walton-on-Thames
Surrey KT12 5LH
Tel.: 01932 227826

Triumph Over Phobia
(TOP UK)
PO Box 1831
Bath BA1 3YX
(No telephone number available)

United States

American Mental Health Foundation
2 East 86th Street
New York
NY 1008
(Written enquiries only)

Association for the Advancement of Behavior therapy
305 7th Avenue
New York
NY 10001
Tel.: 212 647 1890

The Behavior Therapy Center of New York
115 East 87th Street
New York
NY 10028
Tel.: 212 410 6500

Behavior Therapy Institute
San Francisco
Tel.: 415 989 2140

Behavioral Psychotherapy Center
23 Old Mamaroneck Road
White Plains
NY 10605
Tel.: 914 761 4080

Institute for Behavior Therapy
137 East 36th Street
New York
NY 10016
Tel.: 212 686 8778

Long Island Jewish Hospital at Hillside Phobia Clinic
New Hyde Park
NY 11040
Tel.: 718 470 7000 (Hospital number)

Institutes for Neuro-Physiological Psychology:
Dr Larry J. Beuret MD
48u Emerson, Suite 209
Palatine
IL 60067
Tel.: 847 303 1800
and
Mrs Victoria Hutton
6535 North Shore Way
Newmarket
Maryland 21774
Tel.: 301 607 6752

White Plains Hospital Center
Anxiety and Phobia Clinic
Davis Ave., at Post Road
White Plains
NY 10601
Clinic tel.: 914 681 0600
(Mon, Wed, Fri only, 9.00 a.m.–4.00 p.m.

Australia and New Zealand

Triumph Over Phobia
TOP NSW
PO BOX 213
Rockdale
New South Wales 2216
Australia

Institutes for Neuro-Physiological Research:
Dr Mary Lou Sheil
80 Alexandra Street
Hunters Hill 2110
Sydney, Australia
Tel.: 298 796 596
and
Heather Jones
501 North Willowport Road
Hastins
New Zealand
(No telephone number available)

Extra monitoring sheets

Self-monitoring from for changing negative thoughts

Rate anxiety level from 0 to 10 where 0 = not at all anxious and 10 = extremely anxious

Day/date	Negative thought	Anxiety level	Challenging thought	Positive/appropriate thought

Self-monitoring from for changing negative thoughts

Rate anxiety level from 0 to 10 where 0 = not at all anxious and 10 = extremely anxious

Day/date	Negative thought	Anxiety level	Challenging thought	Positive/appropriate thought

Self-monitoring from for changing negative thoughts

Rate anxiety level from 0 to 10 where 0 = not at all anxious and 10 = extremely anxious

Day/date	Negative thought	Anxiety level	Challenging thought	Positive/appropriate thought

Self-monitoring from for changing negative thoughts

Rate anxiety level from 0 to 10 where 0 = not at all anxious and 10 = extremely anxious

Day/date	Negative thought	Anxiety level	Challenging thought	Positive/appropriate thought

Self-monitoring from for changing negative thoughts

Rate anxiety level from 0 to 10 where 0 = not at all anxious and 10 = extremely anxious

Day/date	Negative thought	Anxiety level	Challenging thought	Positive/appropriate thought

Self-monitoring from for changing negative thoughts

Rate anxiety level from 0 to 10 where 0 = not at all anxious and 10 = extremely anxious

Day/date	Negative thought	Anxiety level	Challenging thought	Positive/appropriate thought

Monitoring form for panic attacks

Date	Situation	Anxiety symptoms (0–10)	Coping (0–10)

Monitoring form for panic attacks

Date	Situation	Anxiety symptoms (0–10)	Coping (0–10)

Monitoring form for panic attacks

Date	Situation	Anxiety symptoms (0–10)	Coping (0–10)

Monitoring form for panic attacks

Date	Situation	Anxiety symptoms (0–10)	Coping (0–10)

Monitoring form for panic attacks

Date	Situation	Anxiety symptoms (0–10)	Coping (0–10)

Monitoring form for panic attacks

Date	Situation	Anxiety symptoms (0–10)	Coping (0–10)

Daily self-monitoring form for muscle relaxation exercises

Effectiveness rated from 0 to 10 where 0 = not at all effective and 10 = very effective

	Monday	Tuesday	Wednesday	Thursday	Friday	Saturday	Sunday
☐ A.M.	☐	☐	☐	☐	☐	☐	☐
Effectiveness rating	☐	☐	☐	☐	☐	☐	☐
Comments							
☐ P.M.	☐	☐	☐	☐	☐	☐	☐
Effectiveness rating	☐	☐	☐	☐	☐	☐	☐
Comments							

Daily self-monitoring form for muscle relaxation exercises

Effectiveness rated from 0 to 10 where 0 = not at all effective and 10 = very effective

	Monday	Tuesday	Wednesday	Thursday	Friday	Saturday	Sunday
☐ A.M.	☐	☐	☐	☐	☐	☐	☐
Effectiveness rating	☐	☐	☐	☐	☐	☐	☐
Comments							
☐ P.M.	☐	☐	☐	☐	☐	☐	☐
Effectiveness rating	☐	☐	☐	☐	☐	☐	☐
Comments							

Daily self-monitoring form for muscle relaxation exercises

Effectiveness rated from 0 to 10 where 0 = not at all effective and 10 = very effective

	Monday	Tuesday	Wednesday	Thursday	Friday	Saturday	Sunday
☐ A.M.	☐	☐	☐	☐	☐	☐	☐
Effectiveness rating	☐	☐	☐	☐	☐	☐	☐
Comments							
☐ P.M.	☐	☐	☐	☐	☐	☐	☐
Effectiveness rating	☐	☐	☐	☐	☐	☐	☐
Comments							

Daily self-monitoring form for muscle relaxation exercises

Effectiveness rated from 0 to 10 where 0 = not at all effective and 10 = very effective

	Monday	Tuesday	Wednesday	Thursday	Friday	Saturday	Sunday
☐ A.M.	☐	☐	☐	☐	☐	☐	☐
Effectiveness rating	☐	☐	☐	☐	☐	☐	☐
Comments							
☐ P.M.	☐	☐	☐	☐	☐	☐	☐
Effectiveness rating	☐	☐	☐	☐	☐	☐	☐
Comments							

Daily self-monitoring form for muscle relaxation exercises

Effectiveness rated from 0 to 10 where 0 = not at all effective and 10 = very effective

	Monday	Tuesday	Wednesday	Thursday	Friday	Saturday	Sunday
☐ A.M.	☐	☐	☐	☐	☐	☐	☐
Effectiveness rating	☐	☐	☐	☐	☐	☐	☐
Comments							
☐ P.M.	☐	☐	☐	☐	☐	☐	☐
Effectiveness rating	☐	☐	☐	☐	☐	☐	☐
Comments							

Daily self-monitoring form for muscle relaxation exercises

Effectiveness rated from 0 to 10 where 0 = not at all effective and 10 = very effective

	Monday	Tuesday	Wednesday	Thursday	Friday	Saturday	Sunday
☐ A.M.	☐	☐	☐	☐	☐	☐	☐
Effectiveness rating	☐	☐	☐	☐	☐	☐	☐
Comments							
☐ P.M.	☐	☐	☐	☐	☐	☐	☐
Effectiveness rating	☐	☐	☐	☐	☐	☐	☐
Comments							

Index

Order further books in the *Overcoming* series

Qnty	Title	RRP	Offer Price	Total
	Anger and Irritability	£9.99	£7.99	
	Anorexia Nervosa	£9.99	£7.99	
	Anxiety	£9.99	£7.99	
	Anxiety Self-Help Course (3 parts)	£21.00	£15.00	
	Bulimia Nervosa and Binge-Eating Self-Help Course (3 parts)	£21.00	£15.00	
	Childhood Trauma	£9.99	£7.99	
	Chronic Fatigue	£9.99	£7.99	
	Chronic Pain	£9.99	£7.99	
	Compulsive Gambling	£9.99	£7.99	
	Depersonalization and Feelings of Unreality	£9.99	£7.99	
	Depression	£9.99	£7.99	
	Depression: Talks With Your Therapist (Audio)	£9.99	£7.99	
	Grief	£9.99	£7.99	
	Insomnia and Sleep Problems	£9.99	£7.99	
	Low Self-Esteem	£9.99	£7.99	
	Low Self-Esteem Self-Help Course (3 parts)	£21.00	£15.00	
	Mood Swings	£9.99	£7.99	
	Obsessive Compulsive Disorder	£9.99	£7.99	
	Panic	£9.99	£7.99	
	Panic and Agoraphobia Self-Help Course (3 parts)	£21.00	£15.00	
	Paranoid and Suspicious Thoughts	£9.99	£7.99	
	Problem Drinking	£9.99	£7.99	
	Relationship Problems	£9.99	£7.99	
	Sexual Problems	£9.99	£7.99	
	Social Anxiety and Shyness	£9.99	£7.99	
	Social Anxiety and Shyness Self-Help Course (3 parts)	£21.00	£15.00	
	Traumatic Stress	£9.99	£7.99	
	Weight Problems	£9.99	£7.99	
	Worry	£9.99	£7.99	
	Your child's Fears and worries	£9.99	£7.99	
	Your child's Shyness and Social Anxiety	£9.99	£7.99	
	Your Smoking Habit	£9.99	£7.99	
	Manage Your Mood: Behavioral Techniques to Overcome Depression	£12.99	£10.99	
	P&P	FREE	FREE	
	Total			

Name: _____

Address: _____

_____Postcode:_____

Daytime Tel. No.: _____

E-mail: _____

(in case of query)

How to Pay:

1. **By telephone: call the TBS order line on 01206 255 800 and quote PANIC. Phone lines are open between Monday–Friday, 8.30am–5.30pm.**
2. By post: send a cheque for the full amount payable to **TBS Ltd**, or if paying by debit, credit or Switch card, fill in the details above and send the form to: Freepost FLUL-SJGC-SGKJ. Cash Sales/Direct Mail Dept, The Book Service, Colchester Road, Frating, Colchester, CO7 7DW

Constable & Robinson Ltd (directly or via its agents) may mail or phone you about promotions or products. Tick box if you do not want these from us ❑ or our subsidiaries ❑.

From

The Women's Press Ltd
34 Great Sutton Street, London EC1V 0DX

FRANCES GAPPER

Saints and Adventurers

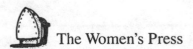 The Women's Press

First published by The Women's Press Limited 1988
A member of the Namara Group
34 Great Sutton Street, London EC1 0DX

British Library Cataloguing in Publication Data available

Typeset by Boldface Typesetters Ltd, Clerkenwell Road, London
EC1
Printed and bound in Great Britain by Hazell Watson & Viney Ltd,
Aylesbury, Bucks.

Acknowledgments

Many women helped me to write this, but especially Ruth Bowen: I relied throughout on her support and encouragement. I was grateful, though it may not have appeared so, for her clear-minded, brave criticism. Dear Ruth, thank you.

Love and thanks also to Gillian Fleming, Sue Bradley, Jenny Sprince, Su Wilkins, Jen Green, Caroline Halcrow, Gemma Davies, Sara Cookson, Sally Purnell, Patience Gapper, Rose Ellis and Siobhan Wall.

I am indebted to Dorothy Carrington for her wonderful book *Granite Island: A Portrait of Corsica*.

What is the human soul? Who are we? How do you respond
in different circumstances? What are your limitations, if
any? Are you a divine being? Are you a shadow of the
infinite or are you some schmuck who's just *here*? Are you
part of the food chain? *That's* what I'm interested in.

Jody Scott

One

On the day my brother died, when I was fourteen, a grey, wet, windy day in late August, my grandmother drowned the cat. I've never told anyone this before. She held him down by his neck in the washing-up bowl until he stopped struggling. We were alone, my mother still at the hospital.

My grandmother is a *mazzere* in the old Corsican tradition – a soothsayer, a seeing woman. She dropped Timmy on the floor, like a wet dishcloth in a pool of water. He looked very dead. My brother's death still seemed unreal to me.

'I saw your brother's soul,' she said, 'in the cat's eyes. I knew it then, for certain, many months ago. Death was eating him.'

My grandmother has brown, wrinkled skin and a hooked nose. She looks like a child's drawing of a witch, dressed all in black, with a headscarf. In Corsica old women like her are quite common; it's only in England they seem peculiar. In her mountain village she was accepted as a wise woman, with power to cure and curse. She went hunting at night in the *maquis*; she tore pigs apart with her bare hands and read the future in their entrails.

Here in England she mends electrical equipment, old rusty things no one else can be bothered to service – record players and dishwashers and radios. She rescues them from scrap heaps and sells them off at high prices. She took a T O P S course in carpentry, but she understands electricity by instinct. She does plumbing too. I think she's wonderful, but I can understand why some people don't like her. My father, for instance. She's very set in her ways.

And she always disliked England. She hated her bedroom, with its pink patterned wallpaper and matching curtains and bedside

1

lamp and my mother's carefully arranged vases of flowers. So she sat up most nights in the kitchen, fiddling with plugs and fuses, muttering under her breath. This used to infuriate my mother.

'Mother, do go to bed. It's past eleven.'

'You did a strange thing, my child, coming to this country. Why did you marry this man?'

'Oh, for heaven's sake, mother.'

'What unnatural impulse possessed you? Why did you leave your home, your family, your native land?'

My grandmother begins to chant softly, one of her weird Corsican peasant songs. 'All songs are about death,' she told me once. Lying in the next room, I can hear everything. The back of my neck prickles, as if touched by a ghostly cold hand. My grandmother's own hands are surprisingly warm, brown and knotted with veins.

A slam as my mother throws the cat out; bangs and crashes as she sweeps the floor and sets the breakfast table.

'Let's not go through all this again.'

'You were not meant to marry. I brought you up to be *mazzere* like myself.'

'I never wanted to be a *mazzere*. That's your way, mother, not mine. You had no right to do that to me. Besides, that's all – '

My mother hesitates, trying to find the appropriate phrase. She speaks English better than any British person, with a pure upper-middle-class accent. You'd never guess where she came from.

'That's all old-fashioned. Old hat. We don't have *mazzere* now. That's all gone out of the window. I'm a married woman – '

A pause. I can picture my mother standing very straight, clenching her left hand behind her back – a characteristic gesture. She sleeps with that hand clenched. She never takes off her wedding ring, not even to do the washing up. My grandmother stole her engagement ring, she maintains, and buried it somewhere in the *maquis*.

'I'm a married woman, with two children to look after. I've neither the time nor the inclination to – '

'Your child is dying. Your son is dying.' My grandmother is half-singing, her voice loaded with doom, fatalism, the burden of ancient sorrows.

2

'Shut up,' my mother screams. 'Shut up, shut up!'

'He is dying.'

'Shut up, you evil old woman. Don't you dare. I'll strangle you with my bare hands. I'll – '

Electric silence.

'He's perfectly all right,' my mother says finally, calm and controlled. 'What are you talking about? He's fine.'

I know my brother is dying, that's quite obvious, just as it's clear my mother knows too and is refusing to see, blinding herself. The whole family structure is toppling, swaying, about to crumple and collapse inwards like a house of cards, her carefully constructed nuclear family, the only safeguard between her and – what?

I know her nightmares. She'll find herself back in Corsica. The dusty, empty streets, the faceless buildings, the blazing sun. My mother in a black dress, sitting behind dark shutters. All the men died young in her family, or shot each other in the vendetta; that began in the nineteenth century with a peach tree growing in the dividing wall between two pieces of territory. In one year, five men died. My grandmother remembers it with pride, she was renowned all over Corsica as a funeral singer.

When my mother was eighteen, her fiancé, Diolé, died of some wasting disease. They had been betrothed for six years, since they were twelve. I know this story by heart; my grandmother retells it often.

'And each year Diolé appeared to grow lighter. He grew thin as if his blood were draining away and the very marrow being sucked out of his bones. And his skin became deathly pale. One day I was at the well, winding the heavy chain to draw water . . .' My grandmother always mimes this bit, throwing her whole body into it, wiping her forehead. I can feel the heat of the sun, hear the chain creaking and the crickets singing, even my hands feel sweaty. 'As I drew up the bucket,' my grandmother says, her voice sinking to a whisper 'as I drew up the bucket . . .' And suddenly she starts back. 'I saw Diolé's face in the water. It was then I knew he would die. I told Pauletta, your mother. She refused to believe me.'

My grandmother lifts her eyes to the ceiling and crosses herself

3

slowly – forehead, heart, right shoulder, left shoulder. Then she sighs and shrugs. 'He died, three months afterwards. Pauletta never drank water again.'

That part used to fascinate me most when I was small. 'She never drank water? What did she drink, then? Lemonade? Did she have Lucozade? Did she have ginger beer?'

Eventually my grandmother had to amend the story slightly. 'Pauletta never drank water again, from that well. But she drank water from the spring, and milk from the cow.'

My mother never refers to this incident, nor to Diolé, and refuses to answer questions. I get the impression she married my father quite shortly afterwards as he was passing through the village on his way to Mount Cinto, on his long search for the yellow horned Corsican/Gallatian butterfly. My father is a world expert on butterflies. We rarely saw him when we were kids: he was always off on some expedition, sailing down the Nile or the Mississippi, climbing cautiously through jungles with his little net and telescope. While my mother was struggling with language books and two small children in Surbiton, he was catching moths in the Cameroons, setting up insect reserves in Burma, writing encyclopaedias, attending conferences and conventions. He's that kind of person – elusive.

I suppose all families have problems, but I envied my schoolfriends. At least their fathers were usually present and more or less in charge. This is very important it seems to me. I don't agree with feminism. Women are too powerful already, they should be kept under control. That's why my father is so hopeless: he evades all his responsibilities. He just stays upstairs all day in his tiny study, with his hundreds of dead butterflies in glass cases and pinned round the walls.

I don't blame him so much now. I suppose we all find our ways of coping and making sense of life. He and I have much in common. I realise this more and more as I get older. As he classifies and arranges his butterflies, I try to pin our family down in some finally recognisable order and pattern. I think this task may be impossible. I remember a lot of things, vividly, but very few of them have any obvious significance, so I don't tell them to people.

4

I'm always hesitant to speak where I may not be understood, unlike my grandmother, who was never bothered by such scruples. My grandmother's name is Clara: clear voices speak through her, she reports what she hears. I used to hear the spirits too. They came whistling round the house about two or three o'clock every morning, crying 'John! John!' – that's my brother's name. My mother slept soundly, with plugs of cotton wool in her ears; she never went to sleep without her earplugs.

The spirits kept me awake, but for some reason they never really frightened me. They were too Corsican, too peculiar to be really convincing: 'over the top', as my mother would say, with their thin, high, frantic voices and little flapping wings. My grandmother's stories had taught me a certain tough insouciance about the spiritual world. When they became too insistent, usually late on Friday nights, I wrapped myself in my eiderdown and ran into the kitchen.

'Granny, I heard the spirits again.'

'Little bags of wind. Little breaths of sour air. Pay no attention, child, they're not calling for you. Hold this screwdriver for me. Now wait. Now turn it around, slowly, slowly. See, the long bolt is leaving his hole. We will be ready to receive him. Keep both your hands very steady. Keep watching.'

She kept me up till dawn sometimes, dismantling equipment, unscrewing, taking it apart – always 'slowly, slowly' – till the table was littered with coils of wire, nuts and bolts, rusty bits of metal. My grandmother had inexhaustible patience. She removed every last screw, stripped things down to their bare essentials. 'This poor refrigerator, he is suffering, the life is trapped in him. Let us release his spirit. Slowly now, gently.'

My father sometimes appeared briefly, looking hassled and distracted, with his hair standing on end, to make himself cups of tea. 'Good, good. Fine weather. Where's the milk? I can't seem to find it anywhere. Who put the milk away last?'

My grandmother ignored him. 'See these wires, let us follow them, one by one. The pink wire, she goes down here. The green wire, up here.'

'Shouldn't you be in bed, Jenny?'

'I'm helping Granny.'

'Oh, I see. Yes. Fine, fine. This milk has gone sour, by the way. We should order some more. Remind me to ask your mother.'

As I remember him, my father was always surrounded by a cloud of butterflies, fluttering around his head, settling on his spectacles and his teacup. This sounds unlikely in retrospect. His disposition was kindly, but his mind was constantly elsewhere, distracted by articles and abstruse theories. Having made his tea, in a vast cracked china cup, and stirred in plenty of sugar, he would shuffle back upstairs.

Did he ever hear the spirits, I wonder? They say everyone in the family does except the dying person. Perhaps he thought they were butterflies. I can picture him, leaning out of the window at dead of night, trying to catch them with his little net.

At dawn there's a sort of pause, an empty space, a gap between the first light and day beginning, before the milkman's van comes whining and clinking down the street and the ceiling creaks as your mother gets up and goes to the bathroom. This time is very quiet, except for the birds singing, and the sky is almost colourless. My grandmother boils up water in a saucepan and makes chamomile tea. Sipping it, she tips her chair back.

'Where I come from,' she says, 'it is a very big place, a very wild place. Where you come from also, child. People say it is beautiful.' She shrugs. 'I don't know about that. The hills make big shapes against the sky. The villages are tiny, like little mice. People are born. They die. It makes no difference. The hills are bigger than death: they are promises of eternity, made by the hand of God. Here in England they have no hills, so they are afraid, like your mother. They never speak of death. They pretend it does not exist.'

All through my childhood, my grandmother was teaching me, showing me different kinds of knowledge and awareness, things I never learned from my mother. 'What does your heart say?' she asked me once. I was only five or six at the time. It was a difficult question to ask a child. 'What does your heart say? Listen to it. Listen.' She put her hand on my chest, and suddenly, with her touch, I could hear all kinds of things. It was like an extra part of

6

me coming to life. 'Listen. What can you hear?' I could hear ordinary things, birds calling and cars going by, but also I could *hear* – this is hard to explain – things far away and silent. My father sitting upstairs reading. My mother in the garden, kneeling among her flowers, her delicate English-garden flowers, so carefully cultivated, with such persistent effort and dedication. Forget-me-nots, heartsease, lilies of the valley. She loves their names.

'What does your heart say? Listen to it.'

The quieter people were, it seemed, the more clearly I could hear them. This makes sense to me now. The quiet people are the most violent, like locked doors. I could hear my own blood too, roaring in my ears like the wind in the trees, or the sea. And it got louder and louder until everything went black. I must have fainted, because I woke up in bed with Mother bathing my forehead with eau-de-cologne.

'They are afraid of death. Your brother is dying. His life is wasting away, wasting away – ' My grandmother spreads out her hands, palms upwards. 'What can be done? Nothing. Who can change the will of God?'

I'm not sure who my grandmother meant by God. She was surprisingly simple and conventional in some respects, so perhaps it was the Christian god, Father, Son and Holy Ghost. Perhaps not. Death was always female in her stories, a woman in black, and the victim was usually a man in the prime of life. He would meet her quite casually, selling fruit at a market stall or begging in the street. I always visualised her as my mother for some reason. A more unlikely person would be difficult to imagine. She never ever wore black or loitered around the market places. She was always brisk and busy, always doing something – making shopping lists, painting the ceiling. She was formidably self-controlled and in control of things, objects – I never once saw her drop or spill anything. Her cupboards were always in perfect order, packets at the back, jars at the front, vegetables wrapped in cellophane. She would have ranged us in similar order given half the chance, all in our separate rooms, safe as dolls in a dolls' house, but fate was working against her.

At twelve my brother stopped going to school. They were giving

7

him tests at the hospital. Then it was drugs – chemotherapy. He was, as my grandmother had always so clearly perceived, dying. He lay on his bed all day, wearing headphones, listening to music. He lay quite still, except for sometimes waving his fingers slightly. I know, because I used to peep through the keyhole. Our house was tall and narrow, winding up from the kitchen to my father's top study, and my brother's bedroom was on the first landing. The door was covered in old tatty stickers and posters, war pictures and aeroplanes, with a little china plaque by the doorhandle saying 'John's room'.

In a dream once I entered his bedroom and saw a skeleton lying there in the same position, stretched out staring at the ceiling. The skeleton was wearing headphones too, but I could hear the music quite loud. It was Beethoven's *Ninth Symphony*.

For a long time the name of his illness was never mentioned, then one day my mother told me. I was just back from school, feeling itchy and hot in my uniform and wanting my tea. She met me at the door with an expression of terrible solemnity, the kind she put on for particular occasions like when I once stole a box of chocolates or when she told me the facts of life. My heart contracted. I felt sick. She took me into the front sitting-room – then I knew it was serious – and drew the curtains before speaking.

The sitting-room was like a small museum, a showcase, used only on special occasions. My mother dusted it religiously once a day and kept the door locked. It contained all the 'best', most grotesque furniture: the red plush sofa, the bidet, various painted screens and gold-lacquered footstools preserved in the family since Napoleonic times and transported with enormous trouble from Corsica, together with a few souvenirs from my father's trips up the Nile – an elephant's foot, a stuffed lizard. I sat gingerly on the edge of a *chaise-longue*. My mother remained standing, very upright, very still and composed. She has an exceptionally sharp outline, even in half-light and shadows. She looked to one side of me, just past my shoulder. 'Your brother has leukaemia,' she said. 'The doctors tell me he will die within a year.' She put both hands behind her back. 'However, that is not true. They have no way of knowing it for certain and I don't believe it. You are not to believe it.'

8

No response being required, I said nothing. My mother had never encouraged intimacy or displays of emotion within the family: she preferred us to keep ourselves to ourselves, English fashion. I felt strangely calm besides; it was hard to imagine my brother really dying. That was my grandmother's belief, my grandmother's storytelling, her drama, her world. My mother was stronger. She could stop anything like that happening; she could close the doors and the windows, seal the walls, keep him alive. My feet felt peculiar, though, as if the floor were dissolving under them. As soon as I could escape, I went to the bathroom. My grandmother was there, squatting by a semi-dismantled washing-machine with five screws in her mouth, frowning intently. I caught sight of my own face in the mirror, dead white, before I was sick in the basin. My grandmother stroked my back and wiped my forehead with a damp flannel. She too said nothing; she was in one of her silent, withdrawn moods. These could last for days, like religious retreats. It was her last resort when some piece of electrical equipment had gone dead: she went silent in sympathy, or companionship. It usually worked in the end.

Shortly after this my brother was taken into hospital. My mother visited him every day. She wanted me to go too. I refused. For one thing, I was too scared; for another, too tired. I was having difficulty in sleeping. Even with all the lights on, I kept waking up every half hour, desperately hungry. And the more I ate, the more I stayed awake. I emptied the fridge every night, devouring whole packets of butter, raw eggs, raw bacon – I had a particular longing for bacon or any kind of meat. My grandmother, absorbed in her machinery, never seemed to notice; perhaps she even approved. It was a very *mazzere*-like thing to do, the equivalent of scouring the hillsides tearing animals to pieces. I was horrified at myself. I felt out of control, voracious, in the grip of wild, unknown forces.

Towards dawn I could usually drop off to sleep, but I had the most peculiar dreams. About getting married, standing in front of the priest in a white veil and wedding dress, with rows of white-clad people behind me. A gold ring was put on my finger. I turned and lifted the veil to see my husband's face. It was my brother.

I can still see his face very clearly, so similar to mine, so

9

unknown. It always disturbed me looking at him. It was like seeing two people blended, one myself, one a total stranger. 'Did you love your brother?' someone asked me once. The question took me aback. I'd never considered it. Love? No. Not at all. I don't think so, anyway. But he was part of my family. He was part of me.

At the hospital they arranged for a bone marrow transplant. He was on a drip, my mother said. He was very weak and spent most of the time sleeping. 'He'll be better soon,' she repeated, 'after his operation. After the transplant.' A hard light of resolution shone in her eyes. It was impossible not to believe her. Modern medicine would outwit the spirits, confound fate. She herself had given five pints of blood. Like the pelican, emblem of Christ. She would live in him. He would live. My grandmother muttered and mumbled in the kitchen corner.

He died during the operation, quite peacefully, they said. The house felt empty and cold. I went upstairs and sat in his bedroom. It was so tidy and well ordered, the books ranged in rows. He had always been ready for death, always waiting for it. My stomach hurt. I could hear my grandmother downstairs, mopping the floor and wailing one of her weird songs. My mother was still at the hospital.

We had reached some kind of resolution, it seemed to me. At this point of crisis, I felt a precarious balance, sitting there on my brother's bed, in the space he had left behind, in his absence. He had chosen death, or the choice had been made for him. He was not a weak person. He was not any kind of real person. He was so thoroughly controlled, in the grip of my family's fate. That's what it means to be haunted, to be overtaken, the spirits eating you alive, from the inside out. That's what happens to men if they won't fight it. And to women? I don't know. In our family, it was always the men – dying, wasting away, succumbing, disappearing. I looked out of the window. My grandmother was kneeling in the rosebed, digging, with Timmy's body beside her wrapped in a black dustbin bag.

That night I slept in my brother's room. It was empty and very quiet. The spirits had gone from outside. I dreamed a lot, mostly about people – my brother, my mother, my father. I still do. I'm

10

still obsessed by them all. They visit me every night, mouthing silent words at me. Or I'm invisible, watching them talk, never quite able to overhear. I had a vivid dream just before dawn. My grandmother came to fetch me; she burst like a whirlwind through my door into my brother's room, seized my arm and wrenched me out of bed. She was stark naked, all wrinkled and bony, with thin legs and sticking-out hip bones. I remember thinking how funny she looked, especially without a headscarf: her hair was all thin and spiky. We went running down the corridor, down the staircase, out of the house. My grandmother went like the wind, I could hardly breathe and my arm was almost pulled out of its socket. Houses whizzed by. Our footsteps made no sound on the pavement. It was still dark, but the dawn was coming in pale streaks across the sky. We passed a milkman, a dustbin van. No one saw us. My legs were exhausted, I thought I was going to die. She was still clutching my arm in a painful grip. At some point my feet left the ground and I was floating, streaming behind her like a flag. She pulled me through an iron gate. It clanged behind us. We were in Richmond Park, under the chestnut trees, by Pen Pond. She let go of me and I fell down. She went leaping out into the bracken on her long brown legs. Some geese flew over, honking. In the distance I could see mountains, and the gate had vanished. There was a heavy, sweet smell. It was the *maquis*, the Corsican undergrowth. I remember seeing the full moon straight above me, hanging enormous in the sky. And then I woke up with my heart pounding, sweating all over.

I grappled with the side lamp and switched it on. There was blood on the sheet, blood on my hands, blood everywhere.

After a few moments of stunned horror, I realised what was happening. It seemed a peculiar time for it. I had foreseen most other possibilities: 'What if it happens in the maths lesson? Or in Assembly? What if I just start bleeding all over the floor?' I had always visualised a great deal of blood, running down my legs, spreading out in enormous pools. My friend Alicia took a more commonsense attitude: 'Don't be silly, it'll only be a few drops at first. We'll have plenty of warning.' I thought of Alicia, who had in fact fulfilled her own predictions just before Christmas: Alicia, always

11

calm, controlled and superior. 'It's such a little thing. I can't think why people make such a fuss. I haven't told my mother. Why should I? It's none of her business.'

The sheets were soaked, bright scarlet. Our family always did things in style; we had a flair for the dramatic. I stripped both sheets and blankets off the bed and dumped them in the laundry basket. Then I went downstairs to the kitchen. It was five o'clock. To my surprise, I found both my grandmother and my mother facing each other across the empty table. My mother's arms were folded; she was gazing blankly into space. My grandmother's hands were outstretched towards her, palms upwards, imploring.

'I saw the child's death, many years ago, in his eyes. The child's death was foretold.'

I stopped in the kitchen doorway, feeling the blood trickling down my legs again. When I returned my mother was speaking, in a strange voice – level, toneless, blank, distant.

'You can do what you want,' she said. 'It makes no difference to me. Go ahead, drown all the cats in the neighbourhood. It will make no difference.'

'You should be wailing and mourning, my daughter. Let your sorrow flow.'

'What's the point?'

'Tear out your hair, like a true woman of our country. Rend your breasts, score them with your nails, your mother's breasts which suckled him. Call on God for revenge.'

'Nobody killed him,' my mother said. 'There's nothing to be avenged. You're living in the past, mother.'

Her voice was so heavy, blank. I can't describe it. It was like a brick wall. In the kitchen doorway, watching, I realised for the first time my mother's power, and my grandmother's, and how powerfully they were opposed. In varied ways but all her life, my mother had been saying 'no', pitting herself against the spirits, against her own past, everything my grandmother stood for. It stops here. No. Shut up and be quiet. I can't hear you. Nothing had changed. She was still rock hard.

I realised, watching them, I would have to choose. Between my

12

grandmother and my mother. An open doorway and a closed door. Equally dangerous. Yes or no.

My first reaction was panic. My first move was towards the cupboard. There was nothing very edible, only glass jars and packets of sugar, flour, etc. I started cramming down sugar very fast, by the handful. It was difficult to swallow, very dry and tasteless.

'What are you doing?' I heard my mother coming swiftly towards me. She gripped my shoulder. 'What are you doing?' she repeated sharply. I turned round, sugar all over my face. 'Eating,' she said contemptuously. 'Eating. I might have known it. Your brother is dead, and all you can do is eat.'

'I've decided,' I said indistinctly through the sugar. 'I've decided.'

'What?'

'I'm going to be a nun.'

'What?'

'When I'm sixteen, I'm joining the Carmelites.'

'Over my dead body.'

I think my mother speaks entirely in set phrases, English phrases. She picks them up on the bus, overhears them in shops, stows them away carefully for future use. Maybe I'm over-sensitive, or over-susceptible, being her daughter, but they never cease to alarm me. She employs them with such force and dexterity, like hand-grenades, bright-edged knives. 'Over my dead body.' She has a certain way of giving life to clichés. An image flashed through my mind: her white, cold corpse outstretched on the kitchen floor, a crowd of nuns beckoning me over.

We stood face to face, the atmosphere fraught with tension. At any moment, I could feel, she was going to slap me. Just in time, my grandmother thrust herself between us.

'Good,' she said eagerly. 'A nun, one of the blessed sisters.'

'You keep out of this, mother, if you please . . . '

'Yes, good. You will be like Blanche, your great-aunt. She became an anchorite after our father's death, she withdrew from the world. Day and night she fasted and prayed in her tiny cell shut away from the light. And she would take no sustenance, only the sacred host. Yes, you will be like her. I see it,' she said, touching

my cheek. 'How old are you? Fourteen. Yes, Blanche was eighteen when she died. A saint, an angel, they preserved her bones for
relics. I have a piece of her elbow in my silver box.'

A strange sound escaped from my mother, a sort of exasperated
hiss. 'Nuns!' she said. 'Don't talk to me about nuns. Elbows,
relics, that's all a lot of gobbledegook.' She turned to me. 'Why
haven't you got a boyfriend? Why can't you be like all the other
girls, normal girls of your age, like your friend Alicia? She's a
nice girl, she's got a boyfriend.'

It was the first time my mother had introduced this subject, but
she had obviously been thinking about it, mulling it over in bitter
silence. I was taken aback. Her attacks always came out of the
blue, unheralded. Why can't you say your six times table? All
your class can say it. Why can't you skip? All the other girls can
skip. Why are you so stupid? Why is your room such a mess?

'I don't know,' I said lamely. My mother's lip curled. In retrospect,
I realise just how strangely she was behaving: like the menopause,
the loss of my brother affected her in all sorts of peculiar ways.

'Come, come,' my grandmother said, urging me away towards
the kitchen door. 'Come, we will find your Aunt Blanche's piece
of elbow.' She opened the door, looked and stopped dead. Her
mouth dropped open. I looked. I nearly fainted. My mother came
up beside us. 'What are you staring at?' she demanded. 'What's
wrong?'

'It's there,' I stammered. 'It's flooding. It's there . . . '

'Where? What?'

'The blood . . . '

'What are you talking about?' my mother said impatiently. But
my tongue had frozen. There was a bitter taste in my mouth, in
spite of the sugar. I could say nothing. Some things you can't even
begin to describe or explain. There was blood on the stairs. That's
putting it mildly. Blood was running down the stairs, pouring
down, streaming. Like water only thicker, and deep red, with
bright reflecting lights, turning darker as it flowed towards us
along the hallway. My grandmother banged the door shut. A little
blood seeped underneath. She stepped backwards. I stepped backwards. We both crossed ourselves.

14

'What's the matter?' my mother cried. 'Have you both gone mad, for heaven's sake?'

My grandmother knelt and muttered a short prayer. Rising, she grabbed hold of my hand. 'Take courage,' she said. 'Come, we will find the source.' I followed, not having much choice, though I did briefly consider trying to escape through the kitchen window. I wondered how you swam in blood, and what it felt like to drown in blood. I thought at least we should wear our Wellington boots, but there was no time, she was already pulling me through the doorway. And the strangest thing happened: the blood parted on either side, leaving a straight path of dry carpet along the hallway and up the staircase.

I walked behind her, like the Israelites behind Moses through the Red Sea, through the terrible sign sent by God to drown the pagans, to obliterate the unblessed. I always felt sorry for the Egyptians and their poor horses. She was talking all the time, in a steady, faraway, storytelling voice. It was like when I was small and scared of going to sleep and she would sit by my bed telling me fairy stories and saint stories. The saint stories were always more exciting. My grandmother told them with utter conviction, as if she were talking about members of our own family. Saint Desolata, who turned into a lion and bit off her pagan father's head. Saint Agnela, who could feed the poor just by crying: the tears transformed themselves into jewels.

'This is a miracle,' my grandmother said as we ascended the stairs. 'Nothing is wrong. You must not be afraid. Exactly such things would happen in Corsica. Yes, all the time.

'Blood is healing,' she added as we crossed the landing. 'Blood is life-giving. You must not fear your own life, the spirit flowing within you. It is given from you. Why should you fear?' The blood flowed past us, soundlessly, not in waves but with its own rhythm, beating out in long pulse strokes steadily from the central source. I could hear my own heart throbbing and the tension in my stomach gradually relaxing. Where the blood lapped against the walls it vanished, leaving no stain.

Something rushed over our heads, something black and flabby with wings, like a cross between a bat and a vulture.

15

'Saint Ranegunde bled for forty nights and forty days,' continued my grandmother. 'Saint Francis of Assisi had the stigmata, he bled from his hands and feet and from a hole in his side. So also did Saint Clare and many of her blessed sisters in Christ. You should consider yourself lucky, child, to be in such company. Blood is a holy sign sent by God.'

The black thing settled on a knob of the staircase, fixing us with one hooded eye.

'What's that?' I said.

'What? Oh, that,' my grandmother said in an off-hand way. 'The devil. Have you never seen him before? Pay no attention, child. He only wants to frighten us.'

The blood tide was ebbing in our wake, retreating backwards upstairs behind us. The hallway carpet was gradually revealed, green and threadbare, looking a bit cleaner than usual. Launching himself heavily into the air, the devil flapped a few feet, then landed with a flat, squashed sound reminiscent of a deflated football. Like the dodo or some other outmoded species, he was apparently incapable of sustained flight. He regarded us sideways, defensively and with hostility. I followed my grandmother hastily into the bathroom.

'Here is the source,' she said, opening the laundry basket. Bending, she took out my bloodstained sheets and blankets and unfolded them carefully, reverently. 'Why should you hide these? Why should you be ashamed? This new blood is the source of life: your own life, the life of your children.'

We both stared at the stains. They looked less frightening than before. It was just ordinary blood, already turning brown. My grandmother sighed. 'Now I am an old woman, I no longer bleed. Still my body changes, but it makes no sign, the blood is held back, hidden away within. In Corsica, for this reason, women of my age are respected and blessed, by our families, both daughters and sons, by the whole village, and people listen when we speak, but here I go unseen, unheard, like the air, like the dust in the street. I may as well save my breath.'

I touched the sheet. It surprised me that I felt no sense of revulsion. I had always imagined my periods would be disgusting and

16

smelly. There was only a faint smell, reminiscent of cow dung. In Corsica they smear cow dung all over the floors to freshen the air. The blood stains made a sort of pattern. Peering more closely, I could almost discern a face – like Christ's face, stamped for eternity on Saint Veronica's towel just before the crucifixion when she wiped the sweat and blood from his brow. It's in the Vatican or somewhere. That's the trouble with being Catholic: it permanently affects your imagination. Signs and symbols abound. The devil on the banisters. Angels round every corner. God's plan for the world. His will made manifest, everywhere, in everything. It becomes exhausting.

'The age of miracles,' said my grandmother, echoing my thoughts, 'is not past. Your old women shall dream dreams,' she added absent-mindedly. 'Your young daughters will see visions. Who knows, I myself may bear fruit again. Children are formed from blood in the womb. The blood grows thick and the child is born. So the Virgin Mary gave birth to our Blessed Lord. So I myself conceived and bore your mother. Come, I shall dry these sheets and put them in my chest.'

My grandmother had a large oak chest under her bed. It was very old and very beautiful, carved with scenes from the New Testament. I was fascinated by these – the angels and the kneeling figures. I used to spend hours gazing at them, tracing them with my fingers, learning every small scene by heart. I imagined them coming alive. In this chest my grandmother stored all her treasures: clothes embroidered with gold and silver, wedding dresses and christening robes, funeral sheets and coffin covers. It had a false bottom, released by pressing the Archangel Gabriel's left eye. Underneath she kept her silver box, containing various relics, and an ancient rusty pistol with nine notches on the handle. I was more interested in the pistol than the box. 'Come, come,' my grandmother urged me across the landing. 'I will hang these sheets from my window. They will dry quickly. Come, we will find your Aunt Blanche's piece of elbow.'

'Oh, can I see the gun? Amaretta's gun?' Amaretta was another of my renowned and legendary Corsican great-aunts. Unsatisfied by her restricted life as a young Corsican woman, fetching water, baking bread, seeing visions and wailing at funerals, she took her dead brother's gun, dressed herself up in his clothes and went out shooting people. She killed nine men before she herself was shot down, in the *maquis*, by her own lover, Léonar. It's a tragic story.

My grandmother picked up the pistol with both hands – it was very heavy – and placed it in my lap. 'Ha,' she said sorrowfully. 'If we were now in Corsica, a man should have died for your brother's life.'

'Nobody killed him, Granny.'

'A man should have died.' My grandmother regarded me with a piercing stare. 'The first man, the first stranger to pass by in the street.'

I took hold of the pistol awkwardly. 'You hold it like this,' she said. 'See' – folding my forefinger over the trigger. At this exact moment, by what has always seemed to me a strange coincidence, the doorbell rang. We both scrambled up. I heard my mother going along the hall. Through my grandmother's open doorway, I saw the devil take off into flight, launching himself down towards her like a great floating vampire. I took aim and fired. The gun was loaded. The devil gave a lurch to one side and vanished. A hole appeared in the front door, shattering one of the coloured glass panes, my mother screamed, the door swung open, a boy staggered inside clutching his arm, and fell. That was how I first met Allibert.

Two

For a long time, all through my childhood, I thought my mother was a martyr and a saint, or at the very least angelically good. Now I realise she was simply mistaken. The word to describe her is naïve. She thought that she was in control, that by moving to England she could escape from the past, create a new world for herself. But no one can leave the past behind, ever. It's a living thing, all mixed up with present and future, a series of recurrent images, of situations and experiences that keep reflecting, repeating and reinforcing each other. We are controlled by our past, by ourselves. My mother's self is essentially helpless in the face of circumstance, stranded in the dark, sitting alone.

Desperation made her over-hopeful. She believed that men – a man – could save her from loneliness and isolation. Her favourite fairy tale was *The Sleeping Beauty*. She used to tell me that story over and over again when I was small, and it always sent me to sleep. I never woke up to hear the ending.

She was unfortunate, perhaps, in marrying my father, whose own isolation was so complete, he never apparently noticed hers, or made any attempt to overcome it. They came back to England in the early 1950s and settled up north, in Stockport, where my mother's perfect upper-middle-class English accent was at first received with hostility. Though eventually the neighbours warmed to her, left cakes on our doorstep and hailed her across the garden wall, she always remained in some sense an outsider, a foreigner. I remember Stockport as a succession of long, grey roads down which my mother walked stiffly, looking straight ahead, pushing the pram, even when it was empty: she used it for the shopping. I disliked being dragged along, forced to hold on to the pram handle. We lived in two distinctly different worlds, my mother and I. By climbing through a hole in the hedge, running down a crazy-paving path and knocking on a green door with the paint flaking off, I could call on Mrs Miller, who was ninety-five years old with a kind, wrinkled face and permanently bent at right-angles, even in bed, and she would give me a mint humbug or a toffee from a tin kept on top of the television. Or by going over the road and down an alley I could find the Loaches, Jane and Judith, who had a big garden with a goldfish pond and a swing; sometimes we played a special game behind the raspberry canes which involved pulling down our knickers and showing our bottoms. My mother had none of these resources, but she had my brother, whom she always kept inside, because he was 'delicate'. I was jealous of him: I wanted to be delicate too. Once I ate five coloured chalks, but it made no noticeable difference, either to my health or to my mother's attitude. I was just sick and then got better. I've always been hopelessly robust. Like most children I wanted to die, either that or to be a princess or to be grown up.

When I was five, everything changed. My father was appointed Chief Lepidopterist at the Natural History Museum and we moved to Surrey.

If my mother was a fairy-tale heroine, then my grandmother was the wicked witch, the old woman spinning in the tower, the evil stepmother. She came over from Corsica on the boat-train, arriving on my mother's doorstep at dead of night carrying only a carpet bag with the barest necessities – two battered saucepans, a knife, a selection of hand tools and her silver relic box. The rest – chaise-longue, etc. – followed later by special delivery.

'Yes, it was her. It was her. It was her,' my mother said, or rather screamed, once, at a moment of crisis and high emotion. 'She ruined everything. She came on purpose to ruin my life. I curse the day she came. I curse her. We could have been so happy –' My mother's voice falters on the word 'happy', dissolves into tears. She covers her face with both hands, slumps into a chair. 'We could have been a nice, normal English family, like all the others. Your brother would never have died. It was her. It was her. She killed him. You would never have – it's her, it's all her fault. *She* turned you against me. *She* made you into this monstrous creature. Don't talk to me. Shut up. Shut up.' My mother jams her fingers in her ears, screws her eyes up tight. 'I'm not listening' she adds, unnecessarily. 'I can't hear you, not a word you're saying. You only want to hurt me. Well, you can't. It won't work.'

The blood episode was never discussed in our family, like most issues. The tide of visionary blood receded, my own flow stopped, my mother presented me silently at arms length with a packet of sanitary towels, and that was apparently that.

I should now explain about Allibert, the boy who fell wounded through the door. Allibert is a minor character, like most men, not particularly interesting, though attractive in his own quietly determined manner. He was distributing newsletters for the local church, Our Lady of Mount Carmel, just up the road. English Catholic churches tend to fall roughly into two categories, unchanged-since-the-nineteenth-century or new wave, post-Vatican II. Our Lady of Mount Carmel was one of the latter. Father John James, the parish priest, was young and eager and full of nervous energy, anxious to make an impact and put across meaningful messages. He organised guitar groups and speakers from other churches and used the New English Bible. The altar was on the same level as the congregation and they stood for Holy Communion, receiving the host by hand instead of having to stick their tongues out, and gave each other the Kiss of Peace.

My mother and grandmother, who disagreed about most things, were united in their opposition to this kind of nonsense, so we attended Saint Cecilia's on the other side of town – a vast, peaceful, empty shell, where Father Carol still said most masses in Latin, with his back to everyone, and services lasted for two hours rather than forty-five minutes, with the Ladies' Choir singing interminably up in the organ loft.

In retrospect, I think they were right. Our Lady of Mount Carmel was too laid-back for my taste, full of liberals and young families. Even Allibert was restless there; he wanted to start

21

another new movement. Father John James meant well, but his concepts were vague and woolly: he believed in loving families, opening our hearts to Christ and being as little children.

'He's not political enough,' Allibert complained. 'He doesn't see all the complexities and the contradictions. What about the Agony in the Garden? What about Christ in the Temple? What about the withering of the fig tree?'

Allibert was small and wiry, with an anxious, intense expression and a restless way of moving from one leg to the other, like a smaller version of Father John James but without the cassock and the kindly smile. What I liked most about him was his lack of intuition. He was like someone from another planet, sent out on a reconnaissance mission, interested in me but distanced, always polite but not really involved on any personal level. However strange my behaviour it never seemed to unnerve him. He took me as I came. At a difficult stage of my adolescence, he was comforting to have around, like a small pet owl. My mother always referred to him as 'that nice boy you shot in the arm', and she was extremely affable towards him, but as a viable male, somehow he failed to make the right impression. She went on bullying me: 'Why haven't you got a boyfriend?'

'I have got one.'

'Who?'

'Allibert.'

'Yes, that's all very well. I mean a proper boyfriend. Like your friend Alicia, she's got a proper one.'

But there was no pleasing her. I tried bringing home other boys, by way of experiment – boys picked up on the street or borrowed for the occasion – but they were never right. 'Yes, that's all very well – ' Once they were actually mine, my mother's enthusiasm cooled noticeably. She regarded them with cynicism and faint disdain, and so they drifted away.

In spite of my mother, Allibert and I established what might be called a committed relationship, never exactly passionate but based on mutual respect. He helped me in the search, the long search, that began after my brother's death and still continues, without any foreseeable ending. I felt my brother's absence physically, as an empty space just below my heart. Often I mistook the emptiness for hunger. Around this time, I began to put on rather a lot of weight.

Allibert's arm was on the mend. He wore it in a sling. My bullet had luckily missed the bone, passing through the fleshy part just below his shoulder. He never asked why I had shot him – one of the many pertinent questions he never asked. He complained vociferously, however, about the tight bandages and the itching. Saturday afternoons and Wednesday evenings we used to sit on my brother's bed, discussing death, or his arm, or sex, or religion. I made various attempts, none very subtle, to entice him into physical contact which he observed with analytical interest, but he remained aloof, having taken a vow of chastity.

After John's death, my mother and father went down to Brighton for a couple of weeks – 'for the air', as my mother said. She was a great believer in air. They booked into a hotel room on the seafront with a white cast-iron balcony. My father disappeared instantly into the local butterfly museum; my mother bought a pair of sunglasses and sat on the balcony reading Mills and Boon books. She had a voracious appetite for romance, especially for romantic heroes – strong and manly, seemingly indifferent, but with concealed depths of tenderness and passion. They were usually doctors or surgeons. I can understand the attraction, sometimes I wished Allibert were a doctor, at least then he might have touched me occasionally.

But the main use of a man is to provide security: men should be life's permanent fixtures, like walls or floorboards, things you take for granted, reliable things. That's why it's so disquieting when they won't be or can't. It's like having no house to live in, no walls, an upsetting lack of sheltering confines.

Sometimes, I like to think, my mother would close her book for a moment, raise her sunglasses and gaze out across the ocean. In the blue distance, on the far horizon, she could just see a few tiny, white, triangular sails. There would be a faint clamour from the beach, children playing on trampolines, and the rhythmic sighing of the waves, washing up and down. If I had been there, sitting opposite her on the white balcony, looking out to sea, I might have

23

glimpsed a mermaid, a woman without a soul, sitting on a rock, combing her seaweedy hair. And singing, a soulless, wordless, wild song of longing. I often see mermaids. In real life, in actual fact, they're quite common. When the sea gets colder, in September and October, they swim in close to the shore. I pointed one out once to Allibert, but he looked in the wrong direction – luckily, perhaps, or he might have been entranced and seduced – and the mermaid gave a flick of her tail and vanished beneath the waves. My mother always refused to look. 'Don't be silly. Mermaids are mythical creatures.'

My relationship with Allibert developed rapidly, I see from my diary. After ten days, on a Wednesday evening in early September, we reached our first crisis. 'He and I are no longer on speaking terms,' I wrote. 'Not on speaking terms', a useful and dignified phrase frequently employed by my mother, who despite her respect for the English lauguage had a tendency to over-dramatise actual situations. She was 'not on speaking terms', she considered, with about half the neighbourhood: the butcher, who called her 'darling'; the milkman, whose whistle she disliked; Mrs Bird from the Catholic Ladies' Sewing Circle. 'Not on speaking terms' – feeling inwardly murderously hostile, but not necessarily not communicating.

In fact, Allibert said a good deal. I remember the infuriatingly level tone of his voice going on and on. He thought that

1. I was sexually frustrated,
2. I should get myself 'sorted out', and
3. I should learn to masturbate.

Both Allibert's parents were Freudian psychotherapists. In addition, his mother was a renowned academic, artist and sculptor, and a socialist feminist. In retrospect, I realise what I was up against; at the time, innocently, I thought it was just him.

I refused point-blank to masturbate. This seemed to me a disgusting idea, even though Allibert offered to read out the instructions. He had borrowed, or removed without asking, a book from his mother's study. It was called *The Modern Woman: Sexual Fulfilment and Sexual Fantasies*, by E. J. Rathbone, M D, gender unspecified. In the first chapter, Dr Rathbone described the various

24

phases of orgasm. One, I remember, was called the 'plateau'. 'Some women never get past that,' Allibert informed me. 'It's the crucial stage.' His own interest, as he tried to persuade me, was entirely clinical, and he had also brought along a briefcase containing his notebook and pencil. 'You needn't be embarrassed. I'll be quite objective.' It was important, he said, for the male to remain aloof and detached, an observer, as instanced by several study cases in the 'sexual fantasies' section. 'I brought the notebook on purpose,' he added. 'When you reach the arousal phase, let me know, then I'll get it out. It could increase your excitement.'

I picked up the book and flicked through; the diagrams were explicit and made me feel faintly queasy. I was still far from reconciled to the female body, in particular wombs and ovaries – the genital bits left me comparatively untroubled. On the flyleaf was a dedication, written in large, sloping, purple letters: 'To Emily, my dearest wife and cherished sexual partner, in token of two decades of pleasure and mutual fulfilment. XXXX'. I read this aloud. Allibert went bright red and grabbed the book. 'My father,' he mumbled. 'He talks like that.'

Allibert's intellectual curiosity remained unsatisfied. I refused to make an exhibition of myself. 'Well, I was only trying to help,' he said defensively. 'Since you obviously have sexual problems.' Like most men, he took his own peculiarities for granted – the vow of chastity, for instance. 'My mother says it's a statement I have to make, a necessary stage in my psychological development.'

Allibert's mother, Emily, was quite a lady, different from mine in almost every possible respect. She had made a film of herself masturbating. 'I'll show it to you, if you like,' said Allibert casually.

'What?' I was torn between horror and fascination. 'But won't she mind?'

'Oh, no. They let me use the cine-camera. I watch it quite often.'

I accompanied him home the following week. His parents lived in a mock-Tudor mansion in south Surbiton, a discreet tree-shaded area almost totally silent, isolated from main roads, railway lines

25

and flight paths. I found this area both frightening and deeply depressing: no kids in the streets, no chip shops, no old people, only barred steel entrance gates and long front drives. Chauffeur-driven cars swished silently past. All the houses had burglar alarms. In Allibert's, this was carried to ridiculous extremes: everyroom was wired up to a central system; the doors had to be kept locked. It took a long time getting upstairs to Allibert's bedroom. He was nervous about relocking all the doors behind us – this had to be done within five minutes, otherwise an alarm went off in the local police station.

It was a vast house, more like a hotel. I was accustomed to deserted corridors and empty feelings, especially since my brother's death, but in our house you could always hear *something* – noises from outside or the kitchen, creaking floorboards, a hoover, a tap dripping, or the bathroom cistern's distinctive high hissing/singing, which incidentally made my grandmother home-sick for Corsica, reminding her of crickets in the *maquis*. In Allibert's house, nothing – no sound. It was like being inside a bank safe. The hallway carpet was dark red, the pile very deep with long, woolly strands. Walking in it was difficult, a strange slowed-up dream-like sensation. Allibert seemed to make better headway; I kept stumbling. The wallpaper was red plush, all the same pattern. There were no pictures, this disturbed me most. Our house was full of pictures, mainly scenes from the lives of the saints – Saint Catherine being nailed to a wheel, Saint Penelope tied to the wild horse. I was beginning to feel very faint. Black spots came floating across my field of vision, small at first, then rapidly expanding. My legs seemed to dissolve and my ears filled up. It was like being underwater, drowning. I could hear voices speaking, very far away and distorted. At this point apparently Allibert was introducing me to his mother. 'What did you think of her?' was the next thing I heard.

'Who?'

'My mother.'

'Oh, your mother? Oh, yes. Very nice.'

'You acted a bit strange.'

'Did I?'

26

'Yes. A bit distant. Embarrassed, maybe. You didn't mind her – ' Allibert made a graphic gesture, with cupped hands.

'What?'

'Being in her bathrobe.'

'Oh, no. Not at all.'

Allibert chewed his little fingernail pensively. 'I think she thinks you've got problems. She had that look on her face.'

I found myself sitting in a vast, soft-cushioned chair, arms outstretched and feet dangling. 'Allibert,' I said. 'Where is this? Where are we?'

'This is my bedroom.'

'I'm not feeling very well.'

'Don't worry, it's a natural enough reaction.'

Allibert's bedroom was in keeping with the rest of the house: like a large hotel suite. A double-bed with the sheet turned down, a circular sunken bath, a chandelier, a television. Impressive but lonely.

'Why is it so dark in here?'

Allibert was holding a small remote-control gadget. He pressed a button and the window curtains shot back with an electric hiss. 'I prefer it,' he said. 'You can see why.'

I walked across the room and looked out. There, a long way down, was a stone courtyard. Perhaps courtyard is the wrong word, since it must have covered about two acres. Flat stone, blind white stone, hard, faceless, stretching east, west and north, bounded on each side by the same immaculate high stone wall. I was used to broken fences, lackadaisical attempts at dividing and partitioning, for although my mother kept her house in such strict order, she relaxed a bit outside. With her hands in the earth, putting in bulbs or weeding, she grew definitely more cheerful; she even looked younger; and she liked to experiment and move things around. She had even made a butterfly garden for my father and though it seldom attracted any actual butterflies, this was a talking point among the neighbours, provoking tentative ecological discussions.

'Who lives next door?' I asked.

'I don't know,' Allibert said gloomily. 'Millionaires. No one

27

lives to the left.'

As my eyes grew accustomed to bleakness and stone, I realised the courtyard was not entirely empty. Here and there appeared big marble shapes, not exactly statues, aborted columns and steps ending in mid-air. Abstracts, I suppose. 'My mother's a sculptor,' Allibert explained. 'She's working on a series; it's called "Landscapes of the Female Psyche".'

I stared at the statues. They didn't remind me of anything female, even symbolically female, though admittedly they haunted my dreams for months afterwards.

'Don't you have a garden?'

'That is the garden.' Allibert paused. 'We used to have a gardener,' he added, 'but he had a mental breakdown and they put him in a home.'

'Oh.'

'He was quite old. I liked him. My mother said his super-ego wasn't sufficiently strong.'

'What was it like, the mental breakdown?'

Allibert pressed his nose against the window pane. 'I don't know. He didn't seem to change much. Only his face got sadder.'

We stayed a long time by the window, side by side, gazing down. The courtyard had a hypnotic effect. I could feel my face getting sadder, like the gardener's. Were all families such lonely places to be? I'd always thought ours was exceptional, but compared to Allibert's, we seemed not to rate so badly. Fair to moderate, on the loneliness scale. Families. Houses. Empty boxes. But I wasn't sure of the alternatives.

'Do you think I'm strange?' Allibert asked me later. We were back in my part of town, walking past the shops. I remember the air seemed lighter and I was thankfully breathing it in.

'Everyone's strange,' I replied. On further reflection this struck me as a profound truth. In my whole life, fourteen years, I'd never met anyone who wasn't. The only difference is, some people think they're normal, that's where all the trouble starts.

'I mean, do you think I'm too intense?'

'No.' It seemed obvious Allibert was too intense; there was no point trying to reassure him. I was watching the sky. Bright blue, with fluffy white clouds, like the pictures I used to draw for my brother when we were small to explain the world. He had had difficulty understanding large concepts.

'Sometimes I wonder,' said Allibert, carefully 'if I might be gay.'

I said nothing. He cleared his throat.

'I think I'm frightened of female sexuality.'

This was the most he'd ever admitted, and perhaps I should have followed up my advantage. But I was fourteen, obscurely resentful and not exactly sure of what the words meant.

We passed a couple of young mothers pushing prams; one was already pregnant again. Allibert stared intently at her stomach. I glanced inside the prams. Two babies, exactly alike: bald, dribbling, with clenched fists. The sight of them gave me a peculiar feeling, between hunger and despair.

'You should have a baby,' Allibert said.

'Why?'

'It might help to resolve the conflicts in our relationship.'

'What conflicts?' I said crossly.

'It might stabilise your emotions. Help you come to terms with, you know – '

'What?'

'Your brother's death.'

'I have,' I said. 'I've completely come to terms with it. Anyway, shut up. Shut up. You didn't know him, and you don't know anything.'

'All right, all right.'

I bought a bar of chocolate and ate it. Allibert waited till I'd finished.

'I'm sorry,' he said.

'That's okay.'

'D'you want some more chocolate?' Allibert liked me to eat and took every opportunity to encourage me: it seemed to cheer him up and clear the air between us.

'Yes, okay then.'

He bought two bars; I ate them both.

D'you want some more?'

'No, I'm going for a walk.'

Allibert's forehead contracted. 'Without me?'

'Yes.'

'I don't think you should.'

'What?'

'You might get lost or something. In the state you're in.'

'What state? I'm fine.'

'Sure you'll be safe?'

'Yes, of course I'm sure.'

He watched me out of sight. I felt guilty at leaving him, like I always did, however we parted, but there are times you have to abandon people. They can live without you, separate and independent. Even men, although as it turned out Allibert had increasing difficulties. I walked off in the direction of home. Passing the municipal cemetery I saw, through the black wrought-iron gates, my mother, her stiff unmistakable outline. She was bent over my brother's grave, in formal mourning posture like a Victorian sculpture, indicating grief, abandonment, widowhood. But not crying.

Three

Like most prophets and visionaries, my grandmother had little concern for social etiquette and normal accepted levels of behaviour. She lived the life of the spirit, however awkward this might prove for other people.

'She only does it to embarrass me. She is impossible. *Impossible*.'

This was after the Avon Lady incident, which turned my mother, like Lot's wife, totally rigid, tears of fury trickling down her cheeks. My grandmother had just bought twenty pots of lipstick/blusher, bright red – the Avon Lady's entire stock – for reasons not fully elucidated.

'It is a good, good colour,' she said excitedly.

'Yes – er, we do find it very popular.'

'It is holy.' My grandmother leant forward. 'The colour of life and death. It is used in my own country, by tradition, for religious ceremonies.'

The Avon Lady maintained a fixed smile, but her eyes rolled helplessly. She got no help from my mother, withdrawn into frozen silence. 'Are you quite sure, dear, you need so much? Most of our customers just buy a single pot.'

But it was pointless talking economy to my grandmother once her eye had fixed on anything she liked, and she could pay besides, cash down for all purchases. She was making £500 a week average; her fridges and ovens appeared regularly in *Exchange and Mart* and the local and national newspapers and she was doing shift work at the garage down the road.

Around this time she began to discard her black dresses,

appearing for tea in boiler suits and greasy overalls. 'Tea time' was my mother's introduction, not so much a meal as a statement of opposing values. My mother wore 'pretty' dresses, paisley-patterned, high-necked and waisted, English style, and served dainty pink-iced cakes. We were never actually permitted to eat these cakes; they were served more as decorations, dolls' house food. Once, greatly daring, I reached out for one, but encountering her furious gaze, faltered and withdrew my hand. I *hated* tea time. Allibert loved it. He basked in all the psychological tension. He adored my mother and her sharp-knived negative atmosphere.

'Of course, she's anorexic,' he said. 'It's her frustrated need for power and control.'

'She's what?' I had never heard this word.

'Anorexic. She doesn't eat; she's starving herself. Haven't you noticed? She's lost about two stone since August. Continuing at the same rate,' Allibert said reflectively, 'that would mean about six stone by Christmas. Interestingly enough, anorexics often die from secondary causes, like colds or pneumonia. More hot water?'

Our Wednesday evening discussions had transferred to the bathroom. I lay in the bath; Allibert sat perched on the side. He controlled the taps. He talked a lot about my mother, but I was only half attending. My own body seemed more of a subject for concern. In direct contrast to hers, it was expanding rapidly: looking down was like gazing over a wide mountainous landscape. The breasts were enormous, one slightly bigger than the other. The word 'belly' was more than appropriate. Overall, I was oblong, filling the bath, bath-shaped. In bed I became flat like a jellyfish, in school I became desk-shaped. It was a curious relief, losing all independent outlines. The only trouble was, I had no role models. None of the saints was overweight. Holiness presumes thinness. I disagreed with Allibert's psychological theories and cynical know-how about my mother's condition. To me it seemed clear she was heading rapidly for sainthood. After all, Simone Weil starved herself to death; no one accused *her* of anorexia. My mother closed her eyes

32

whenever she caught sight of me, accentuating the dying-martyr effect.

Alicia too was thin. Very, very thin. Horrifically thin, and indeed, she was a compulsive watcher of horror films. She adored Dracula in particular, which gave me the shudders: it was the blood theme, too close to home. Alicia liked the final scene, where the ice cracks and Count Dracula disappears underneath. 'Imagine how it feels to drown,' she said. We were down in the cloakroom, the dark womb of the school, the warmest place, where we spent most lunchtimes. It was possible to be more or less private, although occasionally nuns sat spying among the coats, recognisable by their knees.

Alicia, as usual, was examining her reflection in the long cloak-room mirror; I rarely had the courage to examine mine. She liked having me there, for the contrast.

'Imagine the water filling your nose, filling your ears, filling your mouth, filling your eyes.'

Alicia had a natural ear for rhythm and a wonderful memory for poetry. She could recite Tennyson's 'The Lady of Shalott' from beginning to end, and frequently did.

> She left the web, she left the loom,
> She made three paces through the room,
> She saw the water-lily bloom,
> She saw the helmet and the plume,
>   She looked down to Camelot.
> Out flew the web and floated wide;
> The mirror cracked from side to side;
> 'The curse is come upon me,' cried
>   The Lady of Shalott.

At this point Alicia always burst into shrieks of laughter. I never understood why. 'The curse, the curse. You know. Oh God,' sighing, 'you're so stupid.' She also knew by heart 'The Ancient Mariner' and Browning's 'My Last Duchess'. I picked them up too eventually, by force of repetition.

Alicia was, in fact, a genius, By the age of fourteen she was fluent in five languages and super-excellent at mathematics. She understood Einstein's theory of relativity without even looking at the blackboard. It was an obvious trial to her having me for a friend, and difficult for me too, but she had no choice, since everyone else ignored and avoided her. Excellence was *not* encouraged at our school; it was far more important, as the nuns constantly emphasised, to be 'good', which meant normal, ordinary and exactly the same as everybody else. Even passing exams was slightly suspect. There was a long tradition of failing 'O' levels. They were training us to be good wives and mothers, *not*, as Sister Athanasia, the headmistress, said scathingly in Assembly, 'spiritual misfits and academics'. A famous feminist had once attended the school, without being noticed and quashed in time: she was now lecturing at Warwick University. They were determined that nothing of this sort should ever happen again.

But they had problem cases in their own community. One of the younger nuns had a sort of nervous breakdown: she just dissolved into tears one evening in the middle of Compline and couldn't be made to stop for weeks and weeks. Eventually in desperation they put her on the night ferry back to Ireland. The tears dried up as soon as her foot touched Irish soil, 'by a miracle,' she wrote back on a postcard, 'of the Blessed Virgin Mother'. Five years later she founded an order on that very spot, just outside the port. It must have been quite difficult to get planning permission. Then three nuns were discovered sleeping together, a skilled feat in a bed only two and a half feet wide. Two of them, Sisters Adelaide and Veronica, later emigrated to Central America; Sister Carmel, the third, underwent some mysterious operation in the Hospital of the Holy Innocents up in Oxford, where 'troublesome' nuns were sent. She returned 'cured', with an expression of calm serenity. Relieved of her teaching duties, she was confined to the chapel as choir leader. She had an exceptionally pure, high singing voice. In between services she passed her time peaceably enough, lighting candles and blowing them out again.

By good chance we had Sister Christina as our form teacher, an insatiable gossip, and I think she had a certain feeling for Alicia; at any rate she kept us both behind every Friday afternoon, to practise italic handwriting, she said, and archery. Archery had been abandoned back in 1947, when the head girl was shot in the heart – the practice grounds were still fenced off and padlocked, one ancient target remaining, rotting desolately in the rain and wind – and the handwriting lessons never materialised either, but we learnt a good deal about convent life. I began to think seriously of becoming a nun. Sister Christina was strongly discouraging: they were all lesbians and perverts, she said, and mental idiots besides, not one bit of real intelligence between them. She herself was a frustrated career woman. 'I'm wasted here teaching inky-fingered adolescents. I should have been a lawyer by rights. It was my mother, she forced me into this dump. Guilt-tripping me, as usual. God, I can't *stand* women,' she said, snapping a piece of chalk in half.

'Why don't you leave?' I knew this was a stupid question, even before I asked. Alicia gave me a withering glance.

'Why don't I leave?' Sister Christina repeated blankly, gazing across the empy classroom. 'Why don't I leave – And my God,' she burst out, 'it's the *boredom*, you've no idea. You think *you're* bored. Christ almighty. So help me, sometimes I could *murder*. If I could just get my hands round someone's neck,' she said, twisting the air with both hands. I recalled her words the following week when a particularly nasty murder story hit the headlines in our local newspaper, the *Surbiton Gazette*. A three-year-old girl had been decapitated on a stretch of waste ground not far from our school.

However, Sister Christina was by then beyond suspicion, having removed to Arundel Castle in Sussex, 'on retreat'. The second possibility was Alicia, who seemed unusually quiet and withdrawn, her mind obviously occupied. She was always glancing out of the classroom window; the only thing below was a small square courtyard around a goldfish pond. It was autumn. The water-surface was covered with dead yellow leaves. Eleven goldfish were underneath there somewhere, drifting sluggishly in the dark depths; soon they would freeze into hibernation. It seemed sensible of them. I too would have preferred to skip a few months/years of this uncomfortable time of life.

I longed to be a fish, or to be anything apart from me in my horrible body. All my clothes were now at least one size too small, my upper legs rubbed painfully together and it was difficult to move my arms. I was becoming increasingly lethargic: most of my energy went in sweat. I was sweating a lot. Mother had sown bulky cotton pads into all my jumpers, an ingenious idea but hideously embarrassing in practice. Next to Alicia, I looked and felt like King Kong. The misery was containable, mostly, though one evening in the half dusk I tried fumblingly to put words to it. Words had begun increasingly to fail me, another awkward side-effect of adolescence. I was losing the power of speech. When required to answer questions or read aloud, I blushed and stammered, the familiar black specks came floating across my field of vision, my heart pounded till I could hear nothing and see nothing and eventually I would have to excuse myself and sit down. Even in ordinary conversations I had stopped making much sense. Alicia was right, I was stupid. But what could I do about it? Nothing much. Allibert, consulting his mother's textbooks, had reassured me I would 'come through it naturally' sometime between the ages of twenty-one and thirty. It seemed a long time to wait for an uncertain result. Meanwhile, school time was dull and endless. I kept detailed time charts in the back of my exercise books, ticking off the minutes and seconds.

'Oh God,' I said to Alicia. 'I wish I could die.'

We were along in the classroom, pressed up against a lukewarm radiator. I was gnawing my fingers. They were covered in blotches of ink, I remember, as usual. Alicia's fingers were long, white and elegant, similar to those of Elaine, the lily-maid of Astolat, the Lady of Shalott, whom in many respects she resembled.

'Do you really?' she said, regarding me with a faint light of interest. 'Seriously?'

'Yes. I mean – '

'Why don't you, then?' Alicia could sound callous at times, and in fact she was callous. She cared for nobody except her dog, Lancelot. People in general she despised, including all her eight brothers and sisters and both her parents. I was her only friend – at least, I think we were friends – providing some dreary entertainment on occasion.

36

'What?' I said, flummoxed.

'Kill yourself. Why not? I would,' Alicia said, 'in your position,' looking me dispassionately up and down.

I shrank into the radiator. 'You think I'm fat.'

'It's not so much *that*,' she said coldly. 'It's the whole thing, really.'

'What?'

'You. As a total entity, so to speak,' she said, staring at me. She had eyes of a singular, intense blue. She always won our staring competitions: I always lost. I glanced away uncomfortably, feeling like a worm. It was easy to crush me and Alicia's techniques had become highly refined through practice. Having gained her brief victory, she lapsed into despondency. 'Oh God,' she said. 'What's the point anyway.'

We looked out together across the quadrangle. My fingers had gone numb. A shadowy figure was perceptible by the school gates: Hubert, Alicia's boyfriend, in his more or less permanent position. He was unemployed and sunk in deep, robotic despair. Alicia had found this interesting at first but now she was beginning to want something more, something which Hubert, like Allibert, seemed unready to provide. 'He's so *boring*. I get more excitement from Lance. At least Lance thinks I'm sexy.'

Alicia and Lancelot in fact led quite an active sex life, of which I knew a few details. She smeared chocolate around her nipples and he licked it off. He was a large, eager, messy sort of dog, a cross between a dalmation and a springer spaniel. They had a good relationship, grounded in mutual trust and affection, unlike all Alicia's human relationships.

'Come on, let's go home. I've got to walk Lance or he'll piss all over the kitchen floor.'

Hubert stirred slightly as we walked past him in the dusk and made a faint sound, something between a sigh and a moan, like a hollow, decaying tree. He was too depressed to speak. He had been unemployed for two years, his mother had cancer and his father had died from a stroke. A year or so after this, he himself committed suicide, in a peculiarly horrible fashion. Alicia wore black to the funeral and her distant, aloof expression was interpreted

37

as grief, but she was not, I think, particularly upset, certainly not in the least remorseful.

'Yes, all right,' she said sharply as we passed him. 'I'll see you on Saturday. I'm too busy this evening. I've got my homework.'

It was a long walk to the railway station, down a busy main road. When Alicia was in a good mood she would recite poetry, but that night she walked very fast and silently, her long hair floating out behind. We were supposed to wear hats, heavy, solid straw boaters fixed under the chin with elastic, biting into the neck and cutting a painful circle around the head – like Saint Charmian's red-hot iron halo – but mine was lost, as usual, out of the railway-carriage window, and Alicia refused to wear hers, ever. Their absence would have been duly noted, as we left, by Sister Perpetua, ninety years old, sitting perched behind a window like Saint Rapunzel in one of the top classrooms, marking crosses against a register. Five crosses meant a fine. Alicia by then owed the convent some astronomical amount, steadily rising. She was getting monthly statements and veiled sinister threats; they sued her parents eventually, but I think they lost the case, or had to settle out of court.

It was a desolate road. Enormous lorries rattled and banged past. We crossed through a factory yard, then an estate, littered and windswept. Men stood in shadowy alleyways, smoking, their eyes following us non-committally. Children were still out playing hopscotch; they stopped and stared. I was always more unnerved by children. We reached the main road again. Alicia stopped short. In the harsh light she looked other-worldly, fierce and bitter. 'I could be a prostitute,' she said 'any time I want. I will do too, some day.'

After a minute or two of silence, we continued walking. I was feeling miserable, exposed, lost in the world: my usual sensations in Alicia's company. Allibert would have rationalised it, probably, in psychological/historical terms: the post-sixties generation, lack of employment prospects, adolescents in need of an identity, etc. I did try to initiate some tentative discussion about the shadow of nuclear war and despair, but the attempt fell flat. 'Don't talk to me about despair,' Alicia replied scathingly. 'You don't know the first thing about it. I know what despair is.' A pause. 'I know I'm mad and everybody hates me.' Her voice tightened. 'They've tried to send me to a psychiatrist.'

'What?' I said. 'Who?'

'My mother and my horrible father. A bloody Catholic psychiatrist, but I won't go. It won't work. They can't make me.'

Gusts of leaves blew across the pavement. My socks had fallen down, as usual. I hitched them up, wondering what to say next. Alicia was not generally one for confidences and when they came the effect was somewhat stunning, like being slapped in the face. I tried to imagine my mother sending me to a psychiatrist. It seemed to indicate some kind of parental care and concern, shedding a new light on Alicia's parents, who had always appeared so entirely uncaring and emotionally detached from all their children. They had nine: Alicia was the second. Her elder brother had vanished into the world at sixteen, leaving no forwarding address, and the younger children were indistinguishable, a series of little white peaky faces, permanently in retreat behind armchairs or under the kitchen table. Raised voices were forbidden; silence was enforced at mealtimes, except for prayers recited before and after. Her mother was an 'Old Girl' of our school and one of its staunchest supporters. She was chairman of the parents' committee and ran the old school uniform stall at the annual Autumn Fair. Her father was a businessman, but he always seemed to be at home, issuing orders and reprimands or adding to and revising his long list of 'Rules for this House', which he kept pinned up on the kitchen door. No wonder Alicia was unhappy. After Hubert's death, and, more importantly, Lancelot's, she adopted desperate measures.

Having a train pass I could take various routes home. That evening I went via Clapham Junction, where on Platform 10, underneath the steps, there was a small door, barred and padlocked, with a rusty notice which said:

> This door is to be kept locked
> And the room is to remain permanently empty

When they talked about Hell, I always pictured Clapham Junction station and that locked, empty room.

Four

If Allibert had never read *The Well of Loneliness*, our relationship might have developed along more normal lines, but unfortunately he picked it up for 20p in a second-hand bookshop and it changed his life. Beneath his cultivated, cool, male intellectualism and *sang-froid* he could sometimes be very susceptible and *The Well of Loneliness* came at a crucial time, while he was still debating his own possibly ambiguous feelings about Father John James.

We sat together in the Wimpy Bar in Surbiton High Street while he read long sections out loud to me. Fortunately he kept his voice down, mainly, but it rose higher in the emotional bits, embarrassing me intensely. I tried kicking him at intervals, but he persisted.

' "If you come to me, Mary, the world will abhor you, will persecute you, will call you unclean. Our love may be faithful even unto death and beyond, yet the world – ow! – will call it unclean. We may harm no living creature by our love; we may grow more perfect in understanding and in charity because of our loving – " '

'Allibert, *shut up!* '

' " – but all this will not save you from the scourge of a world that will turn away its eyes from your noblest actions, finding only corruption and vileness in you – " '

'*Allibert!* '

' "You will see men and women defiling each other – " Sorry?'

'Yes?' The Wimpy Bar waitress had an unnerving way of suddenly appearing. She was an alarming sort of woman anyway: stunningly beautiful, in her early twenties, with an expressionless face, false eyelashes, painted nails and a sharp tongue. The Wimpy

40

Bar attracted a lot of male customers and she was expert at avoiding their groping hands, carrying her trays high with a swerving walk, manoeuvring between the narrow gaps between tables in which I generally got stuck.

'Yes? What?' she said, flicking her notebook over. Hastily I ordered a number 37, egg and chips, with knickerbocker glory to follow. Allibert was obviously impatient to continue reading.

'Nothing for me, thanks,' he said.

'It's past twelve. There's a minimum order.'

'Oh, very well – ' Allibert raised one eyebrow despairingly, in what he fondly imagined to be a 'camp' expression; he was cultivating his repertoire. 'A cheeseburger.'

'They're off.'

'Well, anything then.'

She tore off the bill, slammed it down and withdrew. I unfolded it. Allibert was growing increasingly mean; these days he expected me to pay for everything. We had fierce arguments over this. He blamed his mother for not breastfeeding and denying him eye contact in the first few months.

'Liver and onions, it says here.'

'You can have them.'

'Okay.'

Allibert picked up the salt cellar very deliberately and held it upside down. It was empty, as usual. 'I'm leaving the church.'

'Gosh.'

'My position has become intolerable. I can no longer reconcile strict observance of the Catholic religion with the dictates of my own moral conscience.'

'Oh. Why not?'

He took a long time to explain. Meanwhile, my egg and chips arrived, and his liver and onions. I ate my way stolidly through them. Most of his arguments went totally over my head, as was generally the case. While he explained the politics of sexuality and how society constructs, and the church supports, false concepts of male and female and narrow constricting role patterns, I was mulling over vague plans for the future. Should I apply to convents? Get married to Allibert? Go away to college? The nuns were discouraging on most fronts and nothing I could do would please Mother; I might perhaps ask my father's opinion. I had not been home for several days. It was the anniversary of my brother's death and I had ominous forebodings. My mother had locked herself in the kitchen. My grandmother had vanished upstairs.

Allibert was talking about power, responsibility and choice. As I started on the knickerbocker glory, he was suggesting I should become a lesbian. I didn't reply. Sexuality of any kind seemed a distant problem, or one I had temporarily managed to resolve by retreating into fat. 'You really ought to consider it,' Allibert said earnestly. The knickerbocker glory was particularly delicious, layer upon layer of totally synthetic cream. I ate it very slowly with a small white plastic teaspoon, savouring every mouthful. Allibert had lapsed into despondency. Homosexuality was to some extent a side issue, he said. What really counted was gender. The future belonged to women. He was thinking of becoming a transexual, the operation was said to be simple. I scraped regretfully at the last bits of cream. Allibert reopened *The Well of Loneliness*. I went to pay. The waitress was painting her nails behind the coffee machine. As she gave me the change, our eyes met. I was disturbed by their sudden intensity behind the false eyelashes.

'You ever go down the Angel?'

'The what?'

'How old are you?' She was still touching my hand. I stepped backwards, nervously.

'I'm fifteen.'

'You look older. Is that your boyfriend?'

'Um, yes.'

'Pity. That's a good book though. My friend lent it me. I've read it four times. Tragic. I like them tragic.'

My key no longer seemed to fit in our front door; it went in all right and twisted round but nothing inside connected. I was just checking I had the right house number when my mother's shadow moved behind the red and blue and yellow glass panes. The door swung open and we faced each other.

'I've changed the locks,' she said. 'Your grandmother's gone mad at last, just as I always predicted. She had an unfortunate streak in her character. You could never trust her. She was – ' My mother paused, deliberating over the right word. 'Volatile. Like most women of her age. I've been enquiring about mental hospitals. She'll have to be strictly confined or God knows what might happen. Come in and *wipe your feet*. Give me that key. I'm burying all the old ones. It's safer. You can never tell.' Her eyes glittered. Extending a skinny hand, she pulled me inside. 'And where have you been?'

'I've been staying round at Alicia's house. I told you.'

'*Oh* yes. *Oh* yes,' she said grimly. '*You*.'

'What?'

'You'd better watch out, my girl.'

I glanced round uneasily for some way of escape. There was none. The air was stale, thick with moral significance and dust, difficult to breathe or see through, she had obviously stopped doing any housework and someone had pasted black paper over the landing window. A pale figure stood silently by the kitchen door, about seven feet tall, glimmering in the dim shadowy light, holding what looked like a sword.

'You shameless hussy,' my mother hissed. 'You treacherous little *slut*. Wallowing in your filthy pleasures, rolling in the common ditches, roaming the highways in your degenerate lust.' As always, I was stuck for a reply, stunned by her phrase-book fluency and command of English. 'You'll get what you deserve, you whore.'

I backed away.

'*You*,' she repeated. 'How dare you. Who are you to – who are you – you – ' Her voice faltered and suddenly she looked uncertain, bewildered, lost, as if she'd just woken up and found herself in a strange place. And I felt like we were both together on top of a very high cliff, blown by the winds – or falling . . .

My mother turned stiffly and stalked away into the kitchen. I tried to follow after, but the pale figure lowered its sword behind her, barring the way. It looked remarkably like the marble statue of Michael the Archangel by the south door of Saint Cecilia's. I refuse to believe it was a *real* angel. It had blank white eyes and a

43

stony expression. Obviously I was forbidden, by some divine law, from following her, so I turned away. Thin letters of flame had appeared over the door lintel, but I had no desire to read them. I went upstairs, looking for my grandmother.

My father rarely appears in this story, as he rarely entered our lives, but during all this time he was writing his great work on the mating habits of *Operophthera brumata*, the winter moth. I've only dipped into it, but the reviews were excellent: *The Times* said it was visionary and poetic, full of delicate insights.

His small study was the lightest room in the house, with a sky-light window through which to observe passing butterflies and stars – he also practised astronomy.

At some point, I think around the time my grandmother arrived in England, he must have stopped sleeping with my mother. They used to share a bedroom on the second landing. Simply by shifting floors he removed himself from not only her but all our family and most human passions, problems and conflicts. Even from mortality, for although he accompanied my mother dutifully to the hospital, he seemed relatively untouched by my brother's death. I remember his detached, thoughtful expression at the funeral changing to eagerness when a butterfly settled on a wreath.

He left my mother free, I suppose, to pursue her own interests, but perhaps she was not interested in freedom, or never felt free. He kept her photograph pinned on his wall, between two butterflies.

His Natural History Museum salary, modest but sufficient, was paid monthly into their joint account – keeping us alive, as I tend to forget. He never spent anything himself, except on books and the occasional bottle of rum.

I visited him sometimes, but we never managed to communicate much. He was awkward on social occasions. 'Good, good. Fine weather we're having. For the time of year, unusual. And you're – Jenny. Yes, of course, of course. Good. A glass of rum? It warms the stomach. I often take a touch myself,' rustling through his papers or staring fiercely at the air just above my shoulder. His eyes never quite focused; one kept drifting off sideways, like a chameleon's eye watching out for flying insects.

44

'Still at school? Applying for college? Oxford or Cambridge? Not decided yet? Maths or science? English literature? Nonsense, nonsense. New-fangled invention. Religion? You mean theology? Humph. Not very sound. But there's a good man at Cambridge. You might do worse. What do your tutors say? The nuns? Oh yes, you go to a convent school. Humph. Your mother's idea. Still, I daresay they teach you the basic elements – Plato, Aristotle, that sort of thing?'

I imagine the academic world is full of men like my father, removed from reality, living in their heads. Though I'm not sure what I mean by 'reality'. 'Removed from reality.' One of my mother's phrases, she often used it to describe my grandmother, and later her own fellow mental patients.

'I've only one piece of advice to give you,' my father said. *'Don't get married. Not under any circumstances. It's a serious* distraction to the brain. Women mean well, but they interfere with one's concentration. Too demanding, too emotional – '

'Your brother is dead,' said my grandmother. 'Your brother is dead, John.' She paused, not looking at me. Delicately, with one long brown forefinger, she touched a flower on the bedcover. It was dark, shadowy; she had closed the curtains. They close all the shutters in Corsica until the dead man is avenged. 'He is dead.'

'Yes, Granny.'

'We know this. Both of us. In our hearts. But your mother's heart is frozen and closed. She will not grieve, she refuses the knowledge. She will destroy herself first. As for your father, psh, what does he know?'

I was having problems breathing. The air in my grandmother's room was even heavier than downstairs. There was an overpowering sweet smell. She had opened all twenty pots of lipstick/ blusher and ranged them on the floor in a circle. Little gaping red mouths. Scented for disguise, as they tell you on street stalls. Made of dead animals – a definite point in their favour as far as my grandmother was concerned.

'Your father would not recognise Death if they met in the street. If she took him by the throat, he would not know her. All women are Death to him.'

Long silence.

'We are *mazzere*,' my grandmother said abruptly. 'All three of us: your mother, myself, you, but above all your mother. She alone has the great gifts: prophecy, the power to call spirits, to bestow and remove curses – all, she has them all. How can she dare to refuse this knowledge? It is a great sin.'

My attention was distracted at this point by a scrabbling, squeaking noise behind the curtains, as though some animal were trying to get in. My feelings of foreboding increased. I hoped my grandmother would keep talking.

'Let me tell you this story,' she said. 'A woman of my village, when I was young – what is that?'

'Nothing, Granny.'

'I heard a sound.'

The scrabbling began again. My grandmother rose and threw back the curtains. It was Katy, the black and white cat from next door. 'Ha,' my grandmother said. 'Yes. Come in, then.' She unlocked the window and the cat twined herself sinuously round, but she hesitated before entering, one paw in the air. She looked at me with her yellow eyes. 'Choose your place,' my grandmother said. 'Sit where you will. A woman of my village was *mazzere*. She had killed many people, both men and women. It was not her own will, you understand. She was commanded from beyond, by spiritual necessity. She killed many people' – my grandmother paused thoughtfully, eyeing the cat – 'in their true selves, their animal selves. For each human being, as I must have told you, lodges his soul for safe-keeping in some animal: a pig or goat, a dog or cat. One day this woman was out walking with her husband and they passed a dog, a white dog, straying in the *maquis*. 'What a fine dog that is,' the woman said, and on irresistible impulse she raised her stick. 'Don't strike that dog!' her husband cried in terror. 'That dog is my soul!' But it was too late: the woman brought her stick down with a swift blow, breaking the dog's neck. It died instantly. The man, her husband, died the next day. And the woman – Pia, my friend – grieved deeply, although honouring the will of the spirits and the ways of destiny. For they had lived

46

together twenty years. They had grown together, two minds and hearts joined, like the ivy and the tree. As you yourself may join with a man, altering the way of your life to his. But you may grow best alone, as the tree grows. Pia made a funeral song for Roberto, her dead husband, and this was long remembered and repeated between us. Even a man like your father came once with a tape machine, but he drank too much wine and we fooled him, giving him another song, inferior to hers, a child's lullaby to store in his dusty archives. In return he taught me the ways of his machine. This was useful knowledge,' added my grandmother reflectively. 'I bore him no grudge. He was an odd man. He came from the north, in search no doubt of his own soul. He was split by desires, drifting, anchored in nothing, like the wind. And Pia's song, I can still recall – '

My grandmother hummed a few bars, adjusting key, then broke into an eerie mournful wail. The back of my neck prickled. It was late August, clouds scudding low across the sky. 'You are the rock, you are the fire,' my grandmother sang. 'You were the strong central column of our house.' She paused. 'Of course,' she said, 'it does not translate very well. English words have no feeling. But you understand, he was many things to her. He was life itself. At the height of her grief, she calls him not "my husband" but "my brother". "You were my brother!" '

The next-door cat had completed her cautious tour of the furniture. Now she yawned, stretched and settled down to wash herself. 'The blood bond,' my grandmother said, with a reverent gesture. 'Between brother and sister, between mother and son. Stronger, deeper their bond than any marriage vow.' And picking up one of the little red pots, she smeared lipstick/blusher all over her hands. I watched in fascination and dread, remembering *Macbeth*, which we happened just then to be studying in English lessons. Macbeth's hands when he's just murdered Duncan, and Lady Macbeth sleepwalking, trying to wash off the invisible blood. But they were British, not Corsican. My grandmother, having once decided on murdering anyone, would have no problems with guilt or remorse.

She bent towards the cat. Everything had gone very quiet. My heart was pounding, remembering Timmy, drowned and buried in our back garden. She was certainly capable of violence when she chose, and of rather more than merely symbolic gestures, but on this occasion she just touched the cat's throat lightly, leaving a streak of red across its white bib.

Harmless, perhaps. But in Corsica the *mazzere*, the hunters of souls, have two selves. A split personality. My grandmother's double, her spiritual self, might have been out walking. Hunting.

Father Carol from Saint Cecilia's died around that time – well, that day in fact – but he was eighty years old and no one suspected anything odd. He was celebrating mass, at six o'clock in the evening. Alone. In an empty church the *Surbiton Gazette* said. But perhaps one woman, dressed all in black, sitting unmoving in the back row? He collapsed with a heart attack just after raising the chalice. It rolled down the marble altar steps, spilling wine, like blood.

Sitting in our shadowy hallway, I read that week's issue of the *Gazette* extremely thoroughly, from cover to cover and backwards again. There was nothing much else to do. Something was obviously due to happen soon – break, snap, erupt.

The angel had disappeared, so had the thin ghostly letters of flame, but it was still impossible to enter the kitchen, my mother having locked herself in. God alone knew what she was doing.

Five

My mother's attitude to sex, birth and the facts of life in general was a curious one. She had evolved it singlehanded through years of silent solitary reflection: I can't imagine my grandmother discussing affairs so purely human and confined to the flesh.

She took her duties seriously as a retailer of information. Too seriously perhaps, for we were sensitive children, my brother and I. Everything she explained to me, I immediately passed on to him. He got more upset. By the time I was five and he was three, we both knew that

1. babies grew inside women's stomachs,
2. giving birth was terribly painful – worse than being burnt alive like Joan of Arc or tortured by the Roman soldiers, and
3. hundreds of women died in childbirth every year.

I drew a picture for Jane and Judith, my friends across the road, of a woman dying in childbirth, mostly done in red crayon. They got upset too – Judith cried – and their mother tore my picture up and threw it in the outside dustbin and told me to draw something nice, like a horse. But in secret later, behind the raspberry canes, we promised each other never to have children. Or get married. Never ever. No matter what.

At nine, I got the next instalment. Facts of life part two, having periods and sex. My mother took me into the front room, the mausoleum room, and closed the curtains – her custom on such serious occasions. She explained sex, which she called 'making love', in the briefest possible terms. It would hurt, too, she said, not so much as birth, but still a lot. Her ram-rod outline, her braced

49

shoulders – my mother has the most unrelaxed shoulders. 'You may find it frightening,' she said, and paused. 'It is frightening. Men are more – uncontrolled than women. They need to make love more often, more violently. Their desire is insatiable (Mills and Boon?). They behave like wild animals sometimes. However, you must remember it is love, and that makes it all right.'

Holding herself so stiff and upright, tensed against the world. No one more guarded, or more vulnerable. Sometimes I can hardly bear to look at my mother. I want so much to protect her, even as a child I wanted to, but I don't know how. And she would never let me.

I suppose she must also have had sexual desires, though she never betrayed any sign of them. And I thought of her – I've mentioned this before – as a saint. A martyr. An angel. In some curious way, I'm still stuck with these impressions/illusions.

They were not mutual. She had always mistrusted me deep down. Hence, I think, her continual nagging, her insistence that I should 'get a boyfriend', clean my face properly, clean out my cupboards, tidy my room, stop eating, etc. Around the time of her breakdown, a year after my brother's death, this attitude intensified, or more accurately her true under-feelings surfaced: hysterical fear and disgust. I became, in her eyes, some kind of wild physical/sexual monster, raving with uncontrolled desires, driven mad by lust, throwing myself at every passing stranger: her shadow self, her complete opposite, the person she had set herself so firmly against ever being or becoming – in sum, as Allibert explained, the sexual female.

'It's not unusual, of course,' he added tactfully. 'Female sexuality is an incredibly frightening thing. We all find it – um – difficult to cope with. But I think your mother has more problems than most, if you don't mind me saying so.'

We sat together in the hallway, casting occasional scared glances towards my mother's kitchen door: two doubtful, confused, bemused, trapped middle-class adolescents. Allibert still maintained a touching faith in psychology and rational understanding: once his personality was properly integrated, he thought, everything would be all right; but I wasn't so sure.

50

'There's a disco tonight,' he said despondently. 'At Our Lady of Mount Carmel. I should go, I suppose. Male bonding rituals, that sort of thing.'

The word disco made me shrink, conjuring up pictures of our peer group, with who we occasionally tried unsuccessfully to mingle. The disco was one of Father John James's enthusiasms, held once a week in the local church hall. The boys wore black leather jackets and drooped around by the snooker table or roared up and down outside on motorbikes; the girls huddled in a corner, giggling hysterically. No one ever danced and the record player usually broke down half way through the evening. The record selection was about ten years old. You could buy Coca Cola at a discount, this was the only advantage, and eat a lot of crisps: cheese and onion, beef and onion, salt and vinegar.

'Will you come with me?'

'I can't,' I said like a coward. 'Someone's got to wait here, just in case.'

We looked again at the kitchen door. 'What's she doing, d'you think?'

Allibert tapped his teeth meditatively. 'Well, obviously,' he said, 'she's seeking attention.'

'Whose attention?'

'God knows.'

I feel uncomfortable now, remembering how we talked about her. Not that parents should be above discussion, but as a couple, however unlikely a couple, we were stronger than her. Since my brother's death she'd been, despite my father, to all real intents and purposes, single. Vulnerable. Alone.

'D'you want a takeaway?'

'Yes. A beefburger.'

'Chips?'

'Mm.'

We lived entirely on takeaways at that time, financed by my grandmother, whose generosity towards me was startling. Often I would find a wad of £10 notes pushed under my pillow or stuffed casually into my coat pocket.

While Allibert was gone, I skipped through the latest copy of the

51

Surbiton Gazette in a desultory fashion. The decapitation murder mystery had now been solved, the child's mother arrested awaiting trial. She had buried her kitchen knife, stained with blood, in the compost heap. While reading this I became aware suddenly of my own mother's presence. She must have unlocked the door very quietly. Now she was standing half sideways, watching me bird-like through one eye.

'It's my birthday next month,' she said. 'The eve of All Souls. They say ghosts are abroad then, wandering in the night. Evil spirits rise out of the ground, wailing, damned for ever in eternal torment. "Who will save us?" they cry. "Who will forgive us?" I don't believe it. That's the kind of story your grandmother would tell, old wives' tales, silly old superstitions. It's so ridiculous, I lose all patience with her. We're living in the modern world. Have you passed your exams yet? What are you taking? Modern languages, I hope. English language, that's very important. Have you got all the right books? Are you in love? Don't fool yourself. No man will every really love you. Love means nothing, it's a word they use to disguise animal desire. Take a realistic attitude, don't *drift* or you'll drift for ever. Keep your eyes open. Plan every move –'

Her voice faltered; she swayed a little.

'I've lost something, I think. Help me look for it. You're my daughter, you should help me. Don't abandon yourself, don't give way to idle pleasures and the lusts of the flesh. It only leaves a bitter taste, dust, ashes and dust. It was something very small I lost, a needle, I think.'

Clearly my mother was 'seriously disturbed', as they say, if not actually cracking up altogether, and I suppose, realising this, I should have taken action – humoured her, phoned the doctor, alerted my father. But I felt curiously detached from it all. I was thinking about going on holiday, preferably a long way away, somewhere hot and sunny. Very hot. Blindingly sunny. Majorca, the Seychelles, southern Italy. Not Corsica – I might meet a relative. Somewhere safe, totally removed from all my family. Australia, or perhaps a desert island. Allibert could come too, if he wanted. I could picture him sitting under a palm tree, wearing

52

swimming trunks and a wide-brimmed straw hat. He would sun-burn easily and probably get bad-tempered. But not my mother. Our romance was over. Gone were my Brighton balcony dreams. Our relationship had deteriorated too far, beyond any hope of tem-porary redemption. Its terms were too clearly defined, too starkly awful.

We, Allibert and I, might order some travel catalogues from the *TV Times*. And with my grandmother's money, maybe we could afford the single air fares. These calculations were abruptly shat-tered. She must have noticed my absence of mind; and Allibert was right, she wanted attention, absolute attention. Translated into screaming fury, she resembled more than ever a very thin bird. I backed up the staircase. I was afraid. She frightened me. She was too real, too alive in her madness. You can maintain a certain safe distance from sane people – they put up barriers, muffle communi-cation – but I could feel her mind, violent, reaching out for me, rending me. Like a bird of prey. She never had any regard for my privacy, even in normal circumstances.

I can't remember what she was screaming, or I've successfully forgotten. In my memory of her, at her worst and maddest times, there's no sound. It's like a silent film. Face contorted, mouth twisted and working, she advances on me. The tragedy queen. Princess Regent of death, mother of darkness, your lost lover and son swallowed by the underworld. Many tragedies could be written around my mother. This sounds cynical. Though I don't doubt she did go mad, and truly despaired, she was also play-ing a part, acting herself into it. By way of escape. Normality, 'sanity', was slowly killing her; she had closed too many doors on herself.

I backed up the staircase. She followed. The house was empty, unfortunately, apart from us; my father was giving his Tuesday afternoon lecture at the museum – not that he'd have been much help – and I had seen my grandmother going out earlier, smartly attired in a new bright red hat and coat. I hoped Allibert might return soon, or Father John James pay us a pastoral visit, or any-body, sufficient to interrupt and distract my mother. A man would have been best. She was only ever mad in female company. At her worst times she could 'switch' into apparent sanity the moment any man appeared.

'Birds must have got in,' my father said, clutching his head. 'Through my skylight window. I can't remember leaving it open. The work of months,' he moaned, 'ruined, ruined, lost to posterity. It's not just the information. Happily I keep all my notebooks locked in a plain safe, along with the Burma snake antidote – one never knows – and my gold medal from the *Société Maréchèse*. But it's the sentences, the bloody sentences. I took such trouble over them. It's the construction, upon which everything hangs. And the nuances,' he cried in despair. 'The nuances! How can they ever be recaptured? Fortunately Collins are behaving like a decent, gentlemanly firm. I've been on the 'phone to Peter Moore. They're prepared to extend my contract. But it's the work involved, the sheer bloody grind. One sentence can take me *hours*, literally *hours*. You'll have to help me, Jenny. I'll dictate aloud, that might encourage the flow, then we'll juggle them around. Can you do shorthand? No, never mind.'

'Daddy,' I said. 'Mother – '

'I can't find your mother anywhere.'

'She's in hospital.'

My father paused, blinking. 'Oh,' he said uncertainly. 'Er – what's wrong? Nothing too bad, I hope.'

'They don't know yet.'

'We must visit her. Yes, yes. Of course. Immediately I've put this room in order. Luckily some of the papers aren't too badly torn. My lecture on *Tortrix viridana* might just be salvageable. I'll need some thin Sellotape.'

'She's had a sort of nervous breakdown.'

'A what? A what?' he said tetchily, picking up bits of paper. 'All this modern jargon. Cant phrases. Speak English, can't you. A nervous collapse. Ah yes. An attack of the vapours. No more than I expected. I've noticed. Yes, yes. She's been feeling very under the weather lately, poor old girl. Since the death, a great shock – er – her son, you know. Your brother that would be. But given time, given time. By the way, that Sellotape, did you say – ?'

54

I went downstairs, where Allibert was warming himself against the hall radiator. The lower ground floor was littered with white paper; my mother had leant over the top banisters, tearing it to pieces and letting it fall.

'Is he okay?' Allibert asked.

'Yes, I think so.'

'How did he take it?'

I described my father's reactions. Allibert nodded wisely. Blocking out, he said. Coping with his distress.

'He isn't distressed.'

'Oh, come on, Jen. He must be.'

'He's upset about his papers, that's all.'

'He's projecting it.'

'I don't think so.'

'Well, anyway,' Allibert said, '*I'm* distressed. And what about you?'

'What?'

'What about yours?'

'My what?'

Allibert sighed patiently. 'Your distress. What are you doing with it?'

I felt irritated by this tactless persistence. Allibert could never let things be. Once he'd got hold of an idea, he worried it to death.

'I'm fine, fine. I was a bit upset at first, maybe,' I said, avoiding his earnest gaze. 'I mean when she fell off the roof – '

'Fell off?'

'But now I'm fine. Did you bring anything to eat? I'm starving.'

Allibert silently unwrapped the takeaways: one double cheeseburger, one beefburger with onion, now cold and congealed.

'I don't feel like mine,' he said, 'somehow, and they're hours old. You can have them.'

'Okay.'

'She asked after you, the waitress.'

'Oh, did she?'

I started eating, desperately stuffing down the food. It tasted of absolutely nothing, dry as dust and ashes. I wanted to stop, but

55

couldn't; some force beyond me was impelling me. Eat, eat. Tear. Swallow.

'You know, your mother,' Allibert said. 'As I came round the corner, she looked like a bird. An enormous bird. I thought she was, at first.'

'What?'

'Flying.'

'Well, she wasn't,' I said crossly through the dust-like beefburger, resenting these supernatural implications. 'And she didn't. She didn't fly; she fell. Straight down.'

'Threw herself, you mean?'

'Yes, all right, then.'

'Strange,' Allibert added absently, 'that she didn't break anything. Lucky, really.'

'Nonsense,' I said fiercely. 'People fall hundreds of feet and survive. Every day. Mountaineers, people like that, all the time. It's very common. Three storeys is nothing. My mother doesn't change shape, she's not a bird, she's not a witch – '

Allibert looked surprised. 'I wasn't suggesting – '

'She's just very thin, that's all. The air pressure would have supported her. And, and – '

My throat constricted, I could no longer chew, swallow or speak a word. Food had failed me, the first time ever. I felt like crying. I felt furious. I felt terrified.

'You should go to bed,' Allibert said. 'Otherwise *you'll* have a breakdown. And then what?'

My teeth began to chatter; I clenched them grimly together. He took my arm; I wrenched it away. A cold wind started blowing from somewhere, an icy roaring wind, bitter cold. Our house was empty, deserted. My mother was gone, its centre and mainstay.

'Let go of my arm.'

'You don't look well.'

'I'm fine.'

'You look sick.'

And I was sick – all over the carpet. Bits of double cheeseburger, undigested, were recognisable. I was sick again. Allibert handed me some tissues.

56

'Come on,' he said soothingly, 'come and lie down.'

'I can't, I can't lie down'

'Come upstairs.'

'I can't. Someone has to watch. Keep watch.'

Always a woman, waiting, watching, silent. Sitting alone behind dark shutters. The blazing sun outside, bright, so bright and hot, no one dares walk in the streets at midday. But this is England. Grey and cold.

'Come upstairs.'

Allibert put his arm around my shoulders, supporting me. I felt so weak, drained and light after the sickness. Like when I was small, on the rare occasions I could compete with my brother. My mother would dab eau de cologne on my forehead, change the sheets, put flowers in a vase. She was gentle with me then – thoughtful, delicate in her attentions.

My bedroom was a mess, as usual. Allibert tidied it up – folding clothes, stowing shoes away under the wardrobe – while I undressed and fell into bed. The ceiling revolved above me.

'This is awful,' I said.

'You feel guilty. Responsible for what's happened.'

'Well, yes – '

'That's only natural, predictable even. But you really don't have to. It's *her* breakdown.'

'But I'm so cold . . . '

'Shall I get into bed with you?'

I looked at him, jolted by this novel suggestion. But then, Allibert often surprised me.

'It might keep you warmer.'

'Yes, okay.'

I watched him undressing. His body, which I had never seen until then, was thin, unhealthily pale, with a knobbly back, vulnerable, exposed, as all men's bodies seem to me, unbearably so – but this is projection, no doubt, attributing to a man my own fears of vulnerability, mortality. His body reminded me of my dead brother, white and wasted away. The invalid, the skeleton. Allibert, shivering, got under the sheets with me. His bony arm lay across my breasts. I remembered my mother and her instructions on sex, the main one unspoken but heavily implied: trap the man. Seduce him, trick him into sex, or he'll escape, vanish, dissolve, be lost to you. Pin him down. Get him inside you, swallow him – it's horribly painful, like dying in childbirth, but every good married woman's duty. Only prostitutes enjoy sex, bad women like Mary Magdalen. Either holy sacrament or mortal sin. Nothing inbetween.

My grandmother's view of sex, in so far as she ever spoke of it, was rather more benevolent, certainly more detached, owing less to bitter experience and Roman Catholicism. 'Unknown forces,' she had once said vaguely, *à propos* of nothing obvious. We were mending my bicycle at the time. 'Powers beyond our control. Men and women meet together, in the *maquis*, under cover of darkness. Who can explain the will of God? At dawn they must part; from that time, the first light, they must be strangers to one another. This cable, she leads to the brake – '

Now was the time, if ever, for me to engage in sexual intercourse with Allibert, but nothing in fact happened. When it came to it, I wasn't interested. The unknown irresistible forces were remarkable by their absence. But it was nice having him there; I felt a bit comforted, less alone.

We discussed our relationship. 'It's been good for me,' he said positively. 'I've come a long way in the last twelve months. From being relatively naïve, in emotional terms, and intellectually very defensive, I feel I've progressed, realising the importance of the female side of our nature, the nurturing and physical – animal even – as opposed to the spiritual and intellectual.'

Several objections instantly occurred to me – my mother, for instance, could hardly be described as 'nurturing', while my grandmother might have fitted either side of his definition – but I let them pass. The female psyche seemed a dangerous matter to discuss, given our present circumstances. Anyway Allibert, I had the impression, was really leading up to something else.

'It's the right time for women,' he said. 'They must show the way. The church is dead, a crumbling pillar of patriarchy. We need a new spiritual leader, a woman, someone to sweep away the old order, rewrite the liturgy even, infusing it with the vital principles of feminism. I was wondering about your grandmother, actually . . . '

Six

Following her attempted suicide, my mother spent seven months in the psychiatric wing of Tolworth General Hospital. This wasn't an easy time. Far from ideal as our mother–daughter relationship might have been, when she was gone I felt bereft. Abandoned. A low wind whistled through the downstairs corridor and the doors creaked as if the house had long been ruined and uninhabited. It was late January. I ventured into the kitchen, drew back the curtains. The small garden outside was bleak, neat, well-ordered, like my brother's old bedroom. But there were pieces of something smashed littered by the shed, her terracotta bird feeder; she'd always liked feeding the birds. It gave her, I suppose, a sense of being needed. Power-seeking, Allibert would have defined it. She'd liked feeding me once too, before I got so out of proportion.

Houses absorb, breathe, re-echo human beings. With my mother's disappearance, our house felt more than ever empty. Her anger had at least filled it, fuelled it with some weird spiritual vitality, furnished it with angels and forbidding commands. It was *her* house, only hers, not my father's; and my grandmother had always been a guest, a temporary sojourner.

Around this time, I began writing her life story. Allibert was away with *his* parents on a skiing holiday: they had decided that he was repressing something or submerging something and as a family they needed to 'spend time together'. They had removed him from school, where he was showing disturbing brilliance, especially in his world studies option, theology. Really, as it turned out, they were worried about his religious tendencies, on which they thoroughly cross-questioned him, but I doubt if they learned much. Allibert's Catholicism was a complex sensitive thing, in a state of flux and development, not easily categorised.

I should have been revising for my mock 'O' levels. Sitting at the kitchen table, I wrote:

My mother was born and brought up in Carbini, a village of moderate size in the Sartenais, the southernmost part of Corsica.

I stopped. They were frightening me, all these so-easy words, like my grandmother's stories. I could almost hear my grandmother's low chanting voice. 'They come from beyond,' she told me once. 'We are taken over, we are spoken through. It is not of our own will.' I'd like to believe this. Stories, whether written down or spoken, are so powerful; it's preferable to attribute them elsewhere. Trapping people, as I might so easily trap her, in my own words and stories, my own patterns to explain. Like my father, classifying and arranging his dead butterflies.

I know nothing about her in fact. This becomes clearer to me as I grow older. She's a mystery. So closed off, barricaded, shut away inside. I continued for months, all the time she was in hospital, doggedly writing her life story, but it grew less and less convincing. I invented secret lovers, passionate affairs with bandits and dying men, a double marriage, my mother deceived, an abortion, a miscarriage in the *maquis* – it was totally engrossing. I forgot to sleep, wash, eat. By the end I'd written at least five novels' worth, a weird mixture, a cross between Mills and Boon, Edgar Allen Poe and *Jackie* magazine, but the main influence of course was my grandmother. I was trying, I think, to explain something – my mother's madness, the reasons for her despair, perhaps – but she remained elusive.

'My mother's in a mental hospital,' I told Alicia.
    'You're lucky,' she replied.
    'She tried to kill herself.'
    'I wish mine would.'

60

Alicia's apparent callousness was based on well-justified desperation; Lancelot, her dog, had been 'put down'. Alicia's mother had arranged it, without warning, one Monday afternoon while Alicia was at school. Lancelot had been 'too much trouble,' she said coolly afterwards. 'I'll never forgive her,' said Alicia. 'In fact I'm going to murder her. I'll murder them both. One of these days, one of these days. God, I hate my parents.'

'Well, this *is* an unexpected pleasure,' said my mother in her brightest, most clipped English accent. 'How delightful. And you've come so far, in this fearful weather. You must be *exhausted*. Well now, do take off your coats, make yourselves at home.' Handing us each a cup, she poured out tea with elaborate care. Invisible tea, into pink plastic dolls' cups. I took one gingerly and pretended to drink. '*Do* have a biscuit,' she added, passing round an invisible plate. 'Sorry they're so *stale*. I should have ordered some more. If I'd only known you were coming. By the way, I do beg your pardon, but I didn't *quite* catch your names?'

I nibbled the air, wondering whether or what to reply. Her 'tea parties' had always been intimidating, taken one stage further into unreality, it felt like something out of *Alice in Wonderland*. I needed Allibert to interpret.

My grandmother's attention had wandered. 'All these women are *mazzere*,' she announced, scanning the ward. My mother froze, plastic teapot in mid-air. 'They are imprisoned, who might speak. They have great powers, each one. It is tragic,' my grandmother muttered. 'Terrible to behold, that such women should be silenced.'

'*Do* have some more tea.'

'And you, my daughter – '

'Please don't mention it,' my mother said, swiftly collecting the teacups. 'I've enjoyed your visit *so* much. *Do* come again,' she said, with extreme distant politeness. 'Come any time. Goodbye.'

'Mother – '

'Goodbye. Have a safe journey back. Perhaps we'll meet again sometime. I *do* hope so.' And covering her ears firmly with both hands, she turned round and faced the wall.

My father accompanied me once or twice to the hospital. He never quite grasped the fact of my mother's illness, or she gave him nothing to perceive; in his presence she preserved a bright, shining, smiling silence. I began to realise, then, how angry she was. Pure cold fury glimmered around her, like an all-over halo.

'Your mother seems perfectly all right,' he said. 'Just the same as usual. Obviously there's been some stupid administrative mistake. Typical of the National Health Service.'

The ward was open-plan, partly curtained-off. In the remaining shabby 'day room', thirty or forty women sat numbly staring into space or wandered erratically across the antiseptic black and white vinyl floor. A television flickered, high up on the far wall; a distorted newsreader's face smiled and talked soundlessly. A young woman hovered nearby, picking her nails. She looked a bit like Alicia – the same superior amused expression and aura of potential violence. My father was obviously rattled, anxious to depart. While he was ringing for a taxi in reception a doctor approached us, clipboard in hand.

'Mr Andrews? We think your wife could benefit from – ' he used here a phrase I'd never heard before.

'Talk to my daughter. Talk to her. Yes, yes. Do whatever you think best.' My father flapped his free hand, as if the doctor were some troublesome common species of moth. 'I know nothing about such things. Not my field. No, no. Don't ask me to understand.' Eventually the doctor was successfully deflected on to me.

'Miss Andrews? Sign this form please.' I signed. 'Thank you.'

I was under eighteen; I had no right to be signing forms. And I had no idea then what I was letting my mother in for, and didn't much care either. Like my father, suddenly I was just desperate to leave, to be at a safe distance. So we abandoned her, by fast car. In our general haste, my father got stuck in the swing doors and we left both our coats behind.

Alicia was impressed, however carefully she pretended otherwise, by my mother being in a mental hospital. At last I had acheived something, it seemed, gaining her faint approval. We grew quite close. She was interested, unhealthily so, in mental disturbances.

To most people, I suppose, madness comes as a surprise, or it certainly did in our family, but looking back I see Alicia was even then deliberately courting it. Beginning with anorexia. 'You should try it,' she told me. 'I can't understand why everyone doesn't. It really works. Honestly, it's amazing; I've lost a stone and a half.'

We were walking, symbolically enough, in a graveyard. Alicia's thinness had become dramatic. She bore no resemblance now to the Lady of Shalott, or to any womanly figure. Instead she appeared remarkably like a skeleton, a vision risen from the tomb, keeping me casual company. Even her hair was thinner and her eyes glittered above jutting-out cheekbones. 'You drink lots and lots of vinegar,' she informed me. 'And don't eat.'

I didn't understand. 'It's like dieting,' she explained patiently, 'only you go further. It's quite easy once you really get started.'

'But aren't you hungry?'

Alicia gave me an impatient, disdainful glance. Obviously I was miles behind her, not only in intellect. She and my mother – both adventuring into wild and dangerous psychic realms, uncharted territory.

'They've noticed, of course,' said Alicia darkly. 'Them. Not that they care, really, whether I live or die. But they'll start forcing me to eat, I expect.'

We walked through damp grass and leftover, withered leaves among half-swallowed tombstones. On the far side of the cemetery my brother was buried, but I had no inclination to tell Alicia about this. She was already far too intimately involved with death. Another favourite poem of hers was 'The Unquiet Grave'.

> The wind doth blow today, my love,
> And a few small drops of rain;
> I never had but one true-love,
> In cold grave he was lain.
>
> I'll do as much for my true love
> As any young girl may
> I'll sit and mourn all day at his grave
> For a twelvemonth and a day.

63

The twelvemonth and a day being up,
The dead began to speak –

Alicia and my mother and God knows how many other women –
turned fiercely inwards, eating away at themselves. There must be
other ways, I thought sadly, other methods of coping. I suppose
anorexia is a bit like Catholicism: at least it makes sense, in its own
weird fashion, gives you some kind of system and a goal in life.
Death.

Such a skilful, delicate business, dying can be. Like a courtship.
Death, the ultimate lover. The consummation and ending of
loneliness.

'There he is again,' Alicia said. 'Him.' She gestured. Hubert
was standing by the churchyard gates, slumped, comatose, stupe-
fied. 'He's such a bore. He just can't take a hint.' Coldly scornful.

I regarded Hubert with awe. In my mind he was now more a
symbolic mythological figure than a real person, gaining his stat-
ure simply from being Alicia's 'boyfriend'. My mother's eternal
complaint recurred to me: why didn't I get a boyfriend? 'I mean a
real boyfriend.' But what did she mean? What did 'real' mean? I
had never in fact challenged her on this. Would she have known?

Alicia said reflectively, 'Do you remember Mariana of the
moated grange? In *Measure for Measure*.' We had read this in
class the previous term. I could only recall Isabella – pure, virgi-
nal, self-preserving – and cold Angelo, the provost. Mariana
escaped me. She's a minor character, I discovered later on rereading, but quite nice compared to the rest. She sleeps with Angelo, in
substitution for Isabella, and so he's forced to marry her.

'It might be worth trying,' Alicia said.

Throughout this time of break-up and loss, with our house fallen
into desolation, no 'family life' left to speak of – my brother dead,
my mother mad and my father as usual withdrawn into his own
room upstairs, not to be disturbed – my grandmother seemed
positively happy and cheerful. Normally arthritis crippled her
from January through to March, and she'd had ominous twinges
just before Christmas, but these apparently had receded or vanished

64

and she had now taken up karate, attending a local group every Wednesday evening. I went along once to watch. My grandmother was obviously the star pupil. She had already, after just two months, taken her orange belt and was working for red. The instructor often called her out to the front to demonstrate. She had amazing balance and her leg kicks were vicious, like flick-knives; she practised them assiduously up and down our hallway. Here at home she practised naked, discarding the heavy, white, cotton karate garments, and I marvelled at her sinewy spare old woman's body. 'Sa-*yeh*!' I loved her final proud gesture, arms crossed and slowly lowered.

'Your mother is a true *mazzero*, her calling is divine. It is not of her own will. Such women as she – yes, ah yes – the ignorant will call them mad – '

Alicia wants to make a career in television scriptwriting, specialising in late-night horror films. I think writing will be a good option for her, at least it'll satisfy her more vicious instincts. So far she hasn't actually murdered anyone, though it's come close at times. her parents are still alive, and so am I, but not Hubert. I have an uneasy conscience, still, about Hubert.

We met, Hubert and I, by her connivance, in the municipal cemetery, at eight o'clock on a freezing cold January night. She had promised him she would 'give herself', like Isabella, but instead she gave me. I still consider this was an unforgivable thing to do. It might have done me permanent damage, sexually.

We encountered each other by the Explorer's Tomb, a nineteenth-century mausoleum. I don't want to go into details over what happened. It was neither comfortable nor enjoyable, but somehow inevitable – it felt as if we had no choice. There was a frost that night and I caught a bad cold.

'A man and a woman meet together, at dead of night, in the *maquis*. At dawn they must part. Who can escape the will of God?' It's funny how you fulfil other people's plans and expectations. I wasn't sure whose web I was caught in, whose script I was playing a part in. Women have too much power altogether.

My grandmother was moving out of our house, having purchased a considerable property of her own: Saint Cecilia's church in north Surbiton. The church, like our local council, was cutting costs, merging parishes. Boarded up and deconsecrated after Father Carol's death, Saint Cecilia's came cheap at £10,000.

I remember seeing notice of the auction in the *Surbiton Gazette*; reading it out loud at breakfast. We were eating Weetabix, lots and lots of Weetabix, swimming in milk, loaded with sugar. Our tastes naturally agreed. A distinct light of interest dawned in my grandmother's eyes. She said nothing, but took the newspaper away with her. My father drifted in later, in his dressing gown, with his big china cup – shambling, petulant, complaining about the scarcity of milk. He had always been anxious about milk, but more and more so since my mother's departure. The milkman regularly eluded him. 'We *must* catch him. He came early yesterday. He didn't see my note. Keep a watch, keep a watch.'

Hubert committed suicide early next month, in February, the most common month for suicides. He was depressed anyway; no one blamed me, not even Alicia, but I blamed myself. Guilt is a terrible thing. It was unfortunate that this had been my first sexual encounter. His death confirmed a very deep-rooted subconscious fear. Men's fears about women are light, laughable, compared to how women feel about themselves. I took refuge in warm secure places; supermarkets, especially Sainsbury's, and the Wimpy Bar.

Seven

My grandmother's church purchase went through without any difficulties. Luckily, she didn't need a mortgage, for I doubt if any building society would have backed her. She wasn't exactly buying a 'home', more an amount of discarded spiritual space. A very large amount. I saw the estate agent's description, or rather lack of description, for Saint Cecilia's defied estate agentese – 'compact *pied-à-terre*', 'delightful three-bedroomed family house, ample power points', 'excellent first time buy', etc. The church was summarised curtly as 'potential conversion property', 'close to local shops', with 'interesting features'.

My grandmother naturally did her own survey and conveyancing. Contracts were exchanged and a week after completion, she showed me round.

Long Sunday morning masses of my childhood, the Ladies' Choir aloft singing genteel arias, interminable sermons, Holy Communion – how it all swept back. The air still smelled of stale incense. I half expected someone to demand my church collection. Nothing had changed. She had also bought up the entire contents: wooden pews, chipped plaster statues, rickety black iron candleholders, the altar.

We toured the church clockwise, following the Stations of the Cross, dusty reliefs depicting the progress of Our Lord's Passion. Passing each one, my grandmother genuflected with a muttered prayer. So did I, automatically. The church still felt like a holy place, deconsecrated or not. A discreet candle signals God's presence, flickering inside a little red glass just above the pulpit. It was lit, I noticed. We arrived at my grandmother's favourite station of the cross, Saint Veronica with her towel, wiping Christ's face, sweat and blood transformed miraculously into a perfect photographic imprint, through God's grace and Saint Veronica's holy loving intentions. It doesn't work ordinarily, however long you press; I used to try with John, my brother, at bathtimes. The towel always remained stubbornly blank. My grandmother became absorbed in prayer. I wandered past the vestry, where she had made makeshift living arrangements – a camp bed, an oil lamp. No different from a bedsit really, except colder. The trouble with churches is their ceilings are so high, all the heat vanishes upwards. My footsteps clanked on iron floor gratings, echoing; every slight sound echoed. In the Lady Chapel I re-encountered an early childhood passion, the most beautiful stained-glass window in the world. The Blessed Virgin of Saint Cecilia's in her blue robe. Blue as the Mediterranean, blue as travel-catalogue summer skies, blue as eternity. I can't imagine anything more awe-inspiring. Chartres doesn't compare.

I began to appreciate the full glory of my grandmother's venture. Anyone can buy a house, a flat – that requires so little imagination – but it takes true vision to acquire a church. How much she owned now. The stained-glass virgin, plaster saints, marble angels. The organ (eighteenth century). A band of painted gold, running round the chancel, '*Et verbum caro factum est et habitavit in nobis*'. And above all space – space to express herself in, to move around in, to *be*. This was so necessary for her.

With my mother in hospital my appetite went very erratic – confused, maybe, with other varieties of desire. I was in the local branch library, checking mechanically through new arrivals, hoping against hope for a new Georgette Heyer, when desperate longings overcame me. Visions of delicious foods – baked beans on butter-drenched toast, fried eggs and bacon, pork chops with apple sauce. My legs collapsed. Someone supported me tottering to a chair and the senior librarian, Miss Smith, brought me a glass of water. Terrible Miss Smith, merciless exactor of fines. On this occasion she was unusually gentle, loosening my scarf and sprinkling water on my forehead, but reckless, ravenous with hunger, I pushed her away and staggered out down the high street.

The Wimpy Bar waitress was already wiping tables. She turned the Open sign round to Closed as I came in and switched off the overhead fluorescent lights, plunging us into semi-darkness. I sat in silence, trying to catch my breath, my heart pounding.

'You're the last,' she said, slapping the menu down. 'What d'you want? Fish is off; so're eggs.'

'132,' I said randomly.

'You must be joking.'

'Anything then.'

'The chef's gone home. I could warm you up a mixed grill, maybe,' she said. 'As a favour. It's not my job, you know.'

'Please.' But by the time she returned with a loaded tray, I wasn't hungry any more.

'Don't you want it?' she said sharply.

'No, I can't manage somehow.'

She gave me a speaking look. 'If it was anyone else,' she said, 'I'd charge. You can't just go ordering things.'

'I'm sorry.'

'Are you ill or something?' she demanded, peering at me suspiciously. She was short-sighted, one of the reasons she often appeared so aloof and disdainful. 'You've lost weight,' she said. 'You should take care. Smoke?'

'No thanks.'

'I'll have one then.' She slid in opposite me. 'Where's your boyfriend?'

'He's away. Skiing.'

Silence. She smoked, while I watched her. She had a mole just to one corner of her mouth and greeny-blue eyes.

'How are you, then?'

'Oh, all right,' I said.

'Thinking about it?'

'What?'

'On, nothing. If you don't know already,' she said, blowing out smoke, 'there's not much point telling you, is there?'

I looked down at a baked potato. Split open, cold and hardened, it appeared entirely unappetising. My hunger had vanished beyond recall. Appetite is such a mysterious thing. It comes from beyond, as my grandmother would say. Baked potatoes used to haunt me in the darkness. They would come floating in front of my eyes, hallucinatory visions. I used to dream about wolves too, and wake up screaming. As a child I was actually a poor eater; a 'picker' my mother called me. 'Finicky.' Wouldn't have fat, couldn't manage gristle, hated rice pudding – it reminded me of frogs' spawn. At one point I began to distrust eggs, having found some blood in a boiled one. My mother *insisted* I should eat them. It became an issue between us. Eggs for breakfast, every breakfast.

'I want to get down.'

'No, you *can't* get down. You'll sit there until you've finished it.'

'It's got a baby inside.'

'No it has not, and don't be silly.'

Rice pudding for lunch. 'Think about the poor children. They'd *love* some nice rice pudding. And what will your teacher say – what will your headmistress say – if you can't eat your food up properly?'

Thinking of my mother, in hospital with her empty teacups and her invisible biscuits and all her powerful mixed-up feelings, her complex emotional untranslatable messages and signals, I pushed the baked potato away. Nowadays, since her illness, eating had begun to seem an enormity, a criminal act almost, heartless and cold. How could I, with a clear conscience, stuff myself?

The Wimpy Bar waitress lit another cigarette. 'You're still at school, though,' she said, 'aren't you?'

I thought about this. *Was* I still at school, officially? Somehow, without exactly meaning to, I had drifted away, due partly to Alicia, partly to fear of the impending 'O' levels, and with a general feeling that nobody cared. And neither did I, but if I was leaving it would be only polite to say something. I should make a definite decision, one way or the other.

Allibert returned from Austria in a terrible state. Three weeks in the company of his understanding, ultra-sane parents had left him a total nervous wreck. I made some attempt to pick up the pieces, but without success. He was in a deep, unreachable panic. I couldn't

70

get a word in edgeways. He needed to talk the whole skiing holiday out of his system.

'It was awful, awful,' he said, pacing nervously up and down my room. 'I can't emphasise too strongly how awful. Everyone about twice my height, all bronzed and healthy and *smiling* all the time. I mean *all* the time. And the *après-ski* – singing rounds and clashing beer mugs and eating open sandwiches and the whole ghastly bonhomie of it all.'

I could see how Allibert might have had difficulties, knowing his preference for friction and tension. When he next paused for breath I suggested visiting my mother in hospital and he brightened visibly.

'You can't think', he said, 'how much I've missed your family. And you too, of course, but – and how's your father?'

'Still upstairs.'

Allibert suddenly went bright red, with a look of recollection. 'If I tell you this,' he said, 'you must *promise* to keep it secret. Never tell anyone else. Ever.'

'No, of course not.'

'A girl came to my room.'

'What?'

'In the ski resort. Birgit, her name was. When I got in late one night. I was drunk, unfortunately. It's most unusual for me, as you know. My parents had taken me to a local wine cellar. My father insisted. He wants me to develop a "discerning palate" .'

'But what *happened*?'

'I got into bed with her. By mistake,' Allibert added hastily. 'Entirely by mistake. It was dark. Luckily, I had my pyjamas on. She was naked.'

'And what happened then?'

'I got straight out again, naturally. I was horrified. Assuming at first I had the wrong bed, I apologised profusely and left the room.'

'Gosh.'

'But realising it *was* my room, I came back and attempted to reason with her. It was hard going at first. She would keep stroking my leg. And cooing at me. But I made my position clear' – Allibert

71

coughed – 'and dropped a few hints about possible homosexual tendencies, and explained about my vow of chastity, and so eventually we had quite a good conversation. She didn't really desire me physically, of course. It was a put-up job. My father, *my father*, had paid her £50 to – er – "make me into a man".'

Allibert's face twitched and he began pacing up and down again, breathing deeply. 'If I weren't so personally involved,' he said, 'it would be quite fascinating really. Such a clear exposé of the whole heterosexual system and its oppressiveness to women. My father wouldn't see it, of course. I wrote him a long letter explaining my position and how betrayed I felt, how manipulated. He refused to understand. We went skiing together. He interpreted it all, predictably enough, in grossly over-simplified terms: angry rejection of the mother, suppressed desire for the father – himself, I suppose he meant. Well, that's part of it, undoubtedly, I freely admit, but then what about *him*? What about *his* submerged desires? It's pretty obvious when you think about it. He's implicated knee-deep. But you can't hold a reasonable conversation with my father. He gets so defensive.'

Allibert pressed his nose against the window-pane. 'It was my eighteenth birthday,' he said bleakly. 'I've never felt so depressed. In those snowy wastes – the mountain peaks seemed symbolic of the harshness of patriarchy. My mother's silent complicity, that was what hurt me most. She always backs him up, always. If only women would realise, they don't *need* men.'

Eventually, impelled by conscience, I paid a brief visit to school. I found Sister Christina in the nuns' staff room, a bleak whitewashed cell down the corridor from the chapel. She was marking exercise books. When I came in she looked up sharply and waited, pencil suspended.

'Er, it's me.'

'So I see.'

'My mother's in hospital.'

'Is she, indeed?'

'She had a breakdown.'

'How upsetting for you.'

72

'So I'm taking' – I swallowed – 'some time off school, if that's all right.'

'Certainly. Go ahead, go ahead. Abandon your education, ruin your future. What do I care? It's a farce anyway, why pretend otherwise? You'll learn nothing at this school. I'm the only woman here with anything remotely resembling intelligence, and no one listens to me, of course.'

I had forgotten Sister Christina's naked impact, her irony and bitterness. People hold many illusions about nuns, *Sound of Music* type fantasies. In real life they don't generally seem very cheerful. When she had finished, returning her attention directly to the exercise books, I wandered back into the main school building to our empty classroom. It smelled of chalk dust and sweaty feet. I cleared my desk out; it was full of old pencil sharpenings. Four years I had wasted here in this ghastly place, this place of terminal boredom. Worse than wasted. I used to hold my breath by the clock to pass the time – three minutes I could manage. Nostalgia gripped me, regret for the past. I think it's hardest to leave unhappy places.

Rootless, I felt now, detached from any sense of belonging. I'd relied on my mother more than I'd known.

Nearing Saint Cecilia's I heard music, and red balloons were tied to the trees outside; my grandmother was apparently throwing a party. I pushed open the heavy door. It was unexpectedly warm inside and crowded. I recognised Mrs Tate from Cedar Grove flats for the elderly waving a bottle of wine and Miss DiMaggio flashed past me at high velocity in her wheelchair. And there was Miss Smith, the librarian, with her face flushed and her bun coming down in long white wisps, arguing volubly by Saint Michael the Archangel. The floor was covered in soft rugs and the wooden pews had been replaced by comfortable-looking old armchairs and sofas. Someone was playing the organ. I recognised the tune: it was *Daisy Daisy, give me your answer do*, but partially drowned by the noise from below. A large group was energetically doing the Hokey Cokey – I remembered it from nursery school.

You put your left leg in,
Your left leg out,
In, out, in, out,
Shake it all about.
You do the Hokey Cokey and you turn around,
That's what it's all about.
Oh! –

I edged nervously towards the south aisle. There was something very disquieting in all this festivity. You expect old ladies to be miserable, sour-faced, bad-tempered, frail and tottering and complaining about their aches and pains, or the cold, or today's youth, the dustbin men or whatever; not drunk, certainly not enjoying themselves. Under the pulpit I collided with a stacked pile of walking sticks and metal frames. 'Doesn't matter, dear!' someone shrieked.

I found my grandmother in the sacristy, half-way up a stepladder. Seeing me, she spat out a drawing pin and told me to get some wine from the fridge. The sacristy was transformed, with posters everywhere – scenic pictures of Corsica, a Monica Sjoo drawing, the great world-mother giving birth. If the nave was warm, here it was sweltering. I removed my coat and jumper.

'It looks different, eh?'

'Well, yes.'

'Good. Good. We are having a celebration.' She waved one hand airily. 'For the opening. The grand opening. Give me some wine.'

The fridge was full of strange bits of equipment, I noticed – test tubes, pipettes, filter paper – and also various cheeses and a half-open tin of luncheon meat. I poured out the wine into paper cups and my grandmother downed hers in three gulps. She was wearing stripy dungarees with leg-warmers and a red tee-shirt.

'You're opening the church?'

'The women's centre,' she corrected. 'It is for all women. A place to gather, to be with each other, to express our spirituality. We must encourage your mother to come here.'

'Er, yes,' I said doubtfully.

74

'This is what she needs. She must leave her husband, that man, he is no good for her. He constricts her spirit. That is why she went mad.' My grandmother rummaged in a drawer. 'I have some forms, here. A founding subscription is £10. Unfortunately, no one is admitted to full membership below the age of sixty-five. Associate membership is £5 only. Pregnancy testing on Saturdays, from ten a.m. till twelve. Karate instruction, Sundays. Women's basic mechanics, Thursday evenings.'

Girls need 'positive messages', they say, about what it means to be a woman. I was getting messages from all sides – negative, positive, mixed. My mother, my grandmother, Alicia. No wonder I felt confused. Meanwhile, actual messages, in envelopes, were arriving daily through our front door. Official brown envelopes with franking machine stamps: 'Give blood, save a life', 'National non-smoking day, March 9', 'Alcohol is the killer'. I read these cryptic statements over breakfast, propping them against the teapot, for reading, as I've always found, goes well with eating. Although it has to be light literature, mindless. Nothing like *War and Peace*. Cereal packets are ideal (thiamine, niacine, riboflavin). I also recommend romance – Barbara Cartland, Mills and Boon – and Radclyffe Hall has a particular affinity with orange cheesecake. Some deep connection exists, obviously, between words and food, visual and literal consumption, but I haven't really thought about this.

The envelopes remained unopened until finally one arrived by registered post. Heart sinking, I tore it open. My mother, it appeared, was 'ready for collection', like a parcel or dry-cleaning. She was 'no longer benefiting' from hospital treatment. Outpatient therapy had been arranged.

The paper slid from my fingers; I felt dizzy and sick. My mother was coming home. She and I, as Allibert would say, were about to enter 'a new phase' in our relationship. I dreaded it.

Eight

So much remains concealed, unspoken, in our family. So many questions unasked. We never talk, for instance, about my brother's death. Why did he die? In my heart, I don't really believe it was leukaemia: that was only a convenient label. She wanted too much from him, needed too much, demanded what he couldn't give. She killed him. But that's only my private theory.

'If only women would realise, they don't need men.' It was easy for Allibert to say. My mother needs them, desperately, hungers for them, covets them; they're her secret terrible addiction. Men – or rather, one man – it's not much to ask, but they slip through her fingers, evaporate upstairs, flow away like water underground. It's unfair, unfortunate, but experiences repeat themselves. You can't do much about it. Patterns become established, wanting, not getting, deprivation. She was deprived in childhood. 'So I myself conceived and bore your mother.' A virgin birth, as my grandmother always insisted. No husband, no father involved. Spontaneous conception: a common occurrence, a tradition among the *mazzere*. You see the same attitude today in England: self-insemination groups, A I D, father unknown, sperm provided anonymously by gay men or laboratory students.

On 28 March she was discharged. I took some daffodils and a change of clothes for her. It felt peculiar, rummaging through her wardrobe, intrusive – she's such a private person. Polishing her shoes, checking a pair of stockings for holes, I grew more and more apprehensive. What rights was I assuming to reclaim her? This remote woman, this stranger. Mrs Pauletta Andrews. My mother.

It might be best, I thought, to return home by some indirect route, via some intermediate place, to give her a chance to readjust. We could visit Hampton Court, a place I've always found especially soothing. The long, straight pebbled walks, the well-ordered formal flowerbeds neatly labelled – *Celosia argentea*, *Achillea filipendulina* – the clipped yew trees. Evidence of how human tragedy is absorbed, swallowed up in time.

As a direct consequence of his skiing holiday, Allibert had joined the Catholic Charismatic Renewal Movement, then sweeping like wildfire through the Inner London boroughs. Father John James was nervously supportative. He printed 500 or so thin blue paper leaflets on his Roneo machine which Allibert helped distribute. I encountered him on the corner of Surbiton High Street, shivering violently, his cagoul billowing around him. It was exceptionally windy and cold weather, though we'd had faint promises of spring.

I scanned a leaflet. It was set out boldly, in question and answer form. 'Do we need something special these days? Look at the world: atheism, wars, hatred, violence, communism infiltrating. Surely *now* is the time for God to act, if we are ready for Him!'

'Of course it's totally reactionary', Allibert said despondently. 'And male dominated like most so-called spiritual movements – Cardinal Suenens is backing it – but what can you expect? You've got to work through existing institutions, subvert the establishment from within. People won't listen otherwise.'

I turned the leaflet over. Charismatics, it said, met together two or three times weekly for prayer, song and Bible discussions, sometimes with guitar accompaniment, and 'SPEAKING IN TONGUES? Has occurred in High Barnet. Mentioned in Acts and by Paul. A gift of the Holy Spirit, breaking barriers of language and culture. Nothing to worry about.'

'Gosh.'

'Yes, well, there you are.'

'Can I come?'

'If you like. It starts with mass.' Allibert waved a leaflet half-heartedly. Passers-by swerved round him.

'Who goes to it?'

'Oh, the usual people, the Mount Carmel lot.'

'Goodness. Sounds interesting,' I said unconvincingly. Conversation with Allibert was getting to be a struggle, he was now so deeply immersed in gloom.

'It's a panacea,' he replied heavily. 'A substitute for real change. Still, there you are, it passes the time. I've no option really. It's different of course for you. Have you read any Mary Daly, by the way?'

'No, I haven't. Who's she?'

'I'll lend you the book. *Beyond God the Father*. It's fairly extremist – radical feminism – very courageous, scholarly.' Allibert sighed. His nose had gone white in the wind and his ears as usual stood out, giving him a sad, earnest expression. Tormented by doubt, unconscious of his own heart-rending integrity, in another age, I think, Allibert would have been a saint.

'D'you think I'm arrogant?'

'On *no*. No, I don't. Really.'

'Less, perhaps, these days. I'm still wrestling with my male conditioning. It's a slow, uphill climb. Everything in our culture confirms it, pressurises me into false role-playing. A man, a man.' He sighed again. 'After all, what does it mean? What is masculinity, *per se* ?'

'Honestly, Allibert, I shouldn't worry about it.'

'The male ego, fragile, narcissistic – Excuse me, sir, would you like a leaflet? – Oh, you're so lucky being a woman. I'd give anything – '

Shortly after I left him, Allibert must have abandoned or dropped his leaflets. The wind caught them, tossed them, blew them all down the high street.

'Collecting' my mother was less simple than I had envisaged. She didn't actively resist, but she didn't help much either; she just sat, or rather her body just sat. Mindless, zombie-like. The duty nurse was balanced precariously on a chair, sticking brown paper over broken windows. They were mostly broken, I noticed, or shattered – white cracks piercing the frosted glass, shooting stars, spiders' webs – and rain was dripping through, spreading in puddles under the radiator.

'What happened?' I asked.

'Don't ask me, I'm only agency. They all went mad, that's what. Last night. Ran wild. They had to call the police in.'

Attempting to cajole my mother into dressing, stories came into my mind, tales my grandmother used to tell. How the Corsican village women, normally so silent and contained, so subservient, hard-working, long-suffering, would periodically, beneath the full moon, run wild. In the evil hours, that forsaken time between midnight and the cock's first crowing, they left their houses, their sleeping children and went hunting. Led by the *mazzere*, the wise woman, wild woman, village witch, they went howling like a ravening wolf-pack through the *maquis*, over the bare moonlit hillsides. Woe betide any man who met them, mad with flesh-hunger; like wolves they would set upon him, tear him to pieces, rend him limb from limb. Once, a young shepherd from Chera, Jean-Antoine Giustini, went after them; he was newly married and foolish. Young fresh brides always made the best hunters, so my grandmother informed me. This was in the last century, when peasant girls were very strictly brought up, confined mainly indoors, with no freedom of any kind before marriage. Giustini's wife, Maria, was just sixteen, a sweet-faced girl, meek and gentle in manner, and they were very much in love with each other. Dreadful screams were heard that night floating faintly from the distant hills. A mass was said the next Sunday for Giustini's soul. All the villagers attended, the women's faces veiled with heavy black lace mantillas. His body was never recovered, only his gold wedding ring and shreds of clothing. Bones, however, kept turning up in unexpected places all over the village – cupboards, chests; and in the *mazzere*'s house, a polished skull (a sheep's skull, she maintained). No sermons were preached, no accusations levelled. Some subjects are best left undiscussed.

We took a taxi from the hospital. My mother was haphazardly dressed and her neck was dirty, which distressed me most. She had always been so neat, clean and meticulous. In the taxi she sat exactly as before, very upright, her eyes fixed vacantly on the dividing glass panel.

If I were an artist, my mother would make such an excellent model. I would paint only her, she would be my sole theme, as some artists paint themselves. Woman sitting. Woman with a blank expression. Widow. Bereaved mother. Or maybe she would be better portrayed through symbolism. As a mountain for instance, a Corsican mountain like those Edward Lear painted, gently sloping at first, chequered with fields and olive orchards, but then shooting abruptly upwards – bare grey rock, vertical towers against the sky, stone citadels. Or a volcano perhaps. 'Series of Volcanoes.' In the morning light, in the evening light. Neither extinct nor yet erupting.

We walked together along the south side of Hampton Court Palace, between the display flowerbeds and the lawns. To our left, beyond iron palings, lay a long canal, then Hampton Court park with its blasted trees, and Bushy Park, wide and utterly flat, open to the sky, with deer herds grazing. So far as England exists here it still is, in Surrey just south-west of London, the legacy or leftovers of past centuries. An unpromising place, no promises made, no miracles likely, little to remember or carry away except postcards for the casual tourist, Anne Boleyn teatowels, badges, Tower of London mugs, lacy plastic bookmarks – flotsam and jetsam.

My mother was still saying nothing. Our feet crunched on gravel. Having gone as far as possible in one direction, down the main walk, we were faced across a dry moat with the Thames. It was flowing swiftly, carrying pieces of driftwood and dead leaves. Willow trees on the bank bent over, trailing their long branches like arms. Without warning, I felt unbearably sad. Until that moment, misery had seemed containable. My mother looked impressively detached, regal and dignified, gazing across the river. She would have made a good queen, I think, one of Henry the Eighth's. She could have faced torture, the rack and the axe, no problem. Her own death she could easily have faced.

We made a round tour – the Tudor tennis courts, the knot gardens, the vine. Only the maze was closed, locked up until Easter, and we didn't enter the palace. By silent consent we remained outsiders, drifting around the peripheries. I felt sapped of energy, drained and exhausted. I can't cope with emotion, that's for certain. My body reacts badly to it. In the vine house I stared hungrily

80

at twisted bare branches, visualising the grapes as they'd by in summer, swollen and purple, sold off for exorbitant prices. Everything has a price in England. In Corsica olives lie ungathered beneath the trees, while the arbutus bushes produce millions of berries to ripen and rot among clusters of their own flowers. Lettuces grow wild too, and carrots and cabbages, and the asphodel bulbs are edible, asphodels that light acres of land in the spring.

The Hampton Court vine was planted in 1768 and is the largest Black Hamburg vine in Britain. The girth of its stem at ground level is seven feet and some of the branches are a hundred feet long. This information was printed on a noticeboard, to which I directed my mother's attention, and she looked politely at it. Still, in spirit she felt miles away, and just five minutes later in fact she disappeared. She just vanished. She had been right behind me, passing on our left the art gallery with a special exhibition as I recall on 'Renaissance Perspectives', then suddenly I sensed a kind of vacuum and there, when I checked, she wasn't. I looked up the paths, down the long avenues. Nothing.

My face must have registered concern, for a guard approached. 'My mother's gone,' I said helplessly. He was a kind, mild and ineffective man. Together we searched behind statues and trees and pieces of ornamental topiary. I kept glancing nervously upwards, dreading to see her on the palace roof, spreading her arms, falling. The palace chimneys, impressive patterned brick affairs, are not, so the guard informed me, Tudor or Elizabethan, but a later Victorian introduction. This fact has remained with me, permanently branded on my mind, ever since.

Our search faltered to a halt. People, he consoled me, often got lost, children especially. It was only a matter of time; they usually turned up. Had I tried the teashop? I tried the teashop, the postcard shop, the lavatories, the old kitchens. I ran wildly across the inner pebbled courtyards and through the palace. Gloomy portraits, misty, distorting mirrors, the floorboards polished and slippery. The King's Bedroom, anterooms, the armoury. That desperate search seems in memory like a dream and, indeed, I repeated it in dreams many nights after. 'I've lost my mother. My mother is lost, she's lost, I can't find her.' As dusk fell and they were locking up, I left a scribbled note at the main exit and crossed, dazed, through busy traffic, hooters and blinding headlights over Hampton Court Bridge, over wasteland, through a swing gate into Bushy Park.

The wind sighed, branches creaked. There was an almost-full moon, light of a kind, but the ground was uneven and I kept stumbling. Pausing for rest, I saw lights travelling steadily in even procession across the western horizon. Aeroplanes, coming in to land at Heathrow Airport. For a second, my heart deceived, I thought they might be angels. I still believed secretly, despite everything, in miracles. Who knew, maybe my mother had been 'assumed' like the Blessed Virgin into heaven. That would solve a lot of problems.

I needed a sign at this point, I felt in very bad need of one. Saint Theresa, when she was dead let fall a shower of roses from heaven. That was thoughtful of her. Relatives need reassuring. And Saint Angela's sister too, she appeared in the middle of a haystack, on a burning hot summer's day, to tell Saint Angela not to worry, not to grieve. But we had received no sign from my brother, by day or night. Perhaps we hadn't prayed enough or had faith enough.

I reached home at eleven o'clock that night, early hours for me. I had got used to sitting up late, chain-drinking endless cups of coffee. A way to avoid sleep, evade dreams and the drifting spirits if they happened to return, their hoarse, rustling voices like dead leaves outside my bedroom window. If they were name-calling, roll-calling again by any chance, I preferred to remain downstairs.

To my surprise, I found my father in the kitchen. I had almost forgotten his existence. He looked distraught and anxious, his hair standing on end. 'Ah, Jenny! I can't seem to recall exactly how this goes.' He was holding, pinched gingerly between finger and thumb, a teabag. 'You do something with it, dip it somewhere. I thought your mother – I've been waiting, expecting her.'

I switched the kettle on, wondering how best to phrase my reply. 'I can't find her', 'She ran away', or 'She's lost'? The truth, as usual where my father was concerned, seemed too direct, too naked. In my mother's role, as I now was, or as his daughter, I felt obliged to protect him from all possible distress, to preserve his cocoon. A family rule. 'Don't disturb your father. Go on tiptoes.'

'I bought her a present.' On the table lay a white oblong paper package. 'An Easter present,' my father explained. 'She likes chocolate.'

Chocolate rabbits. Ten rabbits. Not much, but representing, as it occurs to me now, a considerable effort of imagination and sacrifice of time on my father's part. To buy these rabbits, he must have actually left the house, found his way somehow to the shops, discovered a newsagents or confectioners, chosen, paid in cash – all sorts of things. His adventuring days were over and present-day England was stranger to him than any butterfly jungle; he took taxis to the Natural History Museum and to conferences.

I attempted a brief summary of recent events, but we were still waiting for the kettle to boil and this was obviously the main thing on his mind.

'Ah, yes. Yes indeed,' he replied vaguely. 'They're like that. Women. Here one second, gone the next. Mysterious. Unpredictable. Your mother's like that. It's part of their charm, you know.'

I reflected. This seemed rather unfair to my mother. For so long she had remained motionless in one fixed position, closeted grimly behind the kitchen door. He might have found her then, anytime.

'Stone-cold, stone-cold,' muttered my father, tapping at the kettle. 'Nothing happening here, nothing at all. Dead as a doornail. Jenny, here – you understand electrics.'

With my grandmother's second-best screwdriver, which she had left behind, I took the kettle apart, knowing in advance it was a futile exercise. Like our refrigerator, now stinking of sour milk and rotting meat, the dead television, or the stopped electric clock with both its hands pointing permanently to midnight, the kettle had gone dead for its own reasons, nothing to do with plugs or fuses or any ordinary electrical logic. In such circumstances I knew enough from my grandmother not to meddle, not to interfere, to respect fate and the kettle's own inner decisions. 'This poor kettle, he is suffering, he desires to be gone. Let us release his spirit . . .

I unscrewed the element and dismantled the plug. My father buzzed anxiously by my shoulder, like a large moth frustrated of its candle flame. The kitchen wallpaper, I noticed, was all peeling off. Our house clearly was falling into ruin, self-destructing, steadily collapsing in my mother's absence and following the natural tendency of all things towards oblivion. I could do little to prevent it.

My mother was lost for several days, a time of suspension and waiting around. It was nearly Easter. Between life and death, living and not living. I understood a little how Christ's disciples must have felt. Waiting, trying to sustain faith, but not exactly sure of the outcome. By chance I wandered into our front sitting-room. My mother's secretarial books caught my eye, ranged neatly along one shelf side by side with the English language texts – *Basic Pitman 2000*, *High Speed Typing Drills*, *Office Practice*, *Secretarial Skills*, *The Perfect Secretary*.

I dusted them off and carted them into the kitchen. Her name was inscribed neatly on every flyleaf. She went to evening classes when we were children, at the Pitman Institute, practised assiduously, passed every exam word-perfect. Despite her chronic lack of self-confidence, convictions of total inadequacy, shivering attacks, of pride, the second-worst sin, my mother was never in danger. Success (and she came top of her class) never 'went to her head', it never entered her mind. Failure was always more real, just around the next corner.

I myself up until this time had worn failure lightly. Alicia and I had established roles, fallen into an easy reliable pattern. She got As for exams, I got C, D, H. She had 'a brain', intelligence, fine analytical capacities, a retentive memory; my mind felt like fog or mushy soup. It hadn't occurred to me ever – I hadn't tried – to *work*. No one had suggested it. Sister Christina had a particular resigned expression reserved specially for me, not implying much hope.

Sitting at the kitchen table, where my grandmother used to sit mending her machinery, I copied down my first tentative symbols:

/. /. /.   ⟩. ⟩. ⟩.   ⊿ ⊿ ⊿   ⌐ ⌐ ⌐

84

I became totally absorbed. Concentration, like a white light, pure light, like the Holy Ghost, descended on me. Carefully repeating each 'outline', practising the heavy strokes – B, D, G – the light strokes – P, T, C – I was released, set free. From the world, the flesh, from all mortal trials, demands of conscience and worries. I forgot my mother. I forgot everything. By that evening I had mastered all the basic consonants (lines) and the vowels (dots). I had found, it seemed, my vocation.

Nine

In times of crisis, especially family crisis, it's important to find some escape route, some means of self-preservation, to practise an art or a skill. As, for instance, I learned shorthand and my father persevered steadily, doggedly, unswervingly, determinedly with his later much-acclaimed work on *Operophthera brumata*, the winter moth.

Meanwhile, my mother's absence remained a total mystery; not the slightest sign or the least clue, despite twenty-four-hour police searches. They were dredging the Thames, so Allibert informed me, but found only old broken bedstands, bottles and sunken houseboats. I'm translating here, reading back and deciphering, for I recall everything from that period in shorthand symbols. I had stopped hearing in the ordinary sense. I was seeing speech, not listening to it – a fascinating process. Watching Allibert speak was like reading a comic cartoon strip: his mouth opened and shut silently like a goldfish, the words emerging perfectly formed, all with their proper vowels. Strung out like washing, they floated across the kitchen, dancing, lingering, slowly dissolving and turning fainter like smoke.

As they play music into machines, note-processors, and it translates instantly on screen into light-symbols and spews out the other side, printed on long continuous sheets, my mind had gone mechanical. It's what they call obsession. Useful things, obsessions, when life becomes too bewildering. At last I had found a system, a way of coping, of making order from chaos. And without it I would certainly never have managed what I did – winning the all-England silver cup for shorthand, breaking 280 w.p.m. Perhaps

86

all uncommon achievement requires a certain degree of fanaticism and strange behaviour. I had more freedom in this respect than Allibert, in whose parents' eyes sanity, 'normal development', was *de rigeur*.

Easter came and went; the chocolate rabbits remained. I had felt no temptation towards them whatsoever. It shows how radically my appetites were changing. I had now reached stage two in my shorthand course manual, where you can leave out the vowels, and I was greedily acquiring 'shortforms', shorthand's most extreme condensation, its pure, distilled, heart's essence.

It was Allibert who eventually discovered my mother, by a slow process of deduction and diligent persistence. He bought a large map of the area – Fulwell, Teddington, Hampton – and a smaller, more detailed plan of Hampton Court, and shaded bits in, drew lines and circles and arrows. He got me to recall our exact route. Then, after much reflection, he drew his own separate map. It looked a bit like a weather chart: areas of high pressure, low pressure, black dots, wavy lines from the west. The police ignored it. I can't say whether it made sense; Allibert seemed convinced it did. While he explained it, mainly in dense psychological terminology – 'risk zones', I remember, was one phrase he used – I was practising 'mother' and 'nature', which, strange to say, are exactly the same sign only reversed, mirror images:

Allibert disapproved of my shorthand. I caught him casting dark glances at it. For him, obviously, it carried all the wrong connotations – secretaries, offices, power structures, deflection of female energy, patriarchal brainwashing techniques. He never understood. To me it was a purely abstract pleasure, an end in itself.

As for oppression, to be honest, at this stage I would have welcomed it, of whatever kind, from wherever. A nice office, a nice boring job, a normal family, a *real* father – like Alicia's, for instance. Oppressive. Overbearing. Sexist. Insensitive. But at least *there*. At least participating, making his presence felt, not like my father, just flitting in and out occasionally. It was pressure, oppression, exactly, that I so much lacked. Something solid, some sense of enclosure. Something to push against. Leaving home, 'growing up' – a uniquely difficult task in our family. By the time it seemed appropriate, I had no one much left to leave.

Allibert rustled the map impatiently. He looked harassed. He too was having a hard time. Serious differences with the Charismatics and his 'A' levels, five of them. *And* my mother on top of it all. I should have been more grateful, I suppose. His detective methods may have been somewhat unusual, drawn largely from Jung and Fritz Perls – random dream/thought processes, free association – but they did find her, as the police had failed to. We'd have got there quicker, perhaps, if I had cooperated. I was dreaming every night of labyrinths, monsters, spiders' webs.

My grandmother might have helped too, but she at this time was extremely busy, converting Saint Cecilia's for disabled access and planning a women's literary festival. It was early days then for the Surbiton radical feminist movement and we were very isolated from the London scene – Feminist Bookweek, women-only readings, lesbian separatist publishing houses and printing presses – but my grandmother was thinking roughly along the right lines. Several of her old ladies had started writing their memoirs and one a science-fiction novel.

My father was also beyond communication, even more so than usual. An article had appeared in the *New Scientist*, challenging his research methods, written by Professor J. Beasley of the San Carolina Institute, his arch-enemy. High cries of rage, inarticulate despair, echoed from above, interspersed with a low booming, moaning sound, jungle-like – my father in pain – and rum bottles piled up by the outside dustbin.

I was thinking of translating the Bible into shorthand. This seemed to me a brilliant, original idea, but in fact it's already been done, by Sir Isaac Pitman. His version, open at Saint Paul, Corinthians I, Chapter 13, 'Though I speak with the tongues of men and angels – ' is displayed under glass at Pitman's College, near Russell Square tube station, in the entrance hall. It's worth a visit.

'Don't you think, in your family,' Allibert ventured, 'there might be some – er – similarities? Parallels? Certain – er – habits of distance, of detachment? Apparent insensitivity? Not,' he added hastily, 'that you *don't* care, really, for each other – I'm sure – but you suppress it, perhaps from fear – '

'Could be' I replied coldly.

My mother was in the Hampton Court maze, in the very innermost circle, sitting on a bench. She must have climbed over the locked turnstile. The maze itself, I'm sure, gave her no trouble. She would have gone straight to the centre.

Getting her out, 'rescuing' her, presented more problems. To me then the maze appeared nightmarishly vast, labyrinthine, very like my presaging dreams. In fact, it's quite small. Allibert, with his usual courage and armed with a guidebook and his maps, went in. For about two hours he walked round and round; sometimes he was almost there, at a hedge's distance, within sight of her through the close-packed yew needles, but then curiously he would go astray, take the wrong turning and walk out again. He made eleven fresh starts from the entrance. My mother sat immovable, statuesque.

I was mounted umpire-like on a cast iron structure, a sort of stepladder, from which the usual maze-keeper shouts instructions at closing time to the lost and confused. I could have helped more, given more clues, but I felt so much an outsider, voiceless and peripheral. A juddering sound came in gusts with the wind. Far up, far away, I saw helicopters circling. I thought it might be the police, still searching, on the lookout for my mother. They might winch her up, whirl her away. I waved violently, but to no purpose; the helicopters came no closer. They were, as I realised later, B B C Television filming the boat race.

Finally Allibert, by persistence and luck, reached the maze centre. He sat down beside my mother, putting his arm around her, and she didn't seem to mind.

'One drop. One small drop only,' my grandmother said. 'This reveals all. One drop of this chemical. Now place it carefully, slowly, on the glass. See, and the liquid changes, it clings together, it forms into tiny grains. You are not with child – '

89

My grandmother's fame was spreading as a pregnancy tester; women came from far and wide. I assisted at her Saturday morning sessions, held in the vestry. My job was to make coffee and wash out the jam jars, the pipettes, the conical funnel. *Not* using washing-up liquid (gives a false positive). A separate bowl for the coffee cups. Rinse the slide, fold the filter paper. Sun flooded through the vestry windows, lighting up long streams of dust, making invisible the electric fire bars. Trees waved outside in the old graveyard, now reclaimed from brambles.

We operated on a no-appointments system; after each consultation I rang a bell, the tiny claw-mouthed brass communion bell. I had always wanted to be an 'altar boy', announcer of mystic rites, signaller of miraculous transformations. Blood into wine. Christ's body into bread. Take and eat. The Catholic priests, walking living symbols in their heavy vestments – white for Easter, red for the feasts of martyrs. The alb, the chasuble. My grandmother, in her stripy dungarees, was a less awesome, more human figure. Her methods were straightforward, her approach firm. She advocated the rhythm method of contraception or the cap. She encouraged natural childbirth and, where possible, single motherhood. 'The man, your husband, ah yes – ' A dismissive wave. 'Pay no attention. He knows nothing, this man. Listen to your own heart only.' For unwanted pregnancies she had various options, including a list of clinics in the last resort.

My mother, recaptured, was now at home, come home to us, but it didn't feel so. It felt as if she was still away somewhere, drifting, wandering, free-floating around the universe. Her eyes were blank, wide, staring. She never slept, that I noticed. She gave me the creeps, the horrors, the old cold prickly feeling on the back of my neck. My grandmother's story feeling. Exactly. She had become fantastic, my mother, a creature of fantasy. As mad people are, as madness sets you free to be. Searching, journeying. Like fairy-tale people.

She was thinner than ever. Mad thin. Not anorexic; anorexia is just play-madness, a dangerous game, an addiction. My mother was not playing; she was in deadly earnest. She had opened a door somewhere and stepped through, crossed a threshold, was seeing now from the other side. Out there.

Allibert put her to bed and there she, or her body, remained, propped against the pillows. I wouldn't touch her. He changed the sheets, gave her baths, spent hours coaxing her to eat. He had borrowed a cookery book from the library, *Food for Stress*. Following its instructions, he concocted delicate omelettes and delicious soups. It's a pity men can't be mothers; they would make a much better job of it. As a mother-substitute, a nurse, Allibert was supreme. I remember him holding the teaspoon steady – intensity of concentration.

He had moved into our house. So had other things. From being a lonely, silent, empty place, it was now transformed. Inhabited by birds – budgerigars, canaries, lovebirds, exotic parrots, two owls, a toucan, ten or eleven white doves, a bird of paradise and a capercaillie. They made a great deal of noise between them, interfering often with my shorthand practice. I mention this as evidence in my favour, proof that, like my father, I was trying, for they were my gift to her. I had bought them, in cages originally, from Kingston Market.

But like most gifts, or attempts at giving to my mother, this most dismally failed. Through my carelessness, the birds had all escaped and colonised the kitchen. By no efforts could they be persuaded upstairs. The kitchen floor, the table, all my mother's once clean, once polished, white formica surfaces were now thickly encrusted with bird droppings. Allibert, finicky, did all his cooking under an umbrella. I kept my shorthand space clear.

They were terribly destructive too: the curtains were torn to shreds, my mother's window-sill plants pecked to pieces and scattered. The female budgerigars started egg-laying, for which purpose, lacking egg boxes, they gouged holes in the wall. Deep holes, into solid brick. A lovebird sawed through the electric light flex. The owls nested in a cupboard, baleful eyes glaring. I was keeping the windows open permanently, due to the smell, but only the doves flew out, in a swirling clattering mass at sunrise, drifting back at dusk.

My father still visited the kitchen, but mistrustfully and heavily protected. He wore a canvas overcoat, a wide-brimmed hat and for some reason a fine-meshed mosquito-net veil. Jungle precautions. I'm not sure what he wore when visiting my mother, or whether he did, and if so, what passed between them. He was growing wilder, more eccentric with age, or perhaps due to his isolation, his self-imposed intellectual solitude. He looked more and more strikingly like a moth.

He said strange things too, which I recorded automatically in shorthand. My father spoke at around eighty words a minute. Reading back through my notebooks, I realise he was actually confiding in me, and making himself quite vulnerable. He talked a lot about women, in terms as usual of 'they' and 'them' – this weird species. I don't think my father had had much sexual experience before his marriage – or after; his nervousness of women contrasted with his confidence in moths.

I think also he felt on some level abandoned by my mother, or seriously let down. Once, in the far-off idyllic days of their courtship, she had seemed to share his commitment to moths, his ideals, displayed apparent interest in his theories; but once married, she dropped the pretence.

'She wanted children,' my father said, his face reminiscent, regretful behind the veil. 'Children! Ah!' Against his plans, his preferences, children. The first definite point of conflict between them, the first rift, now widened to an unbridgeable chasm. My perspectives were altering. Again. It was her original fault then, her move first, or ours – we came in the way, thrust their lives apart. Another light on the past. Yet one more theory, way of explaining, blaming. Endless permutations.

My father stirred his tea meditatively. Feathers floated softly in the air, remains of a recent dove squabble. The toucan regarded us quizzically sideways. 'You know, dedications,' my father said. 'I don't usually dedicate my books. Acknowledgments, of course, a list of acknowledgments – in alphabetical order or one risks causing offence – ' His voice trailed away. He coughed. For a consistent, steady flow of words, my father was unreliable. He had never been in any sense a dictator.

I wondered where to get hold of some tapes; or maybe I could attend an evening class and learn to type, take exams, get some

92

proper qualifications. Now I was sixteen and had left school. I couldn't rely for ever on my grandmother. I had a feeling I would make a good secretary. I was quiet, for one thing. And tactful, and a good listener in appearance. I could turn my obsession to use. Taking down other people's words, men's words, unthinkingly, precisely, mechanically. This would be, it seemed to me, the greatest happiness.

'She doesn't read my books,' my father said. 'We don't discuss my writing. It's not the sort of thing she likes. And yet, and yet, it makes a living. It's important to me.' He gestured deprecatingly. 'I often think of her, when I'm writing. I write them for her.'

Ten

The desire to live, the instinct of life, where does it come from? My grandmother knew how. Maybe it's a skill that comes with age, not natural or inborn. A flame in people, a small flame flickering, so carefully it has to be fed. In children especially, as my mother tried so hard to keep John alive. To shield him like a small candle from the winds and darkness.

In the darkness, the spirits of death. Howling, drifting on the wind, the lost souls. Spiteful, jealous of the living, still hungry for life. But with cunning, with great daring, they may be fooled. My grandmother still remembered one or two tricks, last-ditch anti-spirit techniques, cases of youngmen and women snatched from death's jaws.

One example was her own dearest friend in childhood, Teresita da Cavalli. For some reason never explained, Teresita stopped eating, ceased taking any pleasure in existence, became dreadfully thin. 'Her life was bleeding away, bleeding away,' as my grandmother described it, waving her hand. Teresita lay on her bed all day in a white gown. Death drew close, very close; everyone could feel her. A heaviness, an oppressive atmosphere, like a thunderstorm impending or snowfall.

The spirits came crying round every night, calling Teresita by name. On the fifth night, a Friday, the village women gathered together, with the *mazzere*, in the downstairs room of the house, and they held a fake funeral. I'm not exactly sure what took place, my grandmother's story varies. At its most alarming, they actually bury Teresita, six feet deep in a wooden coffin. In another version they substitute a number of young chickens, or the chickens are

94

tied in a sack and drowned. The women tear their hair, rend their clothes and breasts and lament. Teresita's mother becomes hysterical. The *mazzere* lights fourteen candles, one for each year of Teresita's life, and solemnly blows them out. Men don't feature in this story; as usual they're somewhere else, in a bed or down the pub. Teresita's mother utters one long final cry of despair. No sound from outside. The spirits have gone, satisfied. In the morning two women dig up Teresita and everyone, including her, eats an enormous breakfast.

'You don't know anything. Anything.' Alicia said. We were in her bedroom. I was visiting her. In the recent turmoil we'd lost touch and I had missed her. She was after all my friend, the closest apart from Allibert, who didn't count. 'Name me,' she said, 'one thing you know about, one subject that I don't know more about.'

She had three mirrors in her bedroom. I could see her reflection, what remained of it, in multiple. She was thinner, I think, than my mother, but still fiercely in control. Studying now simultaneously for 'A' levels and Oxbridge; she had taken all her 'O' levels, thirteen of them, in January. Nobody at school was speaking to her. The nuns disapproved of excellence, success, miracles unaided by prayer. At the end-of-term prize-giving, Alicia was conspicuously ignored. The inscribed books, *Prince Caspian*, Gwen Raverat's *Period Piece*, *Little Women*, *The Song of Bernadette*, went to the 'good' ones, the prefects, the class monitors, the blackboard wipers. I once got *Prince Caspian*, for neat handwriting.

Alicia's attacks came like her confidences, straight out of the blue, allowing no space for reply. She launched instantly into a recital of 'Kubla Khan'.

> In Xanadu did Kubla Khan
> A stately pleasure-dome decree;
> Where Alph, the sacred river, ran
> Through caverns measureless to man
> Down to a sunless sea.

There was no furniture in her room, apart from the mirrors. For lack of a chair, I was sitting on the floor, on the bare floorboards, back against the wall. I felt in need of support. Alicia apparently needed none. There was no bed. I shifted uncomfortably, feeling my weight of fat. In some people's company you can forget your body, more or less, or feel easy with it, but Alicia's glances prevented this.

Having finished 'Kubla Khan' she then re-recited it, without a pause, backwards. This was a new skill of hers.

> Man to measureless caverns through
> Ran, river sacred the, Alph where –

Nonsense poetry, unpoetry. Alicia's face remained expression-less. She betrayed no pride, ever, in her accomplishments. Language is so easy to destroy, once you start. When I was small, I once unravelled my mother's knitting, half a cardigan; I pulled one thread and it all came apart. I got the same feeling of awe and terror listening to Alicia. She could also do 'The Prelude' and most of 'Paradise Lost'.

'Pass me that cup,' she ordered. 'Now watch.' I watched. She made a motion like drinking, then threw up. Very neatly into the cup, not a drop spilt. 'Gosh' – my standard response. 'That's nothing,' Alicia said. 'I can do that any time I want. *They*' – pointing at the floor – 'force me to eat now.'

I had passed 'they' on my way upstairs. Alicia's mother seemed in a pitiable state of fear. Her hands trembled and dripped. As usual she was washing up; I don't think she ever stopped. They should have got a dishwasher. Her hair, I noticed, had turned grey. Alicia's seven brothers and sisters, with their little pale anxious faces, were watching television as I came through: a cartoon programme, *Deputy Dawg*. They didn't seem to be growing up much. I could imagine they would die quite soon. Families are such strange affairs, especially Catholic families. Stranger than fiction. Alicia's small siblings reminded me of the Jellabies in *Bleak House*.

Alicia herself had several fictional predecessors. She was hum-ming now *Soul of my Saviour*, one of the school's regular Assembly hymns.

96

Soul of my savour, sanctify my breast,
Body of Christ be thou my saving guest,
Blood of my saviour, bathe me in thy tide,
Wash me with water, flowing from thy side.

Strength and protection may thy passion be,
Oh blessed Jesus, hear and answer me,
Deep in thy wounds Lord, hide and shelter me,
So I may never, never part from thee.

It's a disturbing sort of hymn, with a dragging heavy rhythm,
very powerful, like the tide sweeping you along. I used to love it,
but then afterwards I always felt very lost and depressed. Like the
hymns to Our Lady, it called up too many, too deep feelings, like
the *Star of the Sea* hymn:

Mother of Christ, Star of the Sea,
Pray for the wanderer, pray for me.

'Do you still have periods?' Alicia demanded. Curiously enough,
I did still, though at irregular intervals. I was having one then; the
tightness, the sharp pulls of pain, felt like a thread connecting me
to something, anchoring me. I felt very heavy. Alicia looked very
light. I could imagine she would be capable, like the saints, of levi-
tation, effortless, accidental, like Saint Teresa of Avila, who had
to weigh herself down with stones. 'Yes, I expect you do,' Alicia
said disdainfully. '*I* don't. I've stopped all that. I expect my
ovaries will wither up now. I don't care in the least. I hope they
will.'

My period pains suddenly increased, shooting across my lower
belly. For relief, I drew both my legs up. 'Don't you want children?'

'Children!' Alicia said, with incredulous disgust. A long pause
ensued. 'Children,' she repeated. 'No thank you. No thank you
very much. There are seven downstairs; you might have noticed
them. As human beings, frankly, they hardly qualify. One's called
Septimus, I believe. Seven! Not counting all the miscarriages. Can
you imagine?'

Alicia put a hand to her throat. 'They have sex *all the time*,' she said faintly. 'Every night. Pretty grim. I suppose it becomes automatic, giving way to your animal instincts. You'll be like that, I expect. I can hear my father sometimes, grunting and twisting around on top of her, like a great fat pig, like the fat pig that he is. I expect she prays.

> – and all the night
> To turn the wheel of false desire: and longings that
>   wake her womb
> To the abhorred birth of cherubs in the human form
> That live a pestilence . . . '

Alicia stretched out her hands, her long, elegant, Lady-of-Shalott hands, now papery white and thin. 'My God,' she said, shuddering. 'Children.'

She went to empty her cup of sick in the toilet. While she was gone I started thinking by chance about my brother. He had wanted children. Maybe he felt deprived of babies, being the youngest, and like Allibert he had strong natural mothering instincts. He liked dolls but my mother refused to give him any, so he adopted mine. We played games sometimes about childbirth, my mother having described this process in graphic detail. The pain involved, the risks – breach births, babies born deformed, Siamese twins. Hundreds of women die every year. For small children, we were remarkably well informed. I can clearly recall my brother writhing about in agony on his bed. 'Cut me open, cut me open! Save my baby!'

We decided to marry. Stupidly he told my mother and she said we couldn't. We planned to get a special dispensation from the Pope, and have sixteen children, including two sets of twins. In a bid to get himself pregnant, my brother ate double helpings of Ready Brek every breakfast. I remember him checking his stomach self-consciously.

These memories, so clear, came as a shock. Since his death, I had hardly thought about him. He went, ceased to be, so completely, leaving only a sort of emptiness.

98

But he was real, my brother. He was real, he was a part of my life, I loved him, he died. So simple, so difficult still to accept. But you can't escape her, truth/Death/fate, wherever you go, however far you travel. 'I'll meet you,' says Death, 'tomorrow.' And to avoid her you travel miles overnight, on foot, through arduous terrain, over treacherous passes, until at last, dusty and footsore, you reach a small, isolated mountain village. And there she is, in the market place. Self-possessed, cool as ever. 'We arranged to meet,' she says.

'All songs are about death,' my grandmother told me once. And all stories perhaps, all true stories. And Death is always a woman. She dresses in black, she wears a headscarf, is quiet and modest in demeanour. You might take her for any village woman. Until she turns and looks at you, with her unwavering clear eyes

In the oldest stories, handed down through generations, barely remembered, Death lives in her own house in the village. A small, whitewashed house set apart from the rest. Men visit her secretly, guiltily, under cover of midnight darkness. Her garden is a graveyard, well tended with many bright flowers and sheltered by soft-sighing poplars, the borderland trees. From her well she draws up sometimes water, the brightest, sweetest water in the village, and sometimes blood. It is immaterial to her whichever. She drinks blood and bathes in it. She might offer you blood for breakfast, big coffee-cups full, pigs' hearts, raw bacon rashers. *Always refuse.*

I had difficulties with this story when I was small. Parts of it seemed so very unlikely. Why did the men visit Death? Why would anyone voluntarily enter Death's house? It was quite safe, my grandmother reassured me, so long as you ate no food. But where did they sleep? In Death's bed; they slept with Death herself. It was safe, but only so long as they kept their eyes shut. 'Tight shut, tight shut.' My grandmother screwed her own eyes up to demonstrate. It was tempting, very tempting, to peep, as Death is such a beautiful woman and she would be giving the men such great pleasure. At this point in the story, my grandmother grew vague; pressed for further detail, she said Death might embrace the men. In her strong brown arms, her beautiful arms.

Nowadays I think it would more likely be the women visiting

Death. Starting with Alicia, followed by a long queue. I like to think I would be elsewhere, out in the wilds with my great-aunt Amaretta and her band of female guerrillas, hunting men, revenging our lost brothers and fathers. Better to inflict death than to court it. I was always very attracted to Amaretta's lifestyle. From certain casual hints, I gathered she and her outlaws, like Death and the men, lay all night in each other's arms, under the round moon on the bare hillsides, or in the *maquis*, the wild heavy-scented Corsican undergrowth. The *maquis* smells like incense, bitter-sweet. It is the scent of all Corsica. Arbutus, myrtle, cistus and lentisk, rosemary, lavender and thyme. Carried on the land breeze it reaches incoming ships, mingled with sea smells, intoxicating. One wakes and sleeps with its fragrance, which is like no other.

I came away from Alicia's house in a state of deep agitation. She was stepping very close, I felt, to the borderline, taking extreme risks, gambling. And though she had stopped menstruating she was still bleeding, as she mentioned in an off-hand way: she was urinating and defecating blood. And she had also stopped digesting: food passed straight through her like liquid or she sicked it up.

She was utterly indifferent to the danger, fearless as ever; but I feared for her, and for myself too. Never had life, never had food seemed so dear to me. In blind panic I bought five Mars bars and ate them all on the spot, outside the newsagents. I felt sick myself after this, but held it down with firm resolution.

I passed the Wimpy Bar without looking in. I hadn't been in for weeks – it was too intense in there, I couldn't cope. She was confusing me, the waitress, with her obscure double-meaning messages. And my own feelings, they were also confusing.

So I went home, hoping to find the kitchen relatively empty. It seemed a long time since I had done any shorthand practice and I longed for that discipline, that pure, clear, abstract world, that world apart. In preparation I had bought some earplugs. To my slight irritation Allibert was there. He had made a lemon cake and stupidly left it unprotected, airing on the inside window-ledge. I flapped two budgerigars off and cut myself a slice. The birds seemed to have increased, in number, variety and size. There were

100

some very large vulture-like ones. They were, in fact, vultures. Allibert borrowed a bird book from the library later and we identified them. Griffon vultures, the European species. I still have no idea where they came from; certainly I never bought them. However, this is really a side-issue.

Allibert was at the kitchen table, his head turned away from me. As I realised after about five minutes, he was crying. Very quietly into a large, greyish handkerchief, without any big show, privately but determinedly, his style of doing most things. He must have been crying for some time: the handkerchief was sodden and his face was all patchy and red. I was horrified. I had so rarely seen anyone give way to tears. In our family it just wasn't done; my mother considered it un-English, especially in men. Quickly, I cut another slice of cake and attempted a tactful retreat, but he had seen me and was now blowing his nose.

'You know what they did,' he said tearfully, bitterly, 'at that so-called hospital, what their "treatment" was? Torturers and bloody murderers.'

'No. What?'

'They gave her E C T. Electro Convulsive Therapy. Against her will. They strapped her down. You know.'

I didn't. Allibert took several deep breaths and then explained. He had culled bits of information from my mother, bits from his parents' textbooks. They strap them to a machine, the mental patients, and send bolts of electricity through them, like in *1984*, an advanced form of torture, except they give you an anaesthetic. I felt, listening to all this, an insane desire to laugh. It's strange how the most serious and terrible things can seem hysterically amusing. When my brother was first told the facts of life he laughed for days.

'I asked my father,' Allibert said furiously, 'what the point of it is, how it's supposed to work, this "treatment". According to him, they don't even know. It's a totally hit-and-miss method. He said, and I'm quoting his *exact* words, "It's a bit like kicking an old television set".'

I crumbled the remains of my lemon cake slice for the doves. 'Gosh'.

'It burns out parts of your brain. So you can't remember things.'

'Well, maybe that could be good,' I said lamely. 'In a way. I mean it might help. If there was something you wanted to forget.'

Recalling the doctor and the form I had signed, although under eighteen, I felt sick. So they had wiped out parts of my mother. Bits of her brain, her past. So would she recover ever? So who was she now?

'Like your mother can't. She's forgotten your brother, totally. As if he'd never been born.'

Eleven

How does the sky stay up, how does it keep from falling on the earth? This was one question, one of the many, that used to bother me when I was small. My mother ignored them; my father gave me only reference book numbers. To satisfy myself and amuse my brother I invented my own world-myths, versions of history.

A woman holds up the sky. Since the beginning of time, for millions of years, this one woman has straddled heaven and earth. She can never relax, not for a moment. She dares not risk letting the sky fall. And she has no hope of rescue. No one else can shoulder her burden. No one else would be strong enough. She sees men pass by sometimes – travellers, adventurers like my father – but they are so tiny, so weak, miniscule compared to her. Like little ants scurrying past on the ground intent on their own business. She is too big for them even to notice. She is five hundred feet high, two hundred feet broad across the shoulders. Her hair is long, brown, all tangled up and matted. Her toenails grip the earth like claws.

My brother, suitably impressed by this story, retailed it to my mother. She said it wasn't true. Atmospheric pressure holds up the sky. Atmospheric pressure. Long words, textbook words, failed to reassure me. All night I lay awake, staring up at our bedroom ceiling. I feared it might fall. If I didn't keep awake it might. Already it had cracks. Each night it seemed to sink lower. This obsession made my brother nervous; we slept in the same bed then. I remember him trying to close my eyes with his fingers. He was a frail child, 'delicate', susceptible to impressions. When I told my

103

stories, he hid under the bedclothes. I felt strong beside him, protective.

But I was frightened too. Some nights the ceiling seemed terribly near. I ached with the mental strain of keeping it up, away from us. Cramp knotted my arms and legs. On bad nights my fears extended over the whole house. All the ceilings were sinking, falling, cracking up, due to collapse. I was a neurotic child, come to think of it. Always I doubted the solidity of things, their endurance capacities. Bricks and mortar, walls, roofs and ceilings, the basics, they gave me no assured sense of security. In one of Allibert's father's textbooks it says houses symbolise wives and mothers in the unconscious mind. This sounds admittedly a bit far-fetched.

Responsibility is what terrifies. Other people. For myself, I knew I would always survive somehow. In cases of earthquake, floods, volcanoes erupting, whatever. It was only my brother I worried about. After we moved to Surrey and were given separate bedrooms, I relaxed a bit, the cramps eased. A time of relative peace, before my grandmother arrived, and the spirits of death soon after.

One of my grandmother's stories, incidentally, matched mine: the same giant woman, the sky-holder. It gave her an exact geographical location, in the southern mountains of Corsica. But in my grandmother's version, the woman escapes. She just walks away one day, leaves the sky to itself. And it stays up, I think.

In early May of that year, my mother's madness year, my grandmother and I went on a picnic. She had discovered the ideal place, on top of her church tower, a flat stone square surrounded by a crumbling, lichen-covered stone wall. Here we ate marmite sandwiches, made with wholemeal bread and soya-bean margarine, and drank rosehip tea from a thermos flask. My grandmother's tastes had changed: for political reasons, she now eschewed all dairy produce. She and her old ladies were now radical spiritual separatists. They had set up a printing press, a women's night-lift service, a refuge for battered aunts and grandmothers, an Older Women for Peace campaign. They held workshops every Saturday, on racism, classism, grandmotherhood, compulsive eating. I attended most of these and took notes: it was good shorthand practice. The discussions sometimes got very heated.

We had climbed the tower to escape the television cameras, the interviewers, the literary agents, the national and international newspaper reporters; my grandmother had no patience with them. She had too many other things on her mind. She was then recasting the bell, the now-famed great golden bell of Saint Cecilia's Surbiton, which chimes E flat. It was made, as few people realise, from scrap metal – bits of old cars, Renaults and Volkswagons.

Shading her eyes, my grandmother gazed into the distance. It was a bright, clear, sunny day, the first real day of spring. From the church tower top we had a panoramic view over Surbiton and most of Kingston and Norbiton. My grandmother, I had the feeling, was looking further, seeing, in her mind's eye, Corsica. She still got nostalgic, hungered sometimes for the old life, for her homeland. 'Where I come from, where you come from also, child, it is a beautiful place. The hills make big shapes against the sky. They are promises of eternity.' Surrey is flat. Pretty in parts, rural even, with its parks and commons, but flat. The religious instinct, I think, derives mainly from hills. 'I will lift up mine eyes unto the hills from whence cometh my help.' I've lived most of my life in flat places, and this discourages faith. And the air too, air has a lot to do with it. In England we breathe very thin air, comparatively. I may be talking nonsense here.

But my grandmother had outgrown, somewhat, her past. She was no longer, if she'd ever been, a simple peasant woman. Or a simple *mazzere* even. And Corsica itself is so different now. Dual carriageways cutting through the *maquis*, high-rise blocks, colour televisions, the tourist trade. Old Corsica, the vanished world, existed only in her memory.

In age the past grows clearer, sharper in outline. The present blurs. It's the best time, in your eighties and nineties, for writing, as my grandmother's old ladies were finding. The best time for being/becoming yourself. Also, the men have mostly died off by then, which simplifies matters.

My grandmother is as old as the century, born in 1900. She lived through two world wars, but it's not these she mainly remembers. Her family suffered no tragedy, no loss through war; by that time, it was already an all-female household. The vendetta, the Corsican family revenge system, had claimed her father and five brothers. Their mother, the widow, had taken symbolic leave of the world, locking herself up in one small shuttered room to grieve, to remember her dead husband, to curse his dead killers. Forgiveness does not come easily to Corsicans. Reconciliation – with others, with oneself, with the past – is very rare.

'She was a true Corsican,' my grandmother said, lowering her hand. 'My mother, your great-grandmother. Upon his death she withdrew from the world. For twenty years, until her own life ended. Here in England' – my grandmother made a scornful gesture over Surbiton – 'how could they understand such a thing?' It was not,' she said with distaste, 'love. This was honour, family honour, duty.'

Family honour. Duty. A fine thing if you can manage it. I chewed my sandwich despondently, wishing she would talk about something else. Seeing we ourselves had so little family left to mention. I've always had a secret yearning to be loyal, but in what way, to whom? To my mad mother, my father upstairs? The last thing they require is loyalty. We all need far more to get free of each other. For survival's sake, to kill each other off. My brother achieved this with most dramatic success. I'm still trying for it in my own way.

And love. Love. I use this word, like my grandmother, as little as possible. Love is so much of an imposition. Such a violent thing to inflict on someone. But love the dead, by all means, be loyal to the dead. It can't harm them.

'Had I remained in Corsica,' my grandmother said sadly. 'Had I stayed there, how simple my life would have been. In the village where I was born, among the faces I knew. Ah, child, when I left that land a great part of me died. Still, one is led. One follows necessity. Since then I am splintered, fragmented.' She touched me on the forehead gently. I touched her hand. I felt like kissing it, but didn't of course, restrained as ever by Englishness, by my

106

mother's inner injunctions. My grandmother's hands – an old woman's withered brown hands, knotted with veins. I thought then for a flickering second of her dying. Drifting away, flying away with the spirits on the wind. It seemed then, still seems, possible to accept her death. Because she's lived so long, I suppose.

I went home and lay down on my brother's bed. I wasn't thinking about anything much. Or feeling much, except very cold, and my hands had gone numb. I remembered Teresita de Cavalli, how she lay on the bed in her long white gown. And the spirits of death came moaning, crying outside. And she almost died. Such a thin line between life and death. So easy to cross over, cross the border. I closed my eyes. They still felt wide open. I was so tired, I was so cold. I was seeing strange things. A white lilac tree. The moon, with clouds blowing over. The sea. Very cold images, nothing comforting. The numbness spread all over me. 'Imagine the water filling your mouth, filling your nose, filling your eyes.' Alicia's drowning games. Then I was in darkness. In a dark land. I saw someone moving ahead of me, walking fast in the dark. My brother. Though he looked taller, older. I had forgotten. He was twelve when he died, no longer a child. I was following him then, running after him. The ground was uneven, tufted with rough grass. It was like Bushy Park and the same feelings as then. Desperation. Loss. There he was, moving ahead silently, always at the same smooth pace. The distance not growing between us, not lessening. I kept stumbling, I was out of breath and sweating, hampered by my flesh, my stupid body. I wanted to call him, but didn't know how. I had never learnt the ways, the spells, how to call/recall the dead. I tried to shout his name but no sound came out. I was voiceless, without power to speak, lost. There was a wind blowing. Dark clouds blew over the moon.

Then he stood still, turned around, stood facing me. A narrow dry ditch between us. It was him, I was certain, almost certain, but his face flickered and kept changing. My mother, my grandmother, a cat's face. My mother again. Then almost his face. Almost. If he would speak, I would be sure. But how do they speak, the dead people? They need blood first, I remember my

107

grandmother saying. Life blood, libation, poured on the ground. Blood of animals or whatever. They drink the blood, then they can speak. But I had none, no blood, none to offer. No instrument to cut myself with. And I had stopped bleeding myself, a fortnight back. Empty, helpless.

The vision faded. I was back in my brother's bedroom. Standing up now, alone, facing myself only in the long wardrobe mirror. He was gone. Lost to me for ever. Dead. Until that moment I had not truly known it, had shielded myself from the knowledge, the pain. It was too much, just felt too much. I can't excuse what followed. I smashed the mirror. I smashed all the windows. Blood ran down my arms. I threw things out, into the garden – books, a crucifix. Such fury I hadn't known I possessed. Such power, strength to break and destroy. But underneath that, helplessness – knowing it was pointless, childish. I could picture Death watching me with an amused smile. Dead, that means no life, ever. It truly means that. Nothing will bring him back. Miracles like Lazarus don't happen these days. No chance ever of resurrection, no hope. So even memories don't mean anything, nor all these words.

Twelve

'I just can't,' I said. 'I just can't.'

Why not?'

'I just don't want to, that's all.'

Allibert and I were talking, our first conversation for weeks. He was making most of the effort. I was reading, or trying to read, an old battered copy of *Woman's Own*. It had an article on compatible starsigns, 'Your Man and You'. Gemini and Virgo. 'A heady combination,' it said. 'When earthy, passionate Virgo clashes with two-faced, airy, electric Gemini, all Hell breaks loose. Fireworks in the bedroom.' My mother is Virgo. I always look up her starsign first, I don't know why; a childish habit. I'm Gemini, so was my brother. Geminis tend to have quite intense relationships. I'm not sure what sign Allibert is.

I started reading the love story. *Free to Love*, it was called. 'Emma was certain that Peter didn't see things her way. Not like David – he understood her and always had. But was it right to go back to him; could she really find her future happiness in the past?'

Allibert removed the magazine from my hands, gently but firmly. 'Jenny,' he said 'you won't find the answers to your life in women's magazines.'

'Why not?' I said crossly. 'Why not? I won't find them anywhere else, that's for sure. I might not be interested in answers, anyway.'

We were back once again in Tolworth General Hospital, the outpatients department this time: a long, crowded, smoky corridor lined on either side with hard red seats. Nurses burst in and vanished through the swing doors, shouting garbled surnames.

The queue wasn't moving noticeably. Nobody else was talking much. Allibert had barely stopped since we arrived. Two kids were playing a chasing game. My arms were covered in strips of Elastoplast, makeshift bandaging. Allibert had a black eye, half-closed now, and fingertip-sized purple bruises all round his neck. I couldn't actually remember attacking him, but there was the evidence.

'If you won't see her now,' Allibert persisted, 'then when? When will you?'

'I don't know, I don't know.'

'She's your *mother*.'

I snatched the magazine back. 'So what?'

'She needs you, Jenny.'

I didn't like this new habit of Allibert's, calling me by name. It seemed superficial and presumptive. Shorthand practice had developed my instincts for privacy, self-respect, consciousness of inner boundaries. Necessary ones. It seemed Allibert was constantly trying to break through these. The more he tried, the stronger they became.

'She's never in her life needed anyone. She doesn't need me now.'

' How can you tell?'

'I just can, that's all.'

Allibert cupped both hands together and stared into them. 'I'll be leaving home soon, anyway,' I added. 'Getting a job.'

'Maybe you need her too.'

'Rubbish.'

Allibert had now taken his 'A' levels, all five, and his parents were pressurising him to start thinking seriously careerwise. They were still concerned also about his lack of a normal adolescent sex life, the suppression of his so-called natural instincts.

'My mother asked me point-blank last Wednesday whether I masturbated. She asked me about my fantasies, what "turned me on". It was very, very embarrassing. She's got an exhibition on now, at the I C A – ' Allibert sighed. 'It's called "Resurgence of the Male", subtitle "Post-feminist Perceptions". It's all penises. I mean nothing but. Blue and green ones. All, I need hardly say, erect. Quite frankly, I didn't know where to look. I went and sat in the restaurant. They do good salads. She's having an affair, I gather. Who with, I don't know. Not a woman, of course, some younger man. I think my father obscurely blames me. He keeps talking about rape now, it's really disturbing, and eyeing up young girls on the street. He's going to Tenerife. He wants me to come too, so we can – quote – "live it up a bit". What that means, I shudder to think. I've told him, I'm planning to follow Saint Paul's journey from Antioch to Macedonia, passing through Pamphylia, Philippi and Ephesus.'

'What did he say?'

'He just gave me rather an odd look.'

Allibert's eye grew more spectacular by the minute, literally, like a sunset, modulating from red to pink to orange to purple and faintly green. Eventually it attracted a passing nurse's attention and they moved him up the queue. I went on reading my *Woman's Own* story. Emma had broken off her engagement to Peter. She had met Derek, an up-and-coming young insurance salesman with a Volvo. She was still feeling dissatisfied, still in search of true love, 'future happiness'. David was still on her mind, the anchor man, the fallback. He was the one, obviously. Emma herself seemed a sketchy character, a faceless, wishy-washy sort of girl. I wished I was her, able to resolve my life in terms of men, 'the right man', husbands. I still yearned, guiltily, after normal life, women's magazine life, conventional existence, no matter what Allibert said and all the disappointments I'd had so far. I had inherited certain expectations, or absorbed them somehow. My mother also was addicted to romance; maybe she read a lot when she was pregnant with me.

My arms were hurting now, considerably. I felt miserable and shaky. The smashed mirror, the windows – had I really done that? Me?

I folded up *Woman's Own* queasily. Allibert was right, Emma's problems bore little relation to mine. Though I could just believe the world did contain people like her, leading successful surface lives, set-formula lives, skating along. Maybe I would manage it someday, pick up the knack. Get engaged, married. Have kids? Directly opposite me, across the magazine table, a young woman was discreetly, as far as possible, breastfeeding her tiny baby. They looked blissful, the two of them, in a world of their own, entranced. I could imagine it was a male, this baby. A little girl was standing close by watching. A very neat, clean child – flowery dress, blue anorak, white socks, plaited fair hair. I was struck by her expression of such transparent agony and outrage. She was sucking her own hand. I felt like crying, just the sight of her, it was so awful.

I exchanged *Woman's Own* hastily for *Country Life*. Flicking through the advertisements, it struck me I would like a large house of my own. A very, very large house, preferably an abandoned castle, with a moat or perhaps a fortress. All to myself. The desire for solitude – absolute, unadulterated – was steadily growing on me. I felt so cramped at home. Needing more space, space to concentrate, meditate, trace my shorthand symbols. I admired my grandmother, how she managed to reconcile sociability and political commitment with her own needs. But then, she didn't have to live with my mother, her daughter. Just the thought of my mother turned me cold all over; my mind went blank and my hands numb, my feet like jellyfish. And then Allibert accused me of being 'uncaring'.

We walked back home together. 'Home', number 38 Princes Road. It now seemed more Allibert's home than mine. He was camping out in my brother's room. I won't go into why, his possible/probable subconscious motives. God knows, he discussed them endlessly enough. He'd escaped from *his* family anyway.

We stopped off at Boots. Allibert had two prescriptions. While we were waiting, he examined the contraceptives. He was still fascinated by sex, in spite of Saint Paul. The Surbiton branch of Boots was getting quite adventurous: they had sheaths in all colours, including stripy ones. And sweet-tasting. I remembered Alicia, with Lancelot and the chocolate. That time seemed in retrospect curiously innocent, now that she'd successfully conquered her body's desires, all earthly appetites.

I looked, resentfully, at the diet 'foods', the one-calorie drinks, watery soups, tasteless crispbreads, half-fat butters, non-sugar jams. This was the kind of thing I *should* be eating. Mouthfuls of nothing. But it would be so hard to give up real food. The alternative was, like Alicia, to keep vomiting it up. Swallow and vomit. Control and reject. Grow slender, grow thin; ungrow rather, dwindle, melt away inside like a wax candle. Oh that this too, too solid flesh would melt. But I wasn't ready yet for dissolution. My stomach kept telling me not. In deep growls, high moans, loud protesting cries. In the most public places. It was extremely awkward. I understood now how possessed people felt, people with demons inside, the kind Christ used to cast out.

I was just thinking, lingering by the diet drinks, how interesting it would be to be thin. To see my rib cage, my hip bones again, as presumably they would resurface. Perhaps it's better to be thin, morally speaking, nearer the bone, the truth. I don't know. Nearer death anyway. Allibert liked me fatter. He was always encouraging me to eat. I liked myself fatter actually. Putting aside all the self-disgust, the feelings of sluggishness and stupidity, I secretly took pleasure in my extra flesh. It felt friendly around me, especially in bed.

I was overwhelmed suddenly by utter exhaustion. Loss of blood, lack of sleep, too much recent emotion. Also, mainly, fear. Fear of going home. There should be a word, a term for this. Home-phobia? I went round the corner into the baby section, a quiet place out of sight. Bibs, ear swabs, cotton wool. Baby baths, mild baby shampoo. I lay on the floor. It felt a great relief. I was wearing a grey dufflecoat, which more or less blended with the carpet. Several people walked by. I suppose they must have noticed me but no one made any obvious sign. Surbiton people are very tactful. You can get away with the most peculiar behaviour. I was thinking about this dream I'd had several nights back, involving the Wimpy Bar waitress and a strawberry milkshake. A very sweet dream. Angels came into it somewhere.

Behind the baby products I could hear Allibert arguing with a counter assistant about Durex's promotion leaflets, which he considered unnecessarily sexist in terminology. Loud sighs of exasperation: 'Bloody Trotskyists holding up the queue', 'Never get served in this place.'

'Mum.' A high, whiny child's voice. '*Mum*. Why is that lady lying on the floor?'

'Shush darling. It's not polite to point.'

'But *why* is she?'

'I expect she's tired, dear.'

Voices coming and going. Hushed whispers. Roars of traffic from the street outside. I began to feel incredibly relaxed, enveloped by a sense of mystical peace. Floating upwards in spirit, leaving behind the awful confusion of everything, my mixed-up existence, rising above it, looking down on it. Like an astronaut floating in dark space, silent space. Heaven above me somewhere. The sweet invisible influence of the spheres, their music. Following their precise pre-ordained paths, in obedience to divine law. The principle of love. I was acquainted vaguely with parts of Dante's *Divine Comedy*. Alicia often recited it, in medieval Italian, with English translation occasionally.

'Jenny, Jenny', Allibert was shaking my shoulder. 'Hello? Are you okay?'

I sat up crossly, brushing his hand away. I felt rudely awakened, muddled and sick, like after too much hymn singing.

'You must have fainted.'

'Go away. Piss off, Allibert. Leave me alone.'

People were now beginning to gather and stare. They looked especially at Allibert's bandaged eye and my ravaged arms. He supported me outside, making soothing smalltalk the while: belated reaction, recent trauma, no wonder. We reached the bus stop.

'Of course, all this connects so clearly with your mother,' he said, 'and your brother's death, still working itself out on some deep level. It's very encouraging, really. I've always been impressed by the richness of your family's subconscious life.'

'Oh, shut up' I said, wrenching free. 'What do *you* know, anyway? You don't know anything about us. You're not one of us. Fuck off, Allibert. Go and be a bloody social worker or something.'

'One of us.' I was appalled at myself. One of whom? What entity? And this language, which I hadn't till then known myself

114

capable of. I had heard the words, of course, but had always kept a strict curb on my own tongue. Like my mother, I handled words at arm's length, respectfully, like fine English bone china. Nothing angered her more than 'bad language', street language, my grandmother's muttered Corsican obscenities. These came flooding all at once into my mind. 'Son of a diseased goat. Daughter of shit.' I could only translate the simplest. 'Go and mount a pig. Go and bugger a dead cow.'

Allibert's stunned, astonished face. The bus drew up; I got on. That was the last I saw of him for several months. But I think it was necessary. I had been avoiding my mother for too long, letting him do all the hard work, taking advantage of his goodwill. He needed a break and we, she and I, were due for some time alone together.

Thirteen

To celebrate the success of my mother's first novel, my grandmother held a big party at Saint Cecilia's. I got extremely drunk, which I think was excusable. For the past year I had been under a lot of strain and pressure. Now this book, this novel/travelogue/journal or whatever, *A Mother Speaks*, was finally 'out', hitting the bestseller charts, flooding the bookshops. My grandmother was euphoric. All her prophecies fulfilled, her intuitions proved solidly accurate. 'Your mother is *mazzere*. She alone has the great gifts.'

I felt dreadful. Besieged by guilt, I wanted to die. It was just beginning to strike me, to filter through, exactly what I had done. Putting my mother in print, making public her most secret voices. I was cursed with a conscience. Unlike my grandmother. I'm always hesitant to blame her, but she did exploit the situation, my mother's multiple schizophrenia. Up to the hilt. It was her peasant-woman's business instincts. Though not greedy by nature, placing more value on spiritual than material things, she just could not resist making money. Books by women, feminist books, she was convinced, rightly, would sell.

Old Hag Press of Saint Cecilia's was thriving. The organ loft, now reachable by an ingenious wheelchair lift system, was crammed with new technology, including a word processor with twenty terminals. They had an open publication policy, would take anything, of however doubtful literary merit, provided the author was (1) female, (2) over sixty, (3) single or divorced, (4) Catholic, lapsed Catholic, or of no recognised religion, (5) anti-racist, (6) radical feminist, (7) lesbian. My mother fell short on most counts, but by

116

a cooperative decision they waived clauses 2, 3, 5, 6, and 7 and accepted her novel. My grandmother, I think, pulled strings. They published it under my name, Jennifer Andrews.

Admittedly, I put it into shape, arranged it into recognisable prose. But the inspiration was hers, the breath of life. She dictated it; I just wrote down the words. Parts were in English, parts in Corsican. Luckily, shorthand is entirely phonetic, so I didn't have to understand it. My grandmother translated later. I suspect her of adding some bits of her own.

It was a strange time, the writing time. Such a strange time. I went partly mad too, I think. In creative sympathy, psychic association. I forgot 'myself', how it feels to be someone, apart from a listening ear and a hand.

Days merged into nights, into days. A kind of semi-dusk prevailed. I sat by her bedside. And she talked. And talked. In all different voices and characters. High voices, little chattering whispering ones, a deep singing wail. I put names to them, provisionally, names all beginning with P. They were quite friendly, some of them, when they deigned to acknowledge my presence. On occasion they addressed me directly: 'Write this down,' 'Cross that out,' 'What have I said?' Apparently it was very important that I should get the words precisely right, not misquote them. They were very exacting. It seemed clear they came from absolutely elsewhere, 'took over' my mother. She, the spirit-medium, remained unconscious of them, propped up glassy-eyed against her pillows. We are taken over, spoken through. It is not of our own will.

She took to wandering at night. In the spirit hours, the dark hours between twelve and three, when most births occur and most deaths. I became quite used to it, her drifting around. Opening cupboards, peering under chairs. Searching still. Accompanied always by the ghostly women, a kind of travelling orchestra, pre-dawn chorus. From all sides of the room they spoke, stereophonic. On an average night we might get ten or eleven. What they hoped to gain by addressing me, me with my shorthand notebook, uncertain spelling, lack of experience in matters spiritual/sexual, I'm not quite sure. Maybe it hardly mattered who. They just needed a go-between.

117

Allibert phoned every evening. He was hurt. He felt I was excluding him. He was right. I was. Caring, conscientious, thoughtful though he might be, his presence would have ruined everything, silenced all our ghosts. I tried to explain this gently, but it was difficult. Allibert had his pride, his egotism, like anyone else. Also he was lonely. He had grown dependent on my mother, in her sickness, addicted to her. Like most 'carers' – psychiatrists, social workers, people who encroach, who intrude, parasites, second-hand livers – he tried by various devious means to reintroduce himself, but I was firm against him. When he got too pressing, I put the phone down. Time felt precious. We had work to do, she and I.

In its first rough draft I think her novel actually read far better. More poetic. Not that it made much sense, but so what? I'm sorry now for having interfered – structured, punctuated, forced it into too-tight literary form. Things should take their own shape. By way of reparation here, unbowdlerised, is some of the raw copy. Two notebook pages.

P. Ask me, who am I? In the dark secrecy of night, I conceive. Alone, lying alone in the locked house. Serpents coil within my womb. Twisting, bright, flickering. Consuming me, sucking me dry. Writhing deep in me. Writhing with delight. Little flickering tongues. My breasts fill, swell, I suck the sweet poison –

P. I reached up and the air lifted me. I flew in the sky. I flew, I grew, I lifted, I filled, I was full of air. Light, delight, laughter. I laughed lightness. I cried rain. The trees reached up, the cloud burst, the bird swarm.

P. A little boy, perfectly formed. A perfect child. Oh, little head, small fingers. I will place you in my glass jar, behind glas –

P. I am lost. My flesh is betrayed. A dark hole, emptiness crying – Aiee – Avenge. Avenge my family. Take the dagger and strike. Strike again – strike deep. Again. Ahh – Again. Again.

P. The child clings in me. Little barnacle, limpet crab. He crept back in me. The cunning child, while I slept, he slipped back. How tight, how tight he grips.

P. Enter me, oh, enter me. Oh, possess me. I grow wide for you.

118

Oh, I long for you. I hunger. Oh, feel me. Touch me, touch. Don't hold away. Oh, come. Here, in here. In, in.
P. No, oh no, it hurts. You bruise me. Your clumsy – too big, too hard. Painful. I close into myself. Anemone. Enemy – forcing me open. I bleed. –
P. Delicate little fish. In the shallows, in the sea, in the waving seaweed. Transparent. Invisible. In the sea –

This sort of thing went on for pages and pages. Notebooks and notebooks. It certainly did wonders for my shorthand, although some bits are indecipherable. The voices would all start speaking at once. Also, my mother distracted me, opening drawers and cupboards, flicking through books. Looking for something, it seemed. Still haunted, obsessed. The tenacity of memory, of spirit, never ceases to amaze me. Allibert was wrong. My brother's death had by no means been excised, cleanly removed, wiped out. Human beings are not blackboards.

The more stupid you are, the more harm you do. The more painful complications certainly you cause. As those doctors did with their 'cures', their therapy. Before the electricity treatment she was okay. Relatively. For a madwoman. Deeply depressed, yes, despairing, suicidal, but at least retaining some vestiges of privacy. Self-possessed in that sense. And where or who is she now? A best-selling novelist. In print, on paper. Sold in thousands. Divided and multiplied. In her third edition.

So, as I say, I got drunk at this party. There was some very wild bacchanalian dancing in progress, not much like the Hokey Cokey. My grandmother had her arm around Miss Smith, the senior librarian. I saw them kissing, which made me feel – a bit strange. How shocked, I thought, my mother would have been. They should have had more discretion at their age, more regard for convention and appearances. My grandmother was now over eighty, Miss Smith only just sixty-five.

I made my way out unsteadily through the heavy wooden swing door and the triple-locked steel entrance gate. They were taking extra security measures, owing to recent intrusions by gutter-press journalists, and war being now openly declared with the Charismatics and the Festival-of-Lighters. A small typed notice was displayed in the church porch, pasted over the old mass and benediction times. It pronounced:

This is a woman-only space. Men are asked to show respect. Children welcome, including boy children up to the age of twelve. Animals also welcome.
Bisexual women not excluded.
Counselling in the confessional. List of workshops in vestry.

True to our Selves,
Loving other women as our Selves,
Smash the patriarchal system. Sisters, unite!

Please ring the bell twice.

The moon hung dimly behind bars of cloud, a crescent moon. I went and sat in the old churchyard, where the vegetables were growing extremely well. Rhubarb in the moonlight. I was tired out. This sensation I always had, of my mother. On my back, in my head. What it means to be haunted. One's family's continual presence. And can you never be free, never be by yourself? Until you get past sixty and they've all died off, hopefully. If death solves anything. Dead people are more powerful sometimes, by their absence, the terrible holes they leave. I was thinking vague thoughts of this kind. And my brother, did he need to escape? Do we still pursue him? Haunt him?

These were chilling considerations. I sat all hunched up on the grass, clutching my knees. To be alive, a living person, as I still undeniably was, how frightening it felt. What an appalling duty.

Someone touched me, a warm hand touching my cheek. It was my grandmother. She had followed me out. 'Ha! My dear. It is cold here, take heed for yourself. This damp grass. What are you thinking of? Your mother?' I nodded. 'She is very well,' my grandmother said confidently. 'Very well indeed. She wakes out of her long sleep. Her spirit at last is released. My heart is glad for

120

her, for my daughter. Each day I give thanks to the Blessed Virgin, for her deliverance. And you, my dear,' – urging me up – 'of what great assistance you have been to her. How proud you should now feel.'

She walked with me over the grass, arm around my waist. I began to cheer up a bit. It was my grandmother's unsquashable optimism which always so beguiled me. She and all her old ladies. Their enthusiasm for life, strength of mind, light-heartedness, innocence. In their dungarees, with their punk haircuts.

'Yes, yes,' she said, 'you will be like Niola, your great-aunt.'

I had never heard of this great-aunt. Sometimes I think my grandmother makes them up, invents new role models for me according to her whim of the moment. I like this habit. It's nice having an extendable family, imaginatively fluid; fixed relatives can be such a pain.

'Yes, you will be like Niola, she was *mazzere*, she was a writer. From an early age this was her vocation. She would write down the women's sorrows, what they had suffered. As it was told to her, yes, in those very words. Just as it was told.'

We passed the east window, the rose window, like a huge eye in the wall. Strains of music filtered through. Shadows danced. Bats veered above the trees, squeaking.

'A grief unspoken, untold,' my grandmother said, 'eats at the heart. Yes, your mother was ill. It was pre-ordained, her great anguish of soul. That she must suffer. Those doctors – madmen and liars – how could they help her? But that is all past. She is no longer watched, she is not in danger. I have shown this, with oil and water together. The oil runs clear now. She is safe.'

I felt then the smallest dawning of hope, light at the end of the tunnel. Her words confirming my own observation, that she, my mother, was back with us, back with herself. Body and spirit joined. I had seen it in her eyes, something returned in them.

Sometimes in the night I would hear her crying. For a long time, often. But I didn't try to comfort her, stop her. It felt necessary, the grief, something she had needed.

So why should I feel so guilty? The writing helped her, speeded her recovery. As for the publishing, the making public – well, she

121

won't ever know. She's unlikely to read it. I'm trying to excuse myself, and for one main reason. I still have a lot of good material left in those notebooks – five novels' worth at least. And it's such an excitement, seeing things in print, under your own name. It does get addictive.

The reviews were a mixed bunch, but on the whole seemed favourable. I pinned the best up on my bedroom walls, butterfly-style.

- 'Painful yet ultimately exhilarating; an account of one woman's journey into selfhood' (*Nursery World*)

- 'Firmly in the English tradition. Recalls the more peculiar excesses of the eighteenth-century female gothic novel, with echoes of Barbara Cartland' (*Wiltshire and Somerset Herald*)

- 'Absurdist fantasy: a refreshing change from the "doom and gloom" school of feminist literature. Unlike most of today's young women, Miss Andrews has no personal axe to grind' (*Gardener's Chronicle*)

- 'Alarmingly solipsistic' (*Surbiton Gazette*).

- 'Christian allegory for our times' (*Pentecost*, the Catholic Charismatic monthly).

- 'The novel's central theme never fully emerges and the style is frustratingly elliptical. Shows promise' (*Gay News*).

I never showed these to my mother. Out of cowardice, or natural enough caution. I wasn't sure that she remembered that time, the madness time, or would want to. Now recuperating, she spent most days in the garden, pulling up weeds and planting things. She had always loved gardening: it seemed to relax her, ease her. She loved flowers. I can see their advantages, perennials at least.

My father's seminal work on butterflies was now drawing to its close. He was writing the appendices, the footnotes.

'It leaves me rather in a vacuum, I must confess. The trouble is, one's knowledge is so very limited. One's general knowledge, so to speak. Where, for instance' – my father coughed, delicately – 'the fair sex is concerned. One gathers some vague impressions. Some parallels spring to mind. Conclusions might be drawn. A small volume of essays perhaps.' He coughed again. 'However, however. Fools rush in. I have so little first-hand experience. Your mother is the only woman, and even there . . . '

Fourteen

Sunlight glittering on the sea, far out. Now the sky clouds over, the water darkens. Waves swell gently up and break, hiss back sucking through shingle. No mermaids today, only the seagulls crying, unearthly sad sound. I've been walking for hours here, along Brighton beach. I'm chilled through and miserable. My pockets are full of stones. I'm still no closer to any resolution or way forward, only to this pain and sadness in me. Which solves nothing really.

A recent dream. I'm walking with Alicia, along by the Thames near Richmond Bridge. The sky is clear blue, the river pure silver. We're holding hands. Sometimes Alicia is incredibly tall, taller than the trees, a giant woman, sometimes small as a child. We're arguing. I want to get in the river and swim. Alicia says, 'We can't do that, the river is polluted with mercury. Look, all the fish have died.' I look, but can't see any fish, dead or otherwise, only the bright-shining silver water. Feeling scared, and aware of Alicia shrinking rapidly by my side, I let go of her hand, I put my arms around her and then she sort of melts into me. I can feel her inside me, all curled up and coiled round, like a baby or a snake. 'You're safe now,' I say – loudly so she'll hear me – 'safe', but with this word suddenly the sun disappeares behind a dark cloud, birds fly over and the river turns red as blood.

In real life I haven't seen Alicia for a while. I just didn't want to. I couldn't bear it any more, the awful sight of her. I got a letter from her last week, written in incredibly tiny writing – she'd read my mother's novel, which she described as 'banal'. She thought her own life/death story would be more 'gripping'.

I'll probably end up writing it. But I've my own life to lead, too.

My brother's death set me free, it set me searching, but who for I don't know, or what for. I would still hesitate to say 'love'. Love is so much to ask from anyone, such a great risk. You gamble everything, yourself, your soul, for a stranger. And then if they die . . .

I'm seventeen, now, and what have I done? Learnt shorthand, survived. Very little, really. I'm not sure what to do next, or where to go.

Possibilities – (1) marriage and/or motherhood, (2) sainthood, (3) secretarial career?

I will have to leave. I can't stay in that house, with that strange woman, my mother, still so secret and self-enclosed. I really have no idea who she is. Maybe one day I'll manage to explain her, find her for myself.

The Demeter and Persephone myth always seemed odd to me, the wrong way round surely. For I'm the one searching, wandering the earth desolate, calling her by name. And in dreams, through all the corridors of our house. But she passes me by without seeing me, like a ghost, without recognition.

I'm not the right person for her. She preferred John to me, always.

I'm not sure if that's true.

Another dream. I'm in the garden with my mother and we're pulling up weeds. Some of these weeds have very complicated roots, going down a long way. My mother says, 'I don't like doing this, it hurts too much.' 'You mean it hurts the earth?' I say. 'No,' she replies, 'as usual you're misinterpreting me, I didn't mean that, I meant love.' Just then I notice some very beautiful red flowers, like poppies, or roses, growing all together in one corner of the garden. My mother tells me they're called 'heart's love' or 'heart's blood'. As she speaks, to my surprise, tears start pouring down my face and splashing on the ground. My mother hands me the watering-can. 'Keep crying,' she says, 'tears are very nutritious.'

If only I'd known her earlier, in Corsica, in her youth, before she met my father and got married. She should never have done that; my grandmother was quite right. Or had children. She was *mazzere*. It was all a terrible mistake.'

Why did she marry him? Because she needed to escape, from her own mother. She was young, hopeful, and he just happened to come along, this butterfly collector. She mistook him for a genuine explorer. So easy to do – meet the wrong person, choose the wrong life.

Gulls crying in the wind, like lost souls. Waves hushing. The sea has so many voices. I'm trying to understand, make sense of things. That my brother died is true, and also not true. We remember him – that's to say he's still a part of us, lives in us.

His death I think destroyed something in her and in me too, it silenced us both. Now we're just starting to speak again, in ghostly voices, in our dreams.

I need words now, language, so much. Ways of speaking to people, to her, to him, and to myself, of exploring what happened, his death and what it meant to us. Meanings. I feel I've missed the point somehow, or wandered away from it. I'd like a way to use the word 'love' again, for that to mean something. Love. I love you. I didn't want you to die.

I imagine having a friend, gentler than Alicia and not so thin. We've come here together, to Brighton for a day out, to enjoy ourselves and get to know each other. We haven't talked much up till now. She's interesting but mysterious. We met in some neutral sort of place, not school, maybe Kew Gardens? Anyway, here we are. She's asking me questions, about my life and what's happened so far, about myself, as if she's really interested. And she wants real answers, the truth. I tell her all about my brother and my mother and father and grandmother. She listens, laughs in all the right places, looks sad at times: but she's still waiting, as if expecting something. For all I've said, it's been only surface-talk and stories. 'Go on,' she says 'And . . . '

Words fail me. I can't speak of the future, it hasn't happened yet. It's wide open, like the sea, boundless. I'm here, I can breathe, I'm warm, I'm alive. 'What do you want?' she asks me – I ask myself. But no, I'm still not sure. I need some miracle or sign, some way forward.

Once I thought I could escape the past, evade grief. Now I go looking for it, collecting pieces of it. Like stones – amber, agate, carnelian – the waves wash up. I remember Saint Agnela, whose tears transformed into precious jewels, water into stone, sorrow for food. That would be useful, if just by crying you could feed yourself. I'm crying now, I don't know why. It's the seagulls, they set me off, so mournful. The tears taste sweet and salt. Why am I crying. I don't know.

Ravinder Randhawa
A Wicked Old Woman

Stick-leg-shuffle-leg-shuffle: decked out with NHS specs and
Oxfam coat, Kulwant masquerades behind her old woman's
disguise, taking life or leaving it as she feels inclined, seeking new
adventures or venturing back into her past.

Divorced from her husband, disappoved of by her sons,
mistrusted by their wives, Kuli makes real contact through a
jigsaw of meetings in the present: with Bahadur the Punjabi punk
who dusts her down after a carefully calculated fall, with
Caroline, her gregarious friend from school days, who watched
over her dizzy romance with 'Michael the archangel', with Maya
the myopic who can't see beyond her weeping heart, and with
Shanti who won't see, whose eyes will remain closed till her
runaway daughter returns to the fold.

A sharply observed first novel set in an Asian community In a
British city – a witty and confident piece of work from a talented
new writer.

Fiction   £4.95
ISBN: 0 7043 4078 X
Hardback   £12.95
ISBN: 0 7043 5032 7

Ellen Galford
The Fires of Bride

A feminist *Whisky Galore* and *Hunting the Fairies* – fantastical, moving and very, very funny.

Off the western coast of Scotland lies the remote island of Cailleach (whose name means 'old woman'). With its ruined convent and ancient stone circle, its population of innkeepers and weavers, seaweed gatherers and garage owners, and its extraordinarily strong local brew, it exerts a powerful influence on those who visit it, particularly women...

Maria, a fugitive artist, is one such visitor. Hesitant guest of Catriona, clan chieftain, GP and witch, she is little prepared for an affair with her or for her involvement with the island's past, particularly with the tenth century illuminator of the heretical *Book of Bride*.

A delirious blend of history and legend, caricature and realism, satire and feeling, *The Fires of Bride* is a worthy successor to Ellen Galford's first novel, the much praised *Moll Cutpurse: Her True History*.

Fiction   £4.95
ISBN: 0 7043 4020 8
Hardback   £8.95
ISBN: 0 7043 5010 6

Stevie Davies
Boy Blue

'One night she dreamed ... of giving birth to a ten-
pound bomb, which slid out from between her legs in a
trail of cold slime, and when she touched it the skin of
her hand stuck to the freezing body. She woke the other
girls in the dormitory with her screams. She would not
survive. She realised this.'

It is December 1944, and Hitler's silent V2 rockets fall over
England. Shells rattle off production lines in factories where
women are now the workforce. Chrissie, just eighteen and
painfully shy, is desperate to quit. She meets and marries Jim, an
airman, and is soon pregnant. As her confinement approaches
she dreads the birth of a boy baby, whom she associates with the
war...

This haunting and exceptional novel is rooted in the experience
of women in a warrior culture; it explores the spiritual cost to
both sexes of the warrior ethos and, in Jungian terms, the price
of man's alienation from the feminine through the motif of the
lost boy-twin.

Fiction   £3.95
ISBN: 0 7043 4031 3
Hardback   £8.95
ISBN: 0 7043 5013 0

JoAnne Brasil
Escape from Billy's Bar-B-Que

**'There were lots of Post-War Babies and Hippies in our
building, it turned out . . . they were always offering to
baby-sit; but Betty Baines wouldn't let them because
they might smoke reefer and start asking 'what is real?'
and stuff like that or start reading *Finnegan's Wake* out
loud even though they said they didn't get it at all . . . '**

After High School, Cecyl escapes from the racist society of
Phoebus, Virginia, to the 'liberal' North of Boston. Yet her
encounters with the Post-War Babies, a group of South
American musicians, and an assortment of room-mates, leave
her perplexed at the barriers by class, sex, race and by people
who won't 'treat each other normal'.

Utterly convinced that everyone else knows something she
doesn't, Cecyl possesses that uncluttered honesty which sees
right to the heart of human contradiction and hypocrisy.

Fiction   £3.95
ISBN: 0 7043 4046 1

Anna Livia
Accommodation Offered

'"There is a woman in Stockwell sinning," insisted
Quercus.
"What's her sin?"
"Despair," said Quercus squeamishly.
"She has been ironing now for three hours, satin sheets
of oyster cream . . . "'

When Polly advertises two vacant rooms in her South London
home, Kim and Sadie move in: bus conductor Kim, and
awkward, gangling Sadie. Tensions develop as the differences
between the three women, their diverse backgrounds and
politics as lesbians, begin to divide them. Fortunately the
household is watched over by the Liberty Boddesses of Hortus,
prepared to risk even divine censure and banishment if they can
help . . .

As all who enjoyed her first novel, *Relatively Norma*, will know,
Anna Livia's is a unique voice and her style a special blend of
humour and seriousness.

Fiction   £3.95 (paperback)
ISBN: 0 7043 3951 X
Hardback   £7.95
ISBN: 0 7043 2857 7

Toni Cade Bambara
Gorilla, My Love

From Sister Sugar on sex to young Hazel on survival in Harlem,
these sixteen stories explode with humour and energy. Written
in Toni Cade Bambara's inimitable style, the effect has been
described as 'like reading jazz'. From uptown New York to
small-town Carolina, from first love to last wishes, her touch
remains absolutely sure.

'Ms Bambara grabs you by the throat. She dazzles, she charms'
Chicago Illinois News

Fiction   £3.95
ISBN: 0 7043 3927 7

Sylvia Townsend Warner
Lolly Willowes

**'I can't take warlocks so seriously, not as a class. It is we
witches who count'**

So says Lolly Willowes, explaining why she broke a lifetime's
service as a maiden aunt, to become a witch – a transformation
which Sylvia Townsend Warner describes in dry, wry lines which
are often very funny indeed.

Lolly Willowes is about spinsterhood – and about family
relationships, conventions and the Devil himself who offers Lolly
peace, independence and civility, to which she is unaccustomed.
Lolly's escape from enforced self-effacement into a sanctuary of
green country, wild flowers, Sabbaths and gentle witchcraft is
superbly entertaining.

'A novel as original in its conception as it is subtle and refined in
its artistry . . . *Lolly Willowes* . . . retains all of the charm and most
of the "relevance" it owned nearly fifty years ago' *Times Literary
Supplement*

'The writing is beautifully sharp and controlled' *Punch*

Fiction   £3.95
ISBN: 0 7043 3824 6